VOGUE HOUSE

VOGUE HOUSE

INSIDE
VOGUE HOUSE

**One building.
Seven magazines.
Sixty years of stories.**

Grant Scott

First published in Great Britain in 2024 by Orphans Publishing
www.orphanspublishing.co.uk

Text copyright © Grant Scott, 2024

Illustrations copyright © Geoff Waring, 2024

A Cataloguing in Publication record for this book is available
from the British Library.

Hardback ISBN: 978-1-903-36027-9

Also available in e-book.

Printed and bound in Great Britain by Clays Ltd, Elcograf S.p.A

MIX
Paper | Supporting
responsible forestry
FSC
www.fsc.org   FSC® C018072

This book is dedicated to Sam and Florence,
and to my parents Penny and Norman.

In memory of Pete Silverton.

Thanks to Geoff Waring for lighting the spark, and
Nick and Jenny Sargeant for the tea and magazines.

Thanks also to Jane Procter
and Miss Timms for letting me into the building.

"When we read a story, we inhabit it.
The covers of the book are like a roof and four walls.
What is to happen next will take place within
the four walls of the story.
And this is possible because the story's voice
makes everything its own."
John Berger

"A magazine must be like a human being,
if it comes into the home, it must contribute.
It can't lie around."
Funny Face

CONTENTS

VOGUE HOUSE, 1958
1–2 Hanover Square, London

Sixth Floor
London's largest photo studio
(With roof garden for outside photography)

Fifth Floor
Offices for *Vogue*, *Vogue* Commonwealth,
Brides and the *Pattern Book*

Fourth Floor
Reception, Accounts, Directors' Offices, *House & Garden*

First, Second and Third Floors and Basement
'To Let'
G-Plan furniture occupy part of the ground floor

2 high-speed passenger lifts

1 slow goods lift

'Supacoust' noise reduction ceiling slabs, 'Vyanide' block board
partitions, polished mahogany doors, (pearwood for directors), all
white painted interiors, heating by radiant electric ceiling panels

Vacant possession: June 1958

Architects: Yates, Cook & Darbyshire
Design Consultants: James Cubitt & Partners

The Magazines
Brides (and Setting Up Home)
GQ
House & Garden
Tatler
Traveller
Vogue
World of Interiors

The Editors
Vogue
Audrey Withers, Editor-in-Chief 1940–59
Ailsa Garland, Editor-in-Chief 1959–64
Beatrix Miller, Editor-in-Chief 1964–84
Anna Wintour, Editor-in-Chief 1985–87
Liz Tilberis, Editor-in-Chief 1988 –92
Alexandra Shulman, Editor-in-Chief 1992–2017
Edward Enninful, Editor-in-Chief 2017–24

Tatler
Tina Brown, Editor 1982–83
Libby Purves, Editor 1983
Mark Boxer, Editor 1983–88
Emma Soames, Editor 1988–90
Jane Procter, Editor 1990–99
Geordie Greig, Editor 1999–2009
Catherine Ostler, Editor 2009–11
Kate Reardon, Editor 2011–17
Richard Dennen, Editor 2018–present

GQ
Paul Keers, Editor 1988–89
Alexandra Shulman, Editor 1990–92
Michael VerMeulen, Editor 1992–95
Angus MacKinnon, Editor 1995–97
James Brown, Editor 1997–99
Tom Haines, Editor 1999

Dylan Jones, Editor 1999–2021
Adam Baidawi, Editor 2021–present

House & Garden
Robert Harling, Editor 1957–93
Sue Crewe, Editor 1993–2014
Hatta Byng, Editor 2014–present

World of Interiors
Min Hogg, Editor 1981–2000
Rupert Thomas, Editor 2000–21
Hamish Bowles, Editor 2021–present

Brides (and Setting Up Home)
Deborah Packe, Editor 1960s
Jean Toogood, Editor 1960s–1970s
Drusilla Beyfus, Editor 1970s–1983
Sandy Boler, Editor 1983–2002
Liz Savage, Editor 2002–19

Condé Nast Traveller
Sarah Miller, Editor-in Chief 1997–2010
Melinda Stevens, Editor-in Chief 2010–21

VOGUE HOUSE

Introduction

T his isn't the story of a building. A building is a static memorial to an architect and its builder and in the case of Vogue House it is a memorial that looks no different today than it did when it was first built in 1957. This is a story about people: people who connected with a building, who worked in it, passed through it and who brought an energy and a purpose to it. The people for whom Vogue House was the stage for their lives, their personal memories and experiences. I was one of those people.

For nine years I worked on *Tatler*. I designed the magazine, wrote headlines, commissioned photographers and illustrators, art directed photographic shoots, created concepts and led the art department. I worked closely with the editor, the writers and section editors, the fashion department, the beauty team, the contributors, the production department, the advertising sales team and the sub-editors. I had previously worked at UK *Elle* magazine in its earliest days during the 1980s with outstandingly talented people but working within Vogue House was different. It had a history, and I was aware of that history before I'd ever set foot in the revolving door that took you into the high-ceilinged ground floor lobby. Working in Vogue House placed you into that history; you became part of its unfolding story, which featured characters and personalities who had each placed their mark on the titles produced under its roof.

I first stepped into Vogue House in 1991. I can't recall which month it was, but it was warm and sunny. In those days the reception was not in the main foyer but on one of the floors above and therefore part of the inner sanctum. A visitor like me had two choices to reach it. You could go via the central, wide, solid white stone staircase, reminiscent of ascending to the balcony of a 1930s Odeon cinema, or you could choose one of the two copper-doored original 1950s lifts, designed for a human fed on a diet of post-war rationing. I chose the stairs. These led to a dark, windowless, wood-panelled corridor that reminded me of a gentleman's club or a rather faded country hotel. Two men – the 'Peters' – in dark blue uniforms and white shirts sat behind a desk, further confirming the feeling of a private club. I took a seat on one of the chairs that ran along the corridor and waited to be interviewed by the editor of *Tatler*. The rest, as they say, is history.

My time on *Tatler* is often described by those who were there as the 'Diana Days'. I have also heard them described as the 'Golden Days' of the magazine, and I can understand why. The 1990s in Vogue House were a wild and wonderful ride – controversial, high-energy and high-impact. The building was filled with an incredible collection of talented people, many of whom just beginning their careers, others well established and intimidating, and some who were coming to the end of their relationship with publishing and magazines. It was a melting pot of experience and ambition. I left *Tatler,* full-time art directing and the building at the end of the last century and in some ways that seemed appropriate. A decade and an era were over for me. Now it is time to turn off the lights for the building itself. All things must come to an end, even in Vogue House.

If you ever find yourself walking between Regent Street and Bond Street (heading south from Oxford Street or north from Piccadilly), you may find yourself crossing Hanover Square. Six streets converge there and many people pass through it, or take refuge in its central garden to escape the bustle of the city surroundings. It remains somewhat of a secret oasis ringed by the splendour of its remaining Georgian buildings.

The development of the land that would become Hanover Square began shortly after the accession of the Elector of Hanover as King George I in 1714 on land owned by Richard Lumley, 1st Earl of

Scarbrough, who sold numerous plots to prospectors to build upmarket townhouses and villas. The kind of homes that would in the future no doubt appeal to Condé Nast readers and feature in the pages of *House & Garden* or *World of Interiors*. In honour of the coronation of the new English king, the area was named Hanover Square. Initially it was home to numerous generals, then noted surgeons, various members of the aristocracy and, in the 1880s, the Royal Agricultural Society. In the central gardens a statue of William Pitt the Younger, the youngest prime minister of Great Britain, was erected and remains in place to this day. Hanover Square was firmly settled by the establishment and the politically conservative. It showed no signs of becoming the home of a building that would one day house the creative energy and eclectic talent that would help shape the country's cultural conversations for sixty years.

There are few buildings in London that have been so important to the national cultural conversation as Vogue House. The old BBC Television Centre in Shepherd's Bush is certainly one, as is Broadcasting House at the top of Regent Street: places where entertainment, knowledge, debate, news and learning were and are devised, created and disseminated. These buildings are embedded into the national consciousness, through their on-air output, as solid bastions of creativity and quality. The Condé Nast HQ is perhaps less well known than its broadcasting counterparts, but arguably no less important.

Vogue House is an imposing modernist building owned by the Church of England that occupies the south-east corner of Hanover Square. Begun in 1957 by Yates, Cook & Darbyshire architects, with the design consultants James Cubitt & Partners onboard, it was completed in 1958. The architects practice had been very active in the 1920s and designed several of the buildings in nearby Regent Street. They also specialised in building racecourse grandstands and were architects for the modernist Odhams Press building in Watford, as well as designing numerous cinemas in the 1930s. In 1952 they moved into an office at 43, Great Marlborough Street, no more than a five-minute walk from their new Hanover Square development. Their architectural background is clear to see in the typography and fascia stonework of Vogue House today, however its original entrance was even more modernist in aesthetic than anything they had designed before, based on clean lines, geometric forms, a grid-based lighting system and the symmetry of two lifts, further emphasized by strong vertical rectangles built into the floor. In its original design it was also missing the now iconic revolving door, which was not installed until the 1980s.

In 1959 Samuel I. Newhouse, known as 'Si', bought the established publishing company Condé Nast for US $5 million as an anniversary gift for his wife Mitzi, who loved *Vogue*. Legend has it that his wife had said to him that morning, "Darling, don't forget to buy me *Vogue* today" and that Newhouse had misunderstood, acquiring the company when she'd just wanted the latest issue of her favourite magazine. This could of course be an apocryphal tale; if so, it would not be the last to be attached to Vogue House. Newhouse may indeed have purchased the company on a whim, as it was to become apparent over the following decades that impulsive decision-making was his signature move; he would go on to earn himself a reputation for brutal and seemingly random dismissals of staff in the US offices. In London, three hundred members of staff moved from Soho's Golden Square into the newly opened building in Hanover Square in 1958. The publisher and its magazines came together in Vogue House, in the building they would inhabit for the following six decades.

The editor of British *Vogue* in 1959 was Audrey Withers, an English journalist and former sub-editor on the magazine, who had taken over the position from the American fashion journalist Betty Penrose in 1940, just after the outbreak of the Second World War. Withers had taken the magazine in a literary direction, whilst also creating an iteration of *Vogue* that recognised women as consumers in their own right, including larger women and those on tight budgets. During the war Withers' *Vogue* also took part in reporting the conflict, commissioning photographers such as Lee Miller and Cecil Beaton to document the reality of wartime Britain, Europe and North Africa. She promoted advanced political and social causes and, alongside its traditional coverage of beauty and fashion, *Vogue* developed a highbrow streak, publishing articles by writers, poets and thinkers including Simone de Beauvoir, Bertrand Russell, Dylan Thomas and Kingsley Amis. British photographers contributing to the magazine included Norman Parkinson and Antony Armstrong-Jones (Lord Snowdon), as well as the American Irving Penn. Despite being a favourite magazine of the ruling classes, Withers' personal style was frugal, preferring sandwiches to expensive restaurants and buses to taxis. Surprisingly for the editor of a fashion magazine, Withers lacked any interest in fashion apart from hats, delegating coverage to others on her staff. However, she knew the importance of good writing and fought hard with *House & Garden* to get Elizabeth David, who wrote for them, to also write on food for *Vogue*.

This sense of internal rivalry between titles would continue to exist within Vogue House throughout the coming decades. Photographers who worked for *Vogue* rarely worked for *Tatler* and vice versa; a similar situation existed between *House & Garden* and *World of Interiors*. The same was true of writers and contributors as each magazine fought hard despite small budgets to get and keep the best talent to themselves.

You will see as you read through this book that there are themes that connect all of the magazines that existed within Vogue House. Tight budgets, a sense of entitlement and restrictive practices are three of these, but another is a distinctly non-politically correct approach to office behaviour. I have not mentioned here every event and situation I've been told of but suffice to say Vogue House definitely had its fair share of employees who pushed the boundaries of acceptable work practices. We may expect to hear of such stories from the 1960s, 70s, 80s and 90s, and I have recounted some of these, but the 1950s were no different, as Withers herself recalled in the biography *Dressed for War* by Julie Summers. She did not get involved in office gossip but was well aware of the finance director with a perchance for young office girls who was once found having sex with one of them under his desk.

Audrey Withers had taken *Vogue* through wartime and the post-war years, but her tenure in Vogue House was limited, as her editorship of the magazine was taken over in the summer of 1959 by Ailsa Garland, previously the fashion editor at the *Daily Mirror*. The following decades would see Vogue led by a series of editors whose passions and priorities saw the title reflect the changing worlds of fashion, style, literature alongside the editor's personal interests.

1959 not only saw *House & Garden* magazine find a new home at Vogue House, but also gain a new lease of life under its editor Robert Harling, who had been appointed the previous year. Iva 'Pat' Patcevitch, the Head of Condé Nast, had followed a recommendation from Ian Fleming, the novelist and creator of James Bond, and Harling's close friend and wartime colleague. Harling revitalised *House & Garden* and produced a magazine which contrasted the traditional and the contemporary, whilst establishing in 1959 a series of books, starting with *House & Garden Interiors and Colour*. However, Harling was also a man of mystery who wore many hats, not only the fedora he was best known for. As well as a magazine editor, he worked as a typographer, advertising executive, sailor, commando, novelist and architectural critic. Obscuring his lower-class origins, Harling had invented himself as a man of action and letters; Fleming commemorated his friend twice in his James Bond novels, once as the Bahamas police commissioner in *Thunderball* and secondly as the *Chelsea Clarion*'s typesetter in *The Spy Who Loved Me*. During the Second World War, Harling had served in the Inter-Services Topographical Department, producing 'pocket target guides' for the commandos, scriptwriting radio broadcasts for the secret 'black propaganda unit' at Bletchley Park and, after the D-Day landings, operating in the field, rounding up Nazi scientists and disarming the German navy in Norway, among other exploits.

Meanwhile, *Brides* magazine was the quiet sister of the trio. Conservative with a small 'c', traditional whilst aware of contemporary fashions, this was the bible for all aspiring brides and the younger female readers of *Vogue*. The staffing of all of the magazines in the building, but *Brides* in particular, was seen by some as a finishing school for young ladies leaving boarding school and was overseen at one point by the enigmatic Miss Barbara Timms, a Vogue House fixture for many years in her smart suits, gloves and pearls, whose background as a Bletchley Park code breaker and Special Operations Executive agent during the Second World War was always rumoured but only confirmed after her death.

During the 1960s and 70s the top floor of Vogue House was dedicated to the Vogue Studios, where an in-house team supported the photographers working for all three titles, producing editorial and advertising images with dedicated photography assistants and darkrooms for processing, printing and retouching photographs. At the other end of the building the basement was home to the monthly growing library of back issues and archives of images commissioned by and featured in the magazines. Photographers such as David Bailey, Brian Duffy, Helmut Newton, Cecil Beaton, Clive Arrowsmith, John Swannell, Peter Knapp, Barry Lategan and Terence Donovan all regularly used the Vogue Studios, creating images that defined the global image of London in the 'Swinging Sixties' and 'Glam Seventies'.

It was not until the 1980s that this original trio of titles was expanded, with the purchase by Condé Nast of *Tatler* and *World of Interiors* magazines and the launch of the established American titles *GQ* and *Condé Nast Traveller* in the UK. The new teams were all based in Vogue House, ensuring that every floor of the building was filled by magazine publishing. The 1980s and 90s were the golden days of the industry, when advertising revenue was at its strongest, circulations at their highest and the voice of the magazines at their most strident. This was a period when Vogue House was full of writers, photographers, designers, editors, stylists and interns who would go on to become household names writing books, presenting television programmes, hosting radio shows and influencing fashion for the coming decades. Members of royalty would regularly drop by the building for fashion advice, celebrities hung out with members of staff and a sense of anarchy was in the air.

As the new century began, the world of magazine publishing took a different trajectory as it was faced with a multitude of challenges outside of its control. By the early 2000s the internet was revolutionising media: from the 'dot com' boom and bust cycle, the arrival of digital photography, fast broadband, to multiple social media platforms, influencers, bloggers and website publishing, traditional magazine publishing was under threat. Sales of magazines began a downward trend that has not stopped, whilst advertising revenue reduced considerably. Titles closed, and staffing teams were reduced in number as their salaries were restricted and budgets constricted. Freelance budgets to commission photographers and writers stagnated and a risk averse environment became evident to anyone involved with publishing in previous decades. The decisions the industry made were often reactionary and seldom successful, despite initial excitement and considerable investment in the latest proffered solution. Magazines started to be referred to as brands to be franchised, and photographs and writing seen as 'content' to be syndicated across the internationally franchised titles. In short, magazine publishing is not what it was and there is no reason to believe that it will ever again regain the creative and commercial heights it once achieved. The fact that in 2023 Vogue House will no longer house its magazines provides physical evidence of that statement.

I am aware that many people have preconceived beliefs about working at Vogue House, and for Condé Nast. Some are well founded, but others are not. The building itself had a rarefied atmosphere and scruffy furniture, and to me it always seemed like a slightly dysfunctional public school, particularly when lining up at 'the hatch' for toast and tea in the mornings. Vogue House was the first place that I came across peanut butter and Marmite on toast! Sons and daughters of the rich, the famous and the well-connected did get jobs there on the basis of conversations over dinner or at drinks parties, and on the basis of what school they attended – they were and are the 'Condé Nostra' without the protection racketeering, criminality and arbitration of disputes with violent outcomes of the Sicilian organisation. But nepotism was not the whole story – it was also a building filled with highly ambitious and talented people, willing to take risks and promote creativity, to challenge the status quo and give a platform to the avant-garde and eclectic. The magazines housed in the building were universally created on the basis of beliefs rather than market research. Mediocrity was not an option.

But that was then, and this is now. In 2024, after sixty years, Condé Nast have left Vogue House, and the Church of England have had to find a new tenant. Could it be demolished or become a theme-led hotel?

Anything is possible. Vogue has left the building that bore its name, but the memories and stories that the walls, ceilings and floors once contained remain with the people who experienced them. Vogue House was never just an office block, it was the stone and brick symbol of quality publishing in the UK. Everyone in publishing knew its name.

Walking across Hanover Square, you couldn't help but look up at its windows and wonder who was in there and what they were up to. To many it was the centre of fashion, glamour, taste and beauty, a place to aspire to work. To others it was a temple to luxury commercialisation, a symbol of privilege and wealth, a monument to nepotism, and to be avoided at all costs. All I can say is that I was employed based on my work, not my family, friends or school, a South London boy who found a desk in the West End with a view of a world I knew nothing about. Vogue House had room for me, and I am honoured to have spent nine years working there. It was never easy, always challenging, demanding and occasionally impossible, but I was always aware that the people I was meeting and the experiences I was having would be some of the most informative in my life.

This book tells the story of Vogue House and the people who trod its floorboards in their own words, and also charts the history of magazine publishing in the UK over a period of technological innovation and social economic change. Condé Nast leaving Vogue House signals an end to an age of publishing that will never return and serves as a metaphor for the industry's decline. So, pull up a chair, sit back and relive the nostalgia, memories and tales of a lost time, entertainingly told by the people who made magazines that defined six decades of popular culture, fashion and lifestyle.

Grant Scott, 2023

Chapter 1: 1960–1970
This is Not an Appropriate
Venue for Introductions

Although Condé Nast moved into Vogue House in 1958, I am going to start my story in 1960. The belief that any cultural decade begins and ends with the stroke of twelve on the final day of the previous year is as inaccurate as it is to believe that cultural change is always the result of one person, group or event. Despite this, it is more convenient to look back and group, label and contain cultural change within ten-year segments. Please accept my apologies, as I am about to do the same, at least chronologically – well, sort of. There are a number of reasons for picking 1960 as a jumping-off point.

As I have previously mentioned, Audrey Withers ended her twenty-year engagement as editor of *Vogue* in the summer of 1959. That feels relevant to me. Withers had led the magazine through the Second World War and a post-war Britain of rationing and make-do-and-mend. Twenty years is a long time for any editor to devote the energies required to produce a magazine every month from blank pages to printed product, let alone through a period of such social and economic challenges. During her tenure she had championed important causes and introduced writers of weight and standing to the magazine, but also, according to her biographer Julie Summers, allegedly destroyed the entire *Vogue* archive in February 1942 in an act of fervent patriotism, urged on by photographer Cecil Beaton, as a response to a government call for paper salvage to help the war effort. In her book, *Dressed for War: The Story of Audrey Withers*, Summers also reveals that Withers had a passion for foreign travel and wild swimming, wrote poetry and often attended concerts and the theatre. Despite this lust for life, two decades on a magazine means approximately two hundred issues, and that can drain the most creative and energetic mind. Speak to anyone who has worked on a magazine and the sense of repetition is a constantly given reason for stepping out of the monthly grind.

Moving into a new building would also have felt like new beginnings, and the dawn of a new decade just two years after the magazines moved from Bond Street and Golden Square may well have given the Condé Nast management a desire to reposition *Vogue* as a more commercial product with a broader appeal, less exclusive and more inclusive. Withers had been suffering from extreme back pain for some time. She had placed a sofa in her office to work from whilst lying down and had even taken the therapeutic waters at a European 'healing spa' to relieve the pain. Eventually she accepted that she had to retire but, not willing to completely let go, she wanted to help find the right person to succeed her. It was a process that would take a whole eighteen months. Having first asked Pat Cunningham, *Vogue*'s fashion editor, who turned the offer down, the Condé Nast management approached several others in the fashion world before turning to Ailsa Garland, the fashion editor of the *Daily Mirror*. It was an appointment that would be short-lived. The general consensus seems to have been that Garland was a square peg in a round hole. Withers stayed on for a year after her official retirement, to guide Garland in her new role, but as is so often the case in publishing there was little love lost between the departing and arriving editors. Withers commented on Garland that "She never in a whole year asked me a single question. I think so often people's behaviour indicates insecurity."

When Garland joined *Vogue*, the *Spectator* magazine reported that she had left the *Mirror* in order to join *Vogue* as part of a greater change of the magazine's focus away from luxury and exclusivity. Garland had wanted a challenge and accepted a pay cut with her new role. Harry Yoxall, Condé Nast UK managing director, wrote rather ominously in his diary in August 1959, "Ailsa Garland, for better or worse, has accepted our offer of the editorship, to join us early next year."

Harry Yoxall had been in charge of British *Vogue* since 1924 and was coming to the end of his time with the magazine and the company. Educated at St Paul's School, London he had won a scholarship to Balliol College, Oxford, but in 1915 joined the army in the 18th Battalion King's Royal Rifle Corps (41st Division) and fought on the Western Front. Yoxall was awarded the Military Cross, endured many near misses and was finally posted to the United States. Returning to England, he took up the offer to attend Balliol, but the war had dulled his passion for learning and, needing to support his wife and family in 1921, he joined Condé Nast Publications in the promotions department. Three years later, Condé Nast, the man not the company, cabled from London, where he had been inspecting British *Vogue*. Nast was not happy with what he found and demanded that Yoxall take charge. In 1934, he was appointed managing director of Condé Nast Publications and from 1957 to 1964, the Vogue House years, Yoxall held the position of chairman.

Despite such an extended period working so close to the fashion industry, Yoxall stated in his memoir *A Fashion of Life* that "I liked, of course, pretty clothes for women (who doesn't?)... But the semi-annual change in fashion, or quarterly change, as it used to be, never gripped my imagination as it does that of some people." Instead, Yoxall's passion was for the mechanics of printing: "Paper, print, engraving, I loved them all ... The scent of printer's ink has always been my favourite perfume." It is strange to consider that someone who had fought gallantly in the First World War was leading Vogue House and its magazines into the permissive, swinging Sixties, but that was the case. Yoxall's focus was on the commercial success of the magazine and his appointment of Garland was intended to bolster this.

I have never met a publisher who has openly encouraged an editor to make a magazine more high-brow and potentially more exclusive, as this usually inevitably means less commercially viable. A magazine's success can be seen from two perspectives, financial revenue or critical acclaim. The two coming together is a rare event. The former, based on sales and subsequent advertising revenue, is desired by the owners and the latter by the editorial staff. However, every editor knows that editorial freedom – and thus the opportunity for critical acclaim – is more achievable if profit is high.

Like Yoxall, Ailsa Garland was also a magazine veteran by the time she took control of *Vogue*. From 1947 to 1950 she had worked as the fashion editor for the *Vogue Book of British Exports*, then from 1952 to 1953 she was editor of the mass-market *Shopping* magazine. In 1953 she became fashion editor for the *Daily Mirror* before joining *Vogue* in the August of 1959.

London in the period from 1960 to 1964 was building the foundations of what was to become 'Swinging London' later in the decade, as photographers, actors, writers, artists, comedians, musicians, models, filmmakers, playwrights and fashion designers from working-class backgrounds began to make their voices known. As Peter Laurie wrote in *Vogue* in 1964, "London is a city of and for the young." This 'New Aristocracy' was not defined by the clipped received-pronunciation accents of the traditional aristocracy, but by voices from industrial towns and cities across the country. It is easy to see Garland connect these new young bucks with her upbringing in Clapham, South London and experience of Fleet Street. One of these was acclaimed photographer David Bailey, and in her autobiography *Lion's Share*, published in 1970, Garland said of him, "Many superb photographers and artists contributed to the magazine under my editorship, but David started at the bottom and rapidly climbed, making a real contribution to the 'look' of the sixties." He unfortunately did not feel the same way about Garland: in his own autobiography *Look Again*, Bailey described her as "an awful woman, who just thought I was an East End yob."

Garland's time in Vogue House was relatively short. She was unhappy with the open plan nature of the offices and her glass-panelled office with walls that did not quite reach the ceiling, denying her privacy. Eventually she was moved at her request into the only room on the floor with traditional walls and a solid door. The loud jazz regularly played by the art editor Max Maxwell may also have been a distraction. She also felt constrained by the restrictive budgets the magazines had to conform to. Despite being a magazine that promoted a life of luxury consumerism and glamour, with many of the female staff wearing white gloves even in the office, those working in Vogue House were expected to work within very tight financial constraints. The budgets were overseen by the legendary Lillie Davies (addressed as the more formal 'Miss Davies'), who held the title of Editorial Business Controller. Each magazine had someone whose role it was to keep a close eye on editorial spending, but Miss Davies was a true legend.

"When the Six Day War broke out in June 1967 between Israel and the surrounding Arab countries, Lillie Davies, the formidable office manager, and an honoured member of AJEX (the Association of Jewish Ex-Servicemen and Women) was deeply anxious. I had spent time in my student days hitchhiking around the Middle East and felt passionately for the Palestinian cause. Without the internet, it was to her radio we had to turn for information. Each lunchtime we met in her office to bend over the portable radio as the news came over. It wasn't that we put aside our differences. We were there in pursuit of them. What we did have was shared concern. When the war abruptly ended with the total Israeli victory, the relief for Miss Davies (we never called her by her first name) was palpable. For me, I was distraught at the thought of the consequences for the Palestinians. Neither of us made any comment. *Vogue* was family and we had each other's interests at heart."
Adrian Hamilton
Vogue

"We came and went under the careful watch of Lillie Davies, the only one left of those who had come to Vogue House in 1958 from Golden Square as the secretary and assistant of then editor, Audrey Withers. Now she was in charge of expenses, travel, even film and processing costs. Her rules were clear. If you

could, you walked. If not, bus routes were produced no matter where you were travelling or the Underground was suggested."
Sandy Boler
Vogue, Brides

"The actress Vanessa Redgrave rang the office to find out where the person was that was meant to be interviewing her. I didn't know how to get to her house, so I took the train and walked because Lillie Davies didn't want to give me money for a taxi. So, I arrived half an hour late."
Polly Devlin
Vogue

"My helicopter bill was to haunt me for the rest of my days at British *Vogue*. I don't think Lillie Davies in accounts ever got over it."
Sarajane Hoare
Vogue

"I think it (Lillie Davies') was the only office where no one was smoking, laughing, discussing, or running through ideas from fashion to literature."
Lucinda Chambers
Vogue

"It was run like the civil service in those days. You had to fill out all these little forms, endless forms to get your expenses through Miss Davies."
Isabella Kullman
Vogue

"I used to get my prints retouched by the *Vogue* retouchers before I sent them in for the magazine to see. I liked Miss Davies, but she was really on the ball when it came to money, and you couldn't overspend so when she got the bill for my retouching,

she wouldn't pay for it and told me to pay out of my own pocket. So, despite my arguments with her I never made any money working for *Vogue*."
John Swannell
Vogue, Tatler, Brides

The interior of the building also belied the glamorous image of the titles that came from it. As model, fashion editor and future US *Vogue* creative director Grace Coddington commented in her autobiography *Grace: A Memoir*:

"The upstairs was a muddle of messy open plan rooms. The furniture looked like it had been dragged from a skip, the floor was done in cork, tired and stained... I chose a wooden floor in pale wood, which nobody else was doing back then. Very narrow, very blonde boards so it looked almost cream... I chose some desks – glass held in a steel rim – and wicker and steel chairs."

This change to the *Vogue* offices was Coddington's first action when becoming fashion director in 1985. According to Coddington, her husband restauranteur Michael Chow thought that there should be a strict rule that no one was allowed to attach more than one photograph of a child, boyfriend or animal to a pinboard. This dictate was commented on by *Vogue* fashion editor (and future editor) Liz Tilberis in her own autobiography: "The fashion department ... consisted of red wooden desks ... and a bulletin board over each desk. The rule was: only one boyfriend picture allowed per board." A corner of the office was partitioned off with plate-glass walls and became Coddington's office, a space that Tilberis says later became known as 'the fishbowl'.

Each decade in Vogue House an icon of the fashion or publishing world emerged, someone who transcended the magazines they worked for, becoming synonymous with styling or journalism. Fashion editor Grace Coddington, or 'Amazing Grace' as she was known, was certainly one of those icons.

"Vogue House was conveniently placed on a corner, half of it looking down on the square below, reminiscent of Impressionist pictures of gardens in Paris, only greyer. It always seemed an oasis of calm until Grace Coddington, then a model with fierce red hair, wearing green tights and the shortest of shorts, appeared carrying a pole and bag on her shoulder, for all the world like Dick Whittington. There was a loud bang of colliding metal as a passing taxi veered into a lamp post."

Adrian Hamilton

Vogue

Coddington was born on the Welsh island of Anglesey to hotelier parents, and her passion for fashion began in her teens, when she would anxiously await the arrival of the next issue of *Vogue*, which would be at least three months out of date by the time it reached her. In 1959, when Coddington was aged eighteen, someone she knew entered photographs of her without her knowledge to a *Vogue* model competition. She won the 'Young Model' category, which resulted in her being photographed by the legendary photographer Norman Parkinson (who later in life became a nationwide household name thanks to his range of sausages named the Porkinson's Banger). The images featured in the October 1959 issue and by 1962 Coddington was on the cover of *Vogue*. However, in 1966, at the age of twenty-six, she was involved in a car accident. It left her with severe head injuries and her eyelid had to be removed, which was later reconstructed through plastic surgery. Despite this she was soon back in Vogue House as a fashion editor working on the magazine, as she later recalled.

"Over lunch with Miss Miller, then editor, it all snowballed, and I went to work at *Vogue* as a junior fashion editor in 1968... my starting salary was £1,100 a year, which was insanely low even then... most of the other girls had private means, because you couldn't live off it. They had to give you luncheon vouchers... the equivalent to approximately £5 today, which at first, I turned my nose up at, but they turned out to be completely essential."

Coddington stayed at British *Vogue* for nineteen years and was responsible for some of the most iconic fashion images of the 1960s, 70s and 80s, casting and occasionally modelling herself in images created by David Bailey, Norman Parkinson, Helmut Newton, Irving Penn and Willy Christie (whom she briefly married), amongst others including the demanding, controversial French genius Guy Bourdin. In 1988 she transferred to US *Vogue* to work with Anna Wintour. It was not until 2016 that Coddington announced that she would finally be leaving *Vogue* to work on other projects.

In her book *Writing Home*, Irish writer and journalist Polly Devlin, who wrote for *Vogue* for many years and who became features editor within six months of her arrival, remembers when she first began working in Vogue House in 1963 for £10 a week: "All the girls in the fashion department know each other, and other girls who work here or at Sotheby's, or at an interior decorator called Colefax & Fowler, and they meet at lunch and talk the same talk. I've also worked out they are rich, though they would rather die than let on." I can confirm from personal experience that little had changed by the 1990s, but Devlin and Coddington's arrival within the building proved the point that it was possible to enter the 'Vogue House Bubble' even if you had not been born close to a silver spoon. However, it was certainly easier if you had been. Future Vogue editor-in-Chief Liz Tilberis was succinct in her autobiography *No Time To Die* with her observations of her fellow *Vogue* employees when she first joined in the 1960s: "The editorial offices were liberally populated with the daughters of the aristocracy and the socially connected rich: young women with double-barrelled surnames, dating young men whom I associated with streets and counties in Britain – Wilton's and Somerset's and Grosvenor's." Tilberis also shared a commonly repeated joke that may or may not be true, "There was a joke about an assistant who announced one day, 'I have to get a real job. Daddy can't afford to send me to *Vogue* anymore.'"

"The day I started I finally found out where my office was and went down to the third floor. It was a big room and as I walked in a tall girl said, "Are you Geoffrey?" and I said, "Yes!" She said,

"My name's Penny and I think I'm your secretary, what do you want me to do?" I said, "Well, the room's empty. We had better order some furniture." She was the daughter of Lady Penelope Plowden, who was very well known in those days, and in no time, I was sharing the office with Pamela Colin, who married Lord Harlech. Many girls then joined *Vogue* to marry a Lord. Pamela got Harlech!"

Geoffrey Aquilina Ross
Vogue

I always wanted to be part of it – even when I was in Ireland, I read the gossip columns and knew all the names of the 'Chelsea Set'. I became a snob. My first revelation of what I had entered into was when I was reading *The Times* and my flatmate, the features editor Jennifer Wolfe, who was rather rich, but I didn't know that, said that she was buying a cottage in Wiltshire for £40,000, when I was earning £10 a week. I said to her "Jennifer, what do you mean? And she said "Well, I've got some money." I said, "How much?" and she said, "Polly, I can't tell you that!" So I said, "Why have you got money?" and she said, "Well, one of my relations is called DuPont!" I knew that was a name that meant something. But the biggest revelation was when my secretary, Susan Pugh, who had left to be replaced by the marvellous Wendy from Orpington, who was pure John Betjeman, was mentioned in *The Times* court circular, which I read. It said that Lady Susan Pugh had become Princess Margaret's Lady-in-Waiting. I had never known that she was Lady Susan."

Polly Devlin
Vogue

As I have intimated, a new editor was soon to take over at the magazine. After five years, Garland felt that the position was too exhausting for her, with its requirements to promote, protect and sell the brand alongside creating the magazine, in addition to the constant interference in editorial affairs by the managing director. I know of very few editors that will not have experienced managerial meddling in the editorial content, design and look of the magazine, with particular reference to the cover image and coverlines, often with little knowledge, experience or explanation for their decisions. It is part of the job that editors and art directors have to accept. However, after an explosive few weeks, including arguments with one of the fashion editors, Garland left in March 1964. Her replacement was Beatrix Miller, known fondly as 'Bea' or 'Queen Bea' and it was she who steered the magazine through the cultural explosion for which the rest of the decade is renowned.

"By the mid-sixties *Vogue* was in full swing. Everything was different, exciting, sometimes dangerous and always alive. It was the advent of a new generation, with Beatrix Miller who came from *Queen* to replace Ailsa Garland. The 60s danced on under this new inspirational editor, whose influence and inexhaustible drive for a different way of seeing things, writing wonderful irreverent captions and frequent 'Revolutions' when she changed everything in the next issue. Summoning people to her office she would turn sideways in her seat to look out of the window, open her powder compact and stare into its mirror. 'Speak' – and that was your chance."
Sandy Boler
Vogue, Brides

"We all received luncheon vouchers, and everyone would go out for lunch every day to use them. Bea Miller would always order the same lunch, because she knew it would be available and she wouldn't have to put her glasses on to read the menu. I think it was always scrambled eggs and smoked salmon."
Geoffrey Aquilina Ross
Vogue

"When Bea Miller came to *Vogue* in 1964, she began to turn the magazine around working against very old-fashioned bosses. I have a letter on a memo sheet from Reggie Williams, who used to run it all saying, 'Yesterday evening, leaving the office, I bumped into a young woman coming out of the lift who was extremely untidy not to say unwashed, she was going into your office, and I went back to find out who this person was. It turns out that she is called Jane Ormsby-Gore (the daughter of William David Ormsby-Gore, 5th Baron Harlech and the believed inspiration for the Rolling Stones song 'Lady Jane') and she's working for you and really, I think you ought to dress anyone coming into the office like that.'"

Polly Devlin

Vogue

After the Second World War, Miller worked with the government agency MI6 in Germany at the Nuremberg Trials, a period of her life that she rarely mentioned, but her journalistic career began at the society magazine *The Queen*. She swiftly started writing feature articles and was promoted to features editor, and in 1956 she moved to New York, where she began working as a copywriter at US *Vogue*. Her progression was impressive and demonstrated a dedication, determination and ambition that was clear throughout the rest of her career.

"Bea Miller was one of the most secretive people in a public position, she seemed to live for *Vogue*, and she cared about every headline, introduction and full stop."

Drusilla Beyfus

Vogue, Brides

"When you get to write about swing macs the second time, it's time to go, the sub-editor had told me. It had begun with a caption, facing that Pterodactyl typewriter, wondering how to say something witty about a beige mackintosh in twenty words. Miss Miller sent me back to my desk, hour after painstaking hour, until I got it right. She was old-school and a perfectionist when it came to editorial details. 'You have to imagine the reader standing there with the gin bottle and a Hoover,' she told me. 'You have a duty to tell her that there is more to life than that.'"

Charlotte du Cann

Vogue

In 1958, *The Queen* magazine had been bought by Eton-educated publisher Jocelyn Stevens, who invited Miller to return to the magazine as its editor. Stevens wanted the magazine to represent the younger side of the British Establishment, sometimes referred to as the 'Chelsea Set' so he dropped '*The*' from the title and it was reborn as *Queen,* a magazine at the epicentre of London's cultural scene. Mark Boxer was its art director (the talented Boxer was to become the launch art director of *The Sunday Times Magazine* before later moving to *Tatler)* and Antony 'Tony' Armstrong-Jones (Lord Snowdon), Princess Margaret's husband was its principal photographer.

The idea of the 'Chelsea Set' was fundamental to understanding the readership for all three magazines in Vogue House in the 1960s. The King's Road, Chelsea had become home to a new breed of fashion designer including Mary Quant, as well as a selection of clothes boutiques where the rock'n'roll stars, trendsetters and young aristocracy shopped. Fashionable restaurants, bistros and clubs were opening along its length from Sloane Square to World's End, whilst the faded grandeur of number 152, 'The Pheasantry', a building midway between both, became a cultural destination for designers, artists, writers, photographers, musicians and graphic designers.

"We were all divided into these cells in the office, you would see the fashion people go by who were friendly enough, but the only time they came in to see me was if they wanted a free new book, which they could have. It was all very friendly and all very nice. I often went to lunch with the other girls, but we had nothing in common, they were all going away for the weekend, and been to the same schools. I was always an outsider, but we were accepted although we didn't have the credentials, we were bohemians and that was very much part of the deal to keep the magazines alive."
Polly Devlin
Vogue

It is not surprising that Condé Nast wanted Miller to take over from Garland. She was editing *Queen*, the coolest established magazine in

London at the time for fashionable women with money, just as the magazine *Town,* under the art direction of Tom Wolsey and control of numerous editors, was appealing to the fashionable men of Carnaby Street and the King's Road. This was a period when the art directors were just as important as the editors in deciding how the magazines looked and whose photographs would appear in them. A magazine without photographs is a book, and the importance of photography to magazines cannot ever be underestimated.

Photographer and illustrator Eric Boman in an article for Vogue.com remembered entering Miller's office at *Vogue* as a young photographer and member of the art department. "The first thing you saw upon entering Beatrix Miller's office was Miss Miller sitting behind her desk in the corner opposite the door, her legs stretched out diagonally so her feet could rest on a high, pillowed side-drawer, a cigarette in her hand, and a smile on her face. As I turned to leave, I saw a banner taped to the wall opposite her desk, made of Xerox copies joined together and browned with age. It read "If we hurry, we'll be late!" – a reminder she had posted, not for her own benefit, but in the hope others would take its message to heart. It only came down when she retired."

Miller's hands-on, elegant but firm approach to commissioning photographers is clearly shown in a piece of archive American documentary film footage captured in the 1970s. In the film Miller is seen in her office in an understated white sleeveless dress and a string of pearls, with photographer Lord Patrick Lichfield. They are discussing a series of layouts featuring Lichfield's fashion images of the author Candida Lycett Green, and a potential fashion shoot to be undertaken the following week. Lichfield, wearing a bright pink denim jacket and dark round sunglasses, sips on a cup of tea whilst holding a cigarette, and as Miller lights her own cigarette plucked from a silver box, she leans back and asks for the pictures to be "poetic and happy, light and lyrical but not whimsical." It is not hard to imagine her driving to work each day in her large white Jaguar, which she called 'Arctic'. Miller's office is calm and orderly, with a standard typewriter, and a 35mm projector for viewing colour transparencies. An interesting cut-away in the clip shows Grace Coddington on the telephone complaining about her photographs being dropped from a story and not being told, a scene and a complaint that is repeatedly relived thirty years later by her in the 2009 film *The September Issue*, a similar behind-the-scenes-at-*Vogue* documentary film. Unfortunately, we do not discover who she was speaking to in the earlier documentary.

The 1960s saw a rapid growth in the interest in photography in the UK and a new school of photographers began to hang out with models, young actors and the rich and famous, becoming just as recognised as the people they were photographing. This increase in photography's presence was fuelled by the 1966 film *Blow-Up*, directed by the Italian filmmaker Michelangelo Antonioni, which premiered in London just two years after Miller, with her art director, John Parsons, took over *Vogue*.

"My Burmese cat was photographed flying high over a leaping Twiggy on a lively session with Helmut Newton. But it was the models who lit up Hanover Square, coming to be seen by the fashion editors and, if good enough, by the editor herself. Jean Shrimpton, Celia Hammond, Tania Mallet, Jill Kennington, the statuesque Veruschka, Twiggy, Penelope Tree, Pattie Boyd, Marie Helvin, Sandra Howard, Susan Murray, Paulene Stone, Grace Coddington and so many others."
Sandy Boler
Vogue, Brides

Antonioni's screenplay for *Blow-Up* revolves around the efforts of a young, successful fashion photographer and his struggle to determine if a series of snapshots he has taken in a public park contain evidence of a murder. The film accurately captures the spirit of the time if not the complete reality of working as a photographer, with the main character supposedly based on the lifestyle, behaviour and backgrounds of *Vogue* photographers such as David Bailey, John Cowans, Terence Donovan and Brian Duffy, with Don McCullin providing the stills that were used in the finished film. In a 2017 interview for *i-D* magazine, *Vogue* model Jill Kennington was clear as to the film's authenticity from her perspective at the time. "For a start, I never stood still like a dumb mannequin, as they do in the film.

The fact that we had to be very stupid was not a real representation. I also never saw any girls end up naked on a studio backdrop paper."

Some scenes in the film were shot at John Cowan's studio; the photographer was Jill Kennington's boyfriend at the time. The German model Veruschka was also in one of the film's most infamous scenes. Veruschka and the photographer, played by actor David Hemmings, engage in an increasingly erotic photographic session, writhing on the floor until reaching a point of cinematic climax only for Hemmings to walk off, leaving Veruschka exhausted and rejected having been used for the photographer's purposes. Such a dismissive and sexist attitude towards women and models in the Vogue Studios is alluded to by Bailey's muse and partner of the time, Jean Shrimpton, in her book *Jean Shrimpton: An Autobiography*. "One of (Terence) Donovan's games was to tickle the girls around the legs with a feather duster. It was all a touch suggestive... The sexist teasing and touching up that went on were enough to give a feminist the vapours... The lads were just having fun, though sometimes it was not much fun being on the end of it." Jill Kennington added her own reflections on Donovan in conversation with Phillipe Garner for the book *Jill Kennington: Model Years*: "I loved working with Terry, though I remember being a bit scared the first time. He and his assistant talked gobbledygook with lots of cockney slang thrown in for good measure; they had a code, so that they could talk about you in front of you."

"Tony Armstrong-Jones (Lord Snowdon) used to come in to see me and sit on my desk with his legs swinging but with his back to me and he would be flirting with the girls in the office, paying no attention to me. He used to come in and seduce the girls."
Geoffrey Aquilina Ross
Vogue

"My first photographic sitting was in one of the Vogue studios. Melanie Miller was the editor styling Jean Shrimpton in a wedding dress and the skirt wasn't full enough. Swift solution – she told me to lie on the floor under the dress, curl myself around Jean's legs and give the dress a shape. It was all about perfection, the

look. Only a few years later I was doing a shoot with Norman Parkinson on my favourite model, Pattie Boyd, then wife of George Harrison (and later Eric Clapton), in a tiny, ruffled night-suit. We looked in at Pattie in the tiny, messy dressing room, hair in massive curlers, long legs akimbo as she finished filing her nails. And photographed her there as she was."
Sandy Boler
Vogue, Brides

"I did hundreds of thousands of fashion shoots. In those days the models did all their own make-up. The thing about this model (Nicole de Lamargé), and by god she was bright, was how she built up her face. Underneath she was dead ordinary – once, I didn't recognise her in the dressing room!"
Brian Duffy
Vogue

"*Vogue* barely covered expenses. It's prestige and always has been. Their line is that it's enough just to be in there. I seem to remember *Vogue's* fee was £15. Photographers often worked for nothing."
Twiggy
Vogue

There were five contracted photographers working in the four Vogue Studios on the sixth floor (this was later increased to five when the tearoom was made into an additional studio, due to the number of stories needing to be photographed), and the building's flat roof was often used as another studio. The roof would sometimes also be used by female members of staff in their underwear as an impromptu sunbathing deck. Presumably this was an improvement on the previous Vogue Studios in Golden Square, which photographer Helmut Newton described in his autobiography as being "Depressing and dusty, with terrible old wooden floors." Newton continued: "I was told that under the grassy square were the bodies of people who had died during the black plague. It was indicative of my whole feeling for the place."

"The Vogue Studios were great, there was always somebody working in one of them. I remember Irving Penn there doing his flower pictures, he'd arrive in his suit and then get into his dungarees to take the photographs. There was Bailey, Parkinson, everybody was there and that created a fantastic atmosphere."
Willy Christie
Vogue

"I saw an ad for a storeroom assistant at Vogue Studios, and I applied so that I could be on the same floor as the photographers. I was sitting in the store room the very first day I saw Bailey. He walked past, and I dashed out to see him walking down the corridor. He was wearing a black polo-neck jumper, a Prince of Wales jacket, black corduroy trousers and Cuban heel boots with a Beatles haircut."
John Swannell
Vogue, Tatler, Brides

"I used to get up at eight o'clock, work in the studio from nine until seven at night, go out and have a bite, come back at nine, develop all the negatives of the day, contact them and go home at 1.30. That's how you learn how to do the job."
Terence Donovan
Vogue, Tatler, GQ

Christie is not the only one to remember the great American photographer Penn working within Vogue House. Coddington also remembered him photographing flowers and the use of the tea room as a studio in her autobiography. "I went up to the Vogue Studios... to hang about in hope of bumping into my hero... he hadn't been given a studio at all but a corner of the tearoom, where he set up his composition on a little table near the window."

"We rarely went out of the Vogue Studios, that only happened if the photographer had a car and then you would drive to

Richmond Park or Wimbledon Common, dependent on which you knew."
Geoffrey Aquillina Ross
Vogue

In addition to the sixth-floor studios, a 10"x 8" large format camera was housed in the basement to copy artwork for use on all of the magazines. This need for extra photographic space is not surprising, as not only were the studios used to photograph editorial stories for the magazines but also advertising campaigns for the brands that appeared in them and newspapers across London needing studio-based images. This sometimes created a conflict of interest: it was certainly the case that advertising work often took priority over images needed for the magazines within the building, presumably because this was additional income for Condé Nast.

"There was a board in Vogue Studios where each day the names of the photographers working that day were posted and the names of those who were to assist them were added. One day I saw that I was assigned to assist the great Cecil Beaton. I was incredibly nervous and went to the toilet. Whilst standing at the urinal Beaton came in and stood next to me. He started to relieve himself and I thought that I had better introduce myself. Without turning to look at him I said that my name was John Swannell and that I was his assistant for that day. Beaton completed his business and proclaimed, 'This is not the appropriate venue for introductions!' turned around and left the room."
John Swannell
Vogue, Tatler, Brides

When David Bailey was invited by the *Vogue* art director John Parsons to see him in 1960, in-house photographers were on two-year contracts and Bailey was offered a staff job for £25 a week. If he had been a contracted photographer, he would have been on £25 for each photograph published, so Bailey declined the offer. Three months later, Parsons cracked and offered him a contract – a story Bailey was still telling in the 1990s as a badge of honour to explain why he got paid more than other photographers. He wanted me to be aware of this the first time I commissioned him for *Tatler*. In his autobiography, Bailey commented on how his contract negotiations upset his friend and fellow photographer Brian Duffy: "John phoned me up and said, 'Alright, we'll give you a contract,' which annoyed Duffy because he'd already signed up as a staff photographer."

It was in the Vogue Studios that Bailey first saw and met the model who, with the help of *Vogue* and Bailey's eye, would define the new direction for fashion in the sixties. Jean Shrimpton was just eighteen and being photographed by Duffy for a Kellogg's cereal advertisement when Bailey stuck his head around the studio door. Bailey described the episode in some detail. "I first saw Jean Shrimpton around the door in Duffy's studio on the top floor of Vogue House... Duffy was using a sky-blue background and you could see the blue sky behind her eyes, as if you could see through her head. When I saw her, I just fell in love with her eyes... I said, "Who's that girl?" Duffy said, "Forget it Bailey, she's too posh for you."

It is impossible to talk about *Vogue* and Vogue House in the 1960s without talking about David Bailey. Many of his iconic images were created for the magazine at that time and remain in our cultural conscience today, but the truth is that those are only a tiny amount of the work he did for the magazine. I once sat in the basement library at Vogue House for a week and flicked, page by page, through every leather-bound issue of UK *Vogue* in chronological order. Page after page, photograph after photograph was credited to David Bailey. However, he was not the only outsider with a camera to bring a working-class sensibility to Vogue Studios in the 1960s. Alongside Bailey were Terence Donovan and Brian Duffy, a threesome described by Norman Parkinson as the 'Black Trinity', while Cecil Beaton, in his 1973 book *The Magic Image*, remembered them as the "terrible three". The straight-talking Duffy put it this way in the documentary *The Man Who Shot the Sixties* made about him by his son Chris: "Before 1960, a fashion photographer was tall, thin and camp, but we three are different: short, fat and heterosexual. We were great mates but also great competitors.

We were fairly chippy and if you wanted it, you could have it. We would not be told what to do."

Having known all three, I can confirm that each could be intimidating and challenging when it came to being commissioned. I did commission Bailey on a number of occasions, and have many stories from these times, all of which concern his ability to 'wrong foot' anyone he worked with and a desire, quite rightly in my opinion, to do his own thing. I spent considerable time with Donovan in his Mayfair studio talking about the state of commissioned photography in the 1990s, but was only able to commission him for *Tatler* once. Sadly, it was a session that did not go well for a number of reasons. Sometimes, fashion shoots fail when the clothes, model and photographer don't connect, and this was one of those situations. I never commissioned Duffy, as he had left photography before I began working on magazines, but I did once interview him, and the recording of that interview demonstrates exactly the same desire to challenge perceptions and knowledge that I experienced working with Bailey. Talking with all three began as a battle until they slowly accepted you, having decided that you were worth talking with. None of them would suffer fools gladly.

Duffy started out after leaving St Martin's School of Art, where he studied dress design because – as he stated in his 2011 book *Duffy: Photographer* – that was "where all the pretty girls were." In 1957, he took five or six of his photographs between two sheets of paper and walked into the Vogue Studios, before meeting with Audrey Withers who promptly hired him. After three months working for *Vogue*, Duffy was sent to photograph the German composer Otto Klemperer, who insisted on being photographed with a Leica camera due to its quiet mechanism. Duffy had never used or owned a Leica before and shot 36 exposures. After the shoot, Klemperer informed Duffy that he had left the lens cap on the entire time. Thinking he was going to be immediately fired, Duffy was called in see Miss Withers, who informed him that his film had been spoiled in the *Vogue* darkroom. The technicians in the Vogue Studios had kindly covered for him. Duffy held his position at *Vogue* under contract until 1962, then worked for fifteen further years for the magazine on a freelance basis. Commenting on his great friend in a 2010 *Sunday Telegraph* article after Duffy's death, David Bailey remembered that "If you said 'Good morning' to Duffy he'd question it, that was his charm, but I could do that Cockney thing with him of defusing it with humour. Cantankerous was a word made for Duffy, it was just his character. You always knew it was never going to be dull with him, because he was always going to pick an argument somewhere down the line."

The third photographer of the 'Black Trinity' was also a Londoner. Donovan was from the East End, like Bailey, and was the son of a lorry driver and a cook. A physically intimidating figure, Donovan sported tightly buttoned Savile Row suits and drove an open-top Bentley around London (as does the main character in *Blow Up*). A Zen Buddhist, black belt at judo and a technically flawless photographer, Donovan was a complex character who was just as at home making iconic images of men's fashion as he was photographing women. But, like Bailey and Duffy, his attitude towards women was very much of the time, jarring with our contemporary understanding of a healthy, professional and respectful relationship between the sexes. As Grace Coddington identified in a 2013 article in the *New York Times*, "He loved photography and cameras and everything to do with it ... So much that nothing stopped him, even getting married ... I walked into his studio and the first thing he told me is that he just got married that day. And I thought, 'What the hell are you doing here at work?'"

On the afternoon of 22nd November 1996, Donovan left a shoot for British *GQ*, leaving his Rolls Royce Silver Cloud parked on the street, and disappeared. Later that night he was found dead in his West London painting studio. The memorial service after his death in 1996, which was recorded as a suicide, was held in the church behind Vogue House. I attended it alongside many of the staff from Condé Nast, as did former Prime Minister Margaret Thatcher and Lady Diana, Princess of Wales, who sat next to each other on the front pew. There is a green commemorative plaque on the front wall of his former studio on Bourdon Street, Mayfair, where he worked between 1978 to 1996, which is just a five-minute walk from Vogue House, and a statue of Donovan outside it in his familiar suit, taking a photograph of Twiggy. Bailey said of Donovan,

"He was a photographer's photographer. All his work was so powerful I could not choose one outstanding image. It was all brilliant. He was an Orson Welles of photography, in every way, in stature, and in his presence."

Bailey continued to work for *Vogue*, *GQ* and occasionally for me at *Tatler* into his eighties, but it would be true to say that the work that he did in the 1960s alongside Beatrix Miller as editor-in-chief, established the tone of voice and visual identity for *Vogue* for the following decades. There are no shortage of stories about Bailey, but these two told by Polly Devlin are, I think, perfect portraits of his Jekyll and Hyde approach to making photographs. In the first, she recalls going up to the Vogue Studios one morning and finding Bailey with Mick Jagger, making the iconic portrait of the singer wearing a giant fur hood, just as Jean Shrimpton came into the studio and did a little dance. In the second, she witnessed the Austrian actor Oskar Werner stamp out of the studio claiming that Bailey was rude. A photographic shoot with David Bailey was always on his terms and to the soundtrack of loud music and his cackling laugh. Bailey's true character and predilections were also well understood by Miller. It is believed that, after a shoot with the American-born model Penelope Tree, the daughter of Ronald Tree, a wealthy Conservative MP and confidant of Winston Churchill, Miller informed Bailey that he was not to go near the young model sexually. A reasonable warning, as he was already married to the French actress Catherine Deneuve at the time. However, Deneuve like Miller was well aware of Bailey's waywardness, telling him when she saw the photographs that "You're going to run off with that girl." He did.

> "Photography was at the heart of the sixties revolution. Indeed, in many ways it was the heart. And *Vogue* had the best names. But it also had the young fashion editors who lived it. Most of journalism, newspaper or magazines is about reporting and making judgements about what you find. The journalist as observer. What made *Vogue* so central to it all in the sixties, and so invigorating to work for, was that you weren't just observing. You were part of the great explosion of ideas and change going on all around you."
> **Adrian Hamilton**
> **Vogue**

If you had the social confidence, like the three working-class photographers Bailey, Donovan and Duffy, it was possible to overcome the feeling of intimidation that Vogue House and its inhabitants exuded over the decades upon those outsiders who came to its doors. For someone from a working-class background in the 1960s that intimidation was deeply rooted in the British class system. In her book *Twiggy: In Black and White* North London girl Lesley 'Twiggy' Hornby recalled her first visit to the building, for a photoshoot with Guy Bourdin, which she vividly describes as "the holy of holies" where "'We work for *Vogue*. You don't,'" were the unspoken words. She describes feeling intimidated by everyone from the receptionist onwards, and feeling so humiliated when she discovered she was booked because of her shoe size – some shoes had been flown in from France and were too small for most English models – that she started to cry.

Jill Kennington shared her own experience meeting Bourdin in the Vogue Studios in a series of conversations with Phillipe Garner. "I first met him in London, in the dressing rooms of the Vogue Studios… There were mirrors in a line down one side of the room for us models, each with light bulbs right around and daylight windows at one end. In addition to a comfortable chair, the opposite wall was taken up with a line of clothes and a few light dressing gowns."

"Reception at Vogue House was originally on the fourth floor. There was no need for an appointment and the place was always busy. Messengers, clothes, deliveries that were directed to the *Vogue* fashion room with its precious clothes cupboard, endless bouquets and aspiring writers. Sometimes animals were brought in for 'extras' on a fashion shoot, even one day the RSPCA to check there was no cruelty or mistreatment involved."
Sandy Boler
Vogue, Brides

"I was assisting on a shoot for Smirnoff vodka with photographer Clive Arrowsmith in the Vogue Studios and we had a live black panther, which arrived in its cage with a handler. I can't remember if we also had a model. Clive and I built ourselves a barricade at one end of the studio in front of the camera, just in case the panther went crazy. The handler took it out of its cage, and it was all very docile until we took the first Polaroid. Then, the thing went absolutely berserk jumping up the wall and all over the background; even the handler didn't know what was going on. Clive and I bolted from the studio and down to the fashion room to tell everyone what had happened."

Willy Christie
Vogue

The fashion editors had the power and the belief that they should dictate how the models should look, but the new photographers emerging in the 1960s challenged these perceptions and began to take control of the style of photography, utilising new camera technology and embracing the anti-establishment thinking of the time. Often, however, there was a meeting of minds between the insiders and the newcomers, as Bailey identified in his autobiography when he speaks of being new to Vogue House and meeting the "very down to earth" fashion editor Shelia Wetton: "I was up a ladder doing the *Vogue* cover shot when she walked into the studio and said, 'What the f***k are you doing up that ladder?' I thought, 'Oh s**t, posh people swear!'

"They had two very senior fashion editors, one of whom was Shelia Wetton, and she was a hoot, she had the bluest language you've ever heard. She was very tall and thin and had been a house model for Norman Hartnell before the Second World War, but my god could she swear."

Geoffrey Aquilina Ross
Vogue

"Some people said that *Vogue* in those days was a bit like a cosy girl's boarding school, with Beatrix Miller as the headmistress, and then there were the teachers who had been there for years like Barbara Timms. Next was the head girl, Grace Coddington, as the

fashion director, and then all the prefects who were the younger fashion editors, such as Elizabeth Tilberis and Mandy Clapperton. Last but not least Lillie Davies, who ran the finances and checked every penny of our expenses relentlessly each month."
Tessa Traeger
Vogue

Of all of the fashion editors, Grace Coddington is the best remembered name from this time in the public's consciousness, perhaps partly due to her creative longevity with the magazine. However, the name that everyone mentioned when I spoke to them about *Vogue* in the 1960s was Marit Allen. Allen was born in 1941 in Cheshire, England to a Norwegian mother and an English father, and a was a pupil at an independent girls' boarding school in Shropshire before attending the University of Grenoble in France. Her fashion career began in 1961 when she took a job as a trainee at *Queen,* where she was promoted to editor and writer for the young fashion section of the magazine, which she used to showcase emerging design talent and innovative photography. When Beatrix Miller joined *Vogue*, she took Marit Allen with her. Allen swiftly established the 'Young Idea' pages, which continued to champion up-and-coming innovative young designers and occasionally she modelled in her own stories. Allen remained at *Vogue* until 1973 and then, encouraged by the film director Nicholas Roeg, moved into designing costumes for successful Hollywood films including *Mrs. Doubtfire, The Witches, Eyes Wide Shut, Brokeback Mountain* and *La Vie en Rose.* Her career as a film costume designer lasted over thirty-three years but she sadly died of a brain aneurysm in 2007.

"I was amazed by the wonderful fashion editors. Unity Barnes – tall, slim and very smart, a different hat and gloves, essential items, every day. Sheila Wetton – a former Molyneux model who only ever wore beige, occasionally grey and had been a well-known model in the Couture Collections when she was young. Melanie Miller, fresh from *Glamour* magazine in New York; and Lady Rendlesham who wore tiny, perilously high heels,

smoked Gauloises – the inspiration for the bright new art students and fashion students of those early years. I arrived with my Jean Seberg cropped hair, black suede flat boots, no hat and no gloves."
Sandy Boler
Vogue, Brides

Whilst some might point to the 90s, and its 'heroin chic' as the decade when models looked unhealthily thin, the fashion was not a new one. When David Bailey took Jean Shrimpton to New York in 1962, to photograph the iconic *Vogue* fashion story 'Young Ideas Goes West', Lady Clare Rendlesham was one of the main fashion editors on the title at the time. Rendlesham, described by Polly Devlin as being "so trim and groomed and clean-edged" had a reputation for not only being tough, but also for being furious if anyone around her put on any weight. Grace Coddington claimed that she had to hide her own pregnancy to avoid Rendlesham's anger. This attitude to how staff looked and what they weighed came to a head in the 1990s, when the HR department staged 'breakfasts' where platters of fruit and healthy food were laid out for selected members of staff as part of an initiative to encourage eating. It was a particularly ill-informed and clumsy approach to deal with the serious issues concerning body image that were beginning to be discussed, and which it could be argued that magazines such as *Vogue* were celebrating.

Perhaps unsurprisingly, given the attitudes to fashion and the body discussed, one aspect of *Vogue* that is rarely celebrated properly is the magazine's rich heritage of food writing. Under Audrey Withers' editorship this was a role filled by Elizabeth David, a British evangelist for seasonal food and Mediterranean cooking, whose writing influenced a generation of cooks, chefs and other food writers, and who introduced olive oil to the UK as a staple cooking ingredient. In 1961 under Ailsa Garland, David's simple approach to food was replaced by the more flamboyant attitude of the American Robert Carrier. Carrier introduced a new sense of culinary indulgence to the magazine, with recipes for medallions of veal parmesan, eggs in aspic and Moroccan steamed lamb gracing his pages. Elizabeth David suggested how to cook; Robert Carrier gave specific instructions on how to execute his creations. Despite their different approaches to the culinary arts, both went on to gain literary and celebrity success, with Carrier regularly appearing on television.

"In 1975 Beatrix Miller, Barney Wan and Judy Britton decided to set me to work on a new series of food pictures with the writer Arabella Boxer. She and I had already met at Barry Lategan's studio and had no doubt that we could work happily together, which we did for sixteen years. After a while Arabella and I got into the swing of things and once a year we would present twelve ideas to Bea Miller for her approval. She nearly always agreed with what we suggested but often requested some kind of sweet dessert to be added to our plan. After I had delivered my picture on the eighth day of the month I would get a call from Bea Miller, who was a woman of few words. She would say, 'Darling, you are a genius' or occasionally 'Do it again, darling, not good enough.' However, Bea was very fair and gave creative people their heads. The *Vogue* deal has always been 'you get paid the absolute minimum, but in exchange for giving us your best work we will give you top quality layout and printing so that your work always looks good'. It was its own reward. Even though I never had a contract with them, it was simply understood that I would not work for any other glossy magazine, although foreign magazines like *Elle* and the colour supplements of the Sunday papers were exempt."
Tessa Traeger
Vogue

A three-year gap followed Carrier's leaving, then in 1967 Arabella Boxer succeeded him as food editor, but she left after just two years claiming that she had run out of ideas. However, she was persuaded to reconsider and in 1975 she returned to Vogue House as *Vogue*'s food editor, remaining in the position until 1991. The youngest daughter of the eighteenth Earl of Moray, Lady Arabella Stuart became Boxer after marrying Mark Boxer, who designed her first book, *First Slice Your Cookbook*, in 1964. You will hear more about the influential art director and editor Mark Boxer later in this book, but suffice to say that Arabella Boxer's food writing and her collaborations with the photographer Tessa Traeger were just as important to the understanding of contemporary food thinking as those of her predecessors. Cementing the importance of *Vogue* to this ongoing conversation concerning a contemporary approach to food, in 1995 Nigella Lawson took on the role of a contributing food writer. Her career since has been unstoppable.

I've touched briefly above on how influential the role of the art director or art editor can be to a magazine. Often overlooked in favour of the editorial side of a magazine's direction, and therefore rarely discussed, the art department is crucial to the look of a magazine. The art director is responsible for the commissioning of photography and illustration through to the overall design, typography and layout of the images and text. In this book I will include the names, backgrounds and influence of those art directors who stood out for their work on the magazines published from inside Vogue House. It is also worth noting that in contrast to the overwhelmingly privileged and connected backgrounds of the Vogue House editorial teams, the art directors often bucked this trend. I have already mentioned *Vogue*'s John Parsons, who was gay at a time when it was difficult and dangerous to be so, but his replacement Barney Wan could just as easily be seen as an outsider. Born in Singapore in 1931, Wan moved to London in the early 1960s and began freelancing as an illustrator at an advertising agency. He then moved on to *Queen* magazine, before being hired as the *Vogue* art editor by Miller. Alongside Miller, Wan continued to work with the photographers that Parsons had introduced to the magazine, art-directing some of the most iconic issues of the late 1960s and early 1970s, as well as appearing in some of photographer Helmut Newton's influential images alongside Coddington. Adopting a sense of creative baton-passing, it was Wan who picked Terry Jones to be his successor in 1972.

"Barney was a treasure. He was the photographer's dream because he had great empathy with photography and pictures. He would always give them space to breathe."
Willy Christie
Vogue

CHAPTER 1: 1960–1970

It was during Barney Wan's time art-directing the magazine that Beatrix Miller was responsible for choosing Donyale Luna for the cover of the March 1966 issue of *Vogue*, the first African-American model to be featured on the magazine's iconic cover, making a statement far ahead of the call for increased diversity across magazine publishing in the 2020s. Miller, an editor noted for always keeping her office door open, was strong and tough but fair, as Lucy Hughes-Hallett, a young member of Miller's features team remembered:

"I think she cultivated that image to an extent – it was her manner to be frightening, but that meant when she passed you in the hall and said, 'That was pretty good, Lucy,' about something you had written, you would be walking on air! She was a patient and helpful editor and read my work very carefully, making really useful comments and suggestions, although her style was pretty laconic. She would write 'ugh!' in the margin for anything she disliked and just a tick meant she was happy with it. Her occasional praise meant it counted ten times more."

Miller's magazine was based on a defined and respectful hierarchy that mostly kept people in check, with older senior editors working alongside the younger members of staff.

"I got a call from Beatrice Miller's secretary: 'Can you come in and have tea with Ms Miller?' she said. I knew to appear promptly when summoned and immediately made my way to her office from the studio at the top of Vogue House. I knocked on her office door, which was adorned with a *YES* or *NO* sign dangling by a string, which set the minimal and clipped tone of her approach to visitors. I strolled into the room and sat down opposite Ms Miller, waiting to hear why she wanted to see me. 'Clive,' she said, holding up the latest *Vogue*, showing me the photograph of model Maudie James. 'This,' she continued in a voice that exuded both admiration and pride, 'is the most beautiful photograph I have seen in *Vogue* for a long time.

I am sending you to see Alexander Liberman (art director of US *Vogue*) with this picture, so that you can work for him.'

"I arrived at the *Vogue* offices in New York and was shown into Mr Liberman's office overlooking the city. Mr Liberman had his back to me and was staring thoughtfully out of the window. 'Hello, Mr Arrowsmith,' he said. 'I have been looking at your work. This photograph, it is *very* beautiful, but your work is far too *exotic* for American *Vogue*. Maybe we can talk in a year or so. Nice of you to come, do please give my regards to Ms Miller.'"

Clive Arrowsmith
Vogue

So far, I have concentrated in this chapter on one magazine in my telling of the Vogue House story, but what about the others in the building? Well, *House & Garden* under the editorship of Robert Harling continued to be the magazine that he had begun to establish in 1957 with his small and dedicated editorial team of approximately thirteen. Following on from the 1959 publication *House & Garden: Interiors and Colour,* Harling worked with members of his team to produce *House & Garden: Guide to Interior Decoration* in 1967 whilst continuing to produce the monthly magazine. Just as the decade had seen an explosion of interest and experimentation in the arts, the world of interior design, furniture design and interior decoration had seen an influx of new ideas from Europe. Young talent was bringing new approaches to the high street, most notably the designer Terence Conran, with his first Habitat shop that opened in 1964 on the King's Road. Harling knew his audience, though, and kept the magazine focused on the traditional whilst lightly challenging his readership with the new and more experimental approaches to interior design. *Vogue* told you how to dress, how to look and what to discuss at social gatherings, whilst *House & Garden* informed you of just how your home should appear.

Harling was to the point when it came to dealing with his staff and saw no reason for anyone to ever be ill and therefore absent from the office. The apocryphal tale is that he once said to a young female secretary, "There's nothing in life which can't be solved by a good f**k or a gargle!" In an obituary for Harling in the *Guardian* in 2008, Fiona McCarthy, merchandise editor and journalist and one of his team in the 1960s, whose grandmother was the Baroness de Belabre, shared her memories of working under him in Vogue House. She describes him running his office "as an amiable harem, extracting his mini-skirted girl assistants one by one for a cappuccino at a nearby coffee bar in Maddox Street" but being "fanatically loyal to his staff [and] a good picker and marvellous encourager of talent." Also on the magazine with McCarthy at the time were a young Hugh Johnson, who would go on to become a formidable wine expert, and Ann Barr, who would go on to write the era-defining 1982 bestseller *The Official Sloane Ranger Handbook*.

Harling's politically incorrect attitude to women in the workplace at Vogue House is further evidenced in a 2015 *Guardian* article by journalist Ian Jack, who noted that "his conversation wouldn't be possible in an office now. Even in 1970 it was unusual; you noticed him for it. 'My glossy' was how he referred to *House & Garden*, the magazine he edited. 'That's a nice little numero' he might say appraisingly of a new secretary. 'Meeting a popsy?' was a typical question if he met you going down in the lift." Jack also commented on Harling's particular style of dress that had changed little over the decades, particularly his black fedora and trousers that were astonishingly tight: " 'I don't know how you make quick getaways in trousers like those,'" his friend Lucian Freud is alleged to have said, bearing angry cuckolds in mind."

Whilst *Vogue* and *House & Garden* both embraced the 'swinging sixties', *Brides* magazine evolved at a much slower pace than its stable mates. It has always been a risk-averse magazine, and although the decade challenged convention in all aspects of life, the desire for a traditional wedding remained strong and so understandably change was less obvious in its pages. Despite this, many of the *Vogue* photographers actually continued their careers there, including David Bailey.

The three magazines being produced within the building shared an essential thread: they were being created for an elite readership, and the advertising reflected the aspiration of the magazines' readers, with classic British brands such as Rayne, Fortnum & Mason and Jaeger believing that *Vogue, House & Garden* and *Brides* readers were their customers. If you have never worked on a magazine, it is worth explaining how the content of a magazine is decided upon. The editor employs a team of people whom they believe understand their readers and live the life that their readers want to lead. On this basis, it is believed that their staff will be the best people to understand what the magazine's audience are interested in, what they want to read and what they want to see. Therefore, the editor will rely on their team to ensure that the content of the magazine is appropriate for its readers, and in turn for the advertisers who pay the bills. Just as a railway magazine will be staffed by railway enthusiasts, so Vogue House was filled with people who reflected the nature of its magazines' readership. Whilst the 1960s was a time when the working class were making themselves known, hoping to break down the social-class obsessions of previous generations, and some were even rising up within Vogue House, there remained an unwavering tradition of employing the connected and public-school educated at Condé Nast. Today we believe that diversity in the background of who is employed on staff will to help to grow a magazine's audience, but this was rarely the case in Vogue House in the 1960s. However, there were some noticeable exceptions.

"I was so pleased to have a job. When I wrote to people for an interview it never occurred to me that I had a budget to commission writers, so I was writing everything for £10 a week. Every once in a while I would go to see this very shy man, who seemed embarrassed about my income, and ask him for an advance to pay my rent or to get luncheon vouchers. I still hold a grudge about this. But it was a very exciting life, I'm not prone to excitement or ever wanted to speak with celebrities; however, whoever I interviewed I kind of made friends with, sometimes I slept with them, but mostly I made friends with them. The actor Maximilian Schell asked me to marry him after an interview, and Gregory Peck asked a girl who interviewed him to marry him also. When I met the man I married, I knew about him as I'd read about him in *Vogue* as a leader of the

'Chelsea Set'. I was always fascinated by grand people, but I never met anyone I fancied in Vogue House."
Polly Devlin
Vogue

"Our hold on reality was often tenuous. Coming across Hanover Square with the items for a joint fashion/features story of dream Christmas presents, a sudden gust [of wind] caught me only just keeping hold of a Russian ikon worth tens of thousands of pounds in a plastic bag, while the fashion editor – and later my wife – clutched a bag into which she had stuffed jewellery worth far more. She was storing the necklaces in the office, she told the manager, until they could be returned to the store next day. The blood drained from his face. Muttering about insurance and gross irresponsibility he reached for the phone. Half an hour later a burly security guard appeared, saying he had to be locked with the goods in the fashion store overnight and my companion was to keep the key. 'But how are you to manage all night?' she asked. 'Don't worry, miss, we're trained for this,' he replied."
Adrian Hamilton
Vogue

Condé Nast may have been an exclusive publisher, but the public's need for the printed page was strong in the 1960s, with 133 daily newspapers and 1,310 weekly newspapers being produced in the UK and Eire in 1961, and *The Sunday Times* recording a circulation of approximately one million copies each week in the same year. In March 2022, the same newspaper posted a weekly circulation of 647,622. Times have changed. Condé Nast titles were targeted at the rich and affluent, and therefore their circulations were not comparatively high, but the magazines were influential. The titles were financially sustainable primarily due to their advertising revenue, which was steady and predictable. Members of staff were not on high salaries, and indeed many did not need to earn vast sums to survive thanks to their family wealth. Many of those employed by the UK Condé Nast magazines in the 1960s, 70s and 80s mentioned to me the meanness of the company when it came to being paid, some of whom I have quoted, but it is also clear that some of those employed were treated differently. In her biography of Antony Armstrong-Jones, titled *Snowdon,* the writer Anne de Courcy reveals that he was setting his own value: "His fees were always the highest the market could bear and sometimes more. A letter from *Vogue* complains of an invoice of nine guineas for three prints. "It's miles more than the (Vogue) Studio charges and even a good bit more than Parkinson."

The *Vogue* brand today is part of a contemporary business plan based on the heritage of the titles, with franchised magazines opening across the world. Whereas, in the 1960s magazine brands were created specifically for defined nationally understood interests, tastes and sensitivities. However, its marketing is nothing new: the aspirational strength of the magazine was already being used to great effect in the 1960s. *Vogue* may have been a magazine designed primarily for an exclusive readership but it did have a connection with a much wider commercial audience.

"One day an American, David P. Davies, appeared in Vogue House and showed me these rather unattractive tights in show-through nylon. This was the future he told me, and I disagreed: 'unhygienic, ladder one leg and the pair were spoilt, expensive and a hideous orange colour.' It simply couldn't work. I took them round endless 'hosiery' manufacturers and was unanimously turned down. Finally, at a chance meeting with John Sainsbury, I persuaded him to take a few boxes. They sold out in a day, and with Mary Quant designing flowery tights, new colours and patterns abounded and legs never looked the same."

Sandy Boler
Vogue, Brides

Vogue readers have always aspired to wear the clothes featured in the magazine, many of which they cannot possibly afford. With the advent of mass-market fashion, copies of couture catwalk looks are readily available but in the sixties cheap high-street or online alternatives did not exist. However, there was a ready-made solution that could give one an association with the *Vogue* name. Dressmaking remained an essential skill for many women during the 1950s, and in a pre-retail-chain high street it offered a way for the latest fashions to be worn via the *Vogue* knitting and sewing patterns.

The *Vogue* Pattern Service had begun in 1899, as a spinoff from *Vogue* magazine's weekly pattern feature. Condé Nast bought *Vogue* in 1909 and in 1914 the *Vogue* Pattern Company was formed, and by 1916 *Vogue* patterns were being sold in department stores. When Condé Nast moved into Vogue House the 'Pattern Book' was given office space on the same floor as *Vogue* and *Brides*. However, in 1961 the Vogue Pattern Service was sold to Butterick Publishing, a specialist pattern company, which licensed the *Vogue* name. *Vogue* Patterns became the only pattern company licensed to produce designs from the world-leading couturiers, establishing a precedent that continues today. The most sought-after patterns were from French designers until the mid-1970s when Italian and English designers, including the popular Bellville-Sassoon, were added. However, styles by Yves Saint Laurent and Hubert de Givenchy are still among the company's bestsellers.

The future can never be controlled or accurately prophesised but with the benefit of hindsight we can often see germs of ideas that may have been planted too early or in the wrong season slowly coming to fruition. The 1990s would see a men's fashion/style magazine produced from Vogue House for the first time, but looking back at an initiative from 1965 proves that there are few new ideas in publishing, including the idea of male celebrities appearing alongside male models in a luxury men's interest magazine. *Men in Vogue* was first published in 1965 attached to the November issue of *Vogue*. The magazine was closely associated with what is commonly described as the 'peacock revolution' in English men's fashion, which could be seen in London on Carnaby Street and the King's Road, Chelsea. It heralded the future explosion of men's magazines featuring celebrities such as actor Edward Fox, footballer George Best and Rolling Stones musician Brian Jones. However, the appointment of its first fashion editor continued the Vogue House non-conformist approach to recruiting staff.

"I was an army officer at Sandhurst, bored witless, and I bought myself out of the army. I returned to London and found myself unemployable, and a girlfriend said, 'I've got you a job, you can't live in London without any money so you're going to be one of the waiters at the Contented Sole in South Kensington. She didn't tell me it was a fish and chip shop – but it was great fun as all of the waiters and waitresses wanted to be actors, as did I. One day I was serving a table of eight charming people whom I was getting on with very well and they said, 'What are you doing in a place like this?' I said that I would take any job to get out of there and they said, 'Why don't you become the men's fashion editor of *Vogue*?' I didn't know *Vogue* or anything about men's fashion, but I said that I'd love to. They said write to Beatrix Miller, which I did. I was invited for an interview with her and in the open plan office she said, 'Anyone ever heard of Geoffrey Aquilina Ross?' and eight people said yes, we had dinner with him recently, but they didn't say I was the waiter! I got the job! And Bea Miller gave me a career."
Geoffrey Aquilina Ross
Vogue

As well as Ross, *Men's Vogue* included on its staff, in the role of shopping guide editor, Christopher Gibbs, the antiques dealer, collector and influential figure in men's fashion and interior design of the time who was often referred to as the 'King of Chelsea'. Robert Harling and Bea Miller were also involved in creating the magazine as a standalone title. However, the title ceased publication in 1970 and instead two to three pages in each issue of *Vogue* were given over to men. *Town* (formerly *About Town* and before that *Man About Town*) had closed in 1968, and the British version of *Esquire* had closed in the 1950s; these closures were blamed on the smaller size of the men's magazine market in the United Kingdom compared to that of the United States, and on the new competition for advertising from commercial television and newspaper colour supplements. Male-focused *Vogue* magazines were subsequently published in Germany and Italy with more success, and in 2006 *Vogue-Man* was launched by Condé Nast, however that too had a short lifespan, closing in 2009 and becoming just a section of the *Vogue* website.

The magazines produced within the walls of Vogue House in the 1960s each had a distinct personality built on the people who created and contributed to them. At that time, Vogue House was a melting pot of talent that accurately reflected a decade where London was the centre of the creative universe for long enough for those involved to build their careers through the pages of the magazines they used as platforms for their exuberant creativity. The next decade would see those talented people further establish their importance, and the magazines they worked on embrace an international perspective.

Chapter 2: 1970–1980
He Twirled his Guns
like a Rodeo Star

The 1970s are often described as the hangover decade that followed the party of the swinging sixties. There is considerable evidence to back this statement up, but there was also enough creativity coming from the UK during the period to construct an argument that it was actually a period of rejection and renewal. The challenge for the titles within Vogue House during the 1970s was how to respond to economic turmoil, political chaos, creative excess and eventual youth anger. This was a decade that went from Prog to Punk, from Zandra Rhodes to Vivienne Westwood, and such magnitude of change requires a magazine to be directly connected to the cultural zeitgeist to remain relevant. In this sense, the 1970s saw the Vogue House magazines struggle to compete with their new strident mass-market magazine rivals such as *Nova* and *Cosmopolitan,* alongside the changing nature of high-street fashion retail.

There are many well-known names whose credentials were established within Vogue House and on the magazines produced there in the 1970s, but one of the most interesting is one of the least known.

Whilst this is not a book about management, the British Condé Nast managing director between 1976 and 1987 is worth recognising not only for his influence on the titles but also for his incredible back story. Similar to Timms, Miller and Harling, Leser's story tied the building directly to the history of the Second World War. Bernard Leser's career with Condé Nast began in 1959, when he launched *Vogue Australia*. As the managing director of British Condé Nast, he was responsible for the launch of *German Vogue* in 1979, buying *World of Interiors* and the purchase of *Tatler* in 1982. He was also responsible for recruiting the young Tina Brown as *Tatler*'s editor. Leser's influence on the building and the future of the titles produced within it was long-lasting. Future *Vogue* and *GQ* editor Alexandra Schuman speaks fondly of her time as a less than competent temporary second assistant to Leser, sitting outside his "cigar-scented wood-panelled office", and his subsequent support concerning her future career; whilst Liz Tilberis comments that "Dear Bernie liked a lovely long lunch and a little nap afterward... the joke was that you knew how you stood according to whether you were asked to an interview in the A.M. or P.M."

Between 1987 and 1994 Leser worked alongside S. I. Newhouse in New York, where he oversaw *Vogue*, *GQ*, *Vanity Fair*, *Mademoiselle* and *The New Yorker*. As such, his influence on the Condé Nast titles on both sides of the Atlantic was important, but it was his life before 1959 that was so incredible and unlike any other member of the Vogue House community. Leser grew up in an industrial town north of Weimar, Germany. His father had been a soldier in the German Imperial Regiment during the First World War, and was awarded the Iron Cross First Class for saving a man's life, before leaving the army to run a knitwear factory. Leser was three when his parents separated and eight when Adolf Hitler came to power. In 1938, the soldier whose life his father had saved became the head of the local Nazi Brownshirts and warned Leser's father to leave Germany as soon as possible, promising that his family would be safe in leaving. However, Leser was expelled from his Jewish boarding school and forced to march through the streets with his classmates, surrounded by jeering Nazis spitting and hurling stones and rotten fruit. As he was under sixteen he was sent home, while many of his less fortunate classmates were sent to the Dachau concentration camp. In 1939, Leser flew to England with his family before travelling on to New Zealand to build a new life.

> "It took Bea two or three years to make *Vogue* into the magazine she wanted it to be which was much, much younger than it was. She would come up with wonderful straplines and say, 'Do something on this.' [Lines] such as 'Come into the garden' or she'd say, 'I've just passed a sign on the road that said, "Diversions Ahead". I want all your features to be "Diversions Ahead".' She was always looking ahead; she was a brilliant editor."
> **Polly Devlin**
> **Vogue**

Bea Miller was still in charge at *Vogue* as the 1970s began but it was in 1972 that an art director joined the team who was to be responsible for ensuring that the magazine looked right for the new decade. In an interview in 2014, Terry Jones told *SHOWstudio*.com that, "Beatrix Miller was amazing. She let me get away with breaking all sorts of rules." That statement not only sums up the freedom that the former MI6 secretary gave her young art director (Jones was just twenty-seven years old when he joined *Vogue*) but the sense of chaos that was in the air throughout the seventies, before it reached its anarchic conclusion thanks to the Sex Pistols and the punk movement. Jones left the magazine in 1977 (to be replaced by the previous art director Barney Wan) and launched his own magazine in 1980, the influential cultural style bible *i-D*.

> "I will love Terry forever because he put my jelly and lips on the cover, but he had a different way of working to Barney. Terry used a lot of type, and used to crop the pictures a lot, which caused a bit of grumbling amongst the photographers. He was great though."
> **Willy Christie**
> **Vogue**

In an *i-D* online article in 2016, Jones spoke of his anarchic approach to design and editorial decisions at *Vogue* during his time as art director, recalling the January 1974 cover featuring Anjelica Huston and Manolo Blahnik shot by David Bailey on a trip to Corsica and the south of France: "Grace [Coddington] and I managed to convince Beatrix Miller this landscape, full length image of Anjelica and Manolo was the best, most exciting and brave cover option...we broke the standard full-face shot."

"Bea Miller was great, she was like someone's aunty, she wasn't like an editor really, but she was powerful. She loved Bailey."
John Swannell
Vogue, Tatler, Brides

In the 1970s magazine publishing became a highly competitive business, and some established magazines struggled to react positively when faced with the cynicism of the times towards fashion and consumerism, which was partly driven by the rise of strident feminism and direct political action. Rather than reacting to new titles that had challenged the status quo, such as the confident, issue-led *Nova*, British *Vogue* instead embraced internationalism and began to feature models from the United States. British models Jean Shrimpton, Celia Hammond and Jill Kennington were replaced by Jerry Hall from Texas, Marie Helvin from Hawaii, Anjelica Huston from Los Angeles, Lauren Hutton from South Carolina and Janice Dickinson from New York, amongst many others. Hollywood was merging with the fashion world as US television shows with A-list stars began regularly appearing on UK television screens, and affordable high-street retailers sprung up catering to those who had previously struggled to access the latest fashions. *Vogue* retained its quirky, eccentric Britishness thanks primarily to the fashion stylings of Coddington and Miller's protégé Liz Tilberis, but red-carpet glamour was definitely to the fore.

One of the photographers most closely associated with the hard-edged, intense-colour, often erotic sexy-glamour of the 1970s was German/Australian Helmut Newton, but another German photographer creating this type of work for British *Vogue* is less well known.

Christoph von Wangenheim was just as controversial as Newton or Guy Bourdin and had a short but influential impact on fashion photography in the decade of excess. Born in 1942, Wangenheim's father was an aristocratic cavalry officer who became a well-known horse rider and gold medal winner at the infamous 1936 Berlin Olympic Games. In 1944, whilst serving on the Eastern Front, Wangenheim's father was taken prisoner and held in a Russian POW camp, where he remained imprisoned for almost ten years, only to be found hanged days before his intended release. Wangenheim studied architecture before turning to photography; in 1965 moved to New York to work as a photography assistant. In 1968 he started his own studio and soon began working for the fashion magazines, including US *Vogue* and the German, French, Italian and British editions. It could easily be said that his images encapsulate the famous New York clubbing, Studio 54-inspired lifestyles and fashions of the era. Sadly, his impact on photography and fashion magazines was cut short in 1981, when Wangenheim was killed in a car crash whilst on holiday.

"'I'll race you!' The venerable fashion photographer (Norman Parkinson) smiles by the lifts as we jump in. I can't remember what else we said, just how immensely tall he was, and how the wager came out of the blue."
Charlotte du Cann
Vogue

In her book *Marie Helvin: The Autobiography,* the model describes an early experience in Vogue House on her first trip to London, when "a cowboy in a Zapata sombrero [...] two pistols tucked into his low-slung belt" forced his way into the lifts going upwards: "He twirled his guns like a rodeo star, grinning at me. As I fled out of the lift towards Grace Coddington, she stopped me in my tracks as she smilingly gestured to the cowboy. 'Have you met our star photographer Clive Arrowsmith?'"

"My first shoot for *Vogue* was with Marie Helvin, who had started seeing Bailey. It was in Studio Two at Vogue Studios, and I had a faux nightclub scene set-up with a piano. I was just about

to start when Bailey arrived with a bottle of champagne and said, 'Am I making you nervous Will?' and laughed his glorious laugh. It was just a lovely gesture."
Willy Christie
Vogue

In the early 1970s the world of couture fashion, which had been the foundation of *Vogue's* annual fashion coverage since its inception, was starting to crumble. The media was sounding couture's death knell. In 1972 the *Evening Standard* newspaper announced that they would not be "spending any more time reporting the funeral obsequies of a moribund institution." This was a time of severe economic downturn, which saw magazine production costs increase and the cost of paper rise dramatically. National strikes, power cuts and industrial unrest plagued the 1970s but issues in the fashion magazine world had already started to sour at the beginning of the decade. There was a global problem with advertising sales, with US *Vogue's* ad sales revenues falling by 40 per cent in the first quarter of 1971; as a response, magazines began to shift from employing full-time staff towards using freelance contracts.

Necessity is the mother of invention, and the couture designers and their financial backers soon realised that there was a new way to keep the world's attention on high fashion – through diversification. The aim was to make luxury brands more affordable, and so the seventies saw an explosion of diffusion lines, with perfumes and toiletries in particular bringing luxury labels within the reach of those not in a position to purchase couture. These diffusion lines were then imitated by a multitude of mass-market clothing and beauty manufacturers and sold through high-street chain boutiques such as Chelsea Girl, Plum, Miss Selfridge and Top Shop.

New technologies in fabric and clothing manufacture, combined with higher efficiency, consistent standards and speed of production, and rigorous construction control allowed consumers access to fashion whatever their income. This raised general awareness of previously niche brands and promoted an interest in fashion for fashion's sake. However, the 1970s also saw the birth of an anti-conformist approach to clothing; the growth of women's rights awareness and demonstrations existed alongside the rise of tribal youth counter-cultures. The 1970s saw street fashion become increasingly important; by the end of the decade it had become the dominant indicator of style trends. All of this was the antipathy of the concept that a fashion magazine was a definer of taste and style.

The 1960s in Vogue House had existed as its own world within a world. The 'Voguettes', as the young women working on the magazine were then known, had been creating a magazine for people like them, or at least for those people who aspired to be a part of, or look as if they were part of, the 'Chelsea Set.' Whilst magazines that had come out of the burgeoning London underground press, such as *Oz, International Times* and *Time Out,* were responding to the needs of the counterculture, the mass-market women's magazines had continued to present unchallenging, safe content aimed at the majority of the population who were not interested in designer-led fashion. The 1970s required magazines to define their audience but also to grow those audiences outside of their recognised tribes.

"The features editors were young and eager. Polly Devlin, Davina Lloyd, Marina Warner, Jill Weldon, Joan Juliet Buck and Adrian Hamilton were part of a new young group who were part of the action as well as reporters [of it], writing and commissioning the best of the new. People forget that in those days we produced sixteen issues a year rather than the twelve published today. March and April, September and October were twice monthly, and we had to type our copy to the exact required length."
Sandy Boler
Vogue, Brides

In a 2016 interview with the British Academy website, Marina Warner recalled her days in Vogue House as a features editor under Miller, comparing it to her own convent education: "I had changed from one entirely female environment to another, with rather comparable figures of authority: the Reverend Mother was quite a model for the Chief Editor of *Vogue*... Beatrix Miller, known to us as 'Miss Miller', was definitely of the same ilk as a Reverend Mother." Under Miller's editorship *Vogue* maintained its intellectual edge, largely thanks to the input of its features editors Polly Devlin, Marina Warner, Adrian Hamilton and Joan Juliet Buck and a wide range of contributors. The magazine included articles on Ibsen plays, Peter Brook's theatrical productions, Ken Russell's films, nouvelle vague directors Jean-Luc Godard and François Truffaut and artists such as Francis Bacon and Allen Jones, amongst many others at the forefront of popular culture. Subjects relating to pollution, conservation and preservation were also given space within the magazine.

"I never considered it a fashion magazine. I was encouraged by Bea Miller to produce good features. The whole situation of upper-class English women was a revelation to me."
Polly Devlin
Vogue

"'Do you like sentences?' asked the writer Annie Dillard of the young man who wanted to be fêted and win prizes. It's the sentences you remember. And learning how to hone them. I watched Antonia Williams in awe tackle the editorial for the latest issue, throwing adjectives and phrases like fireworks onto the page, as she sat before the keys, spreads spilling over the desk, a cigarette hanging from her lips. The features department was a brown wood and glass stage, where the magazine's contributors came in and out of the open door, delivering lines about their copy like characters in a Moliere play: pithy sentences on opera, food, art, books, travel in faraway places. Our own dramatic relationships would be acted out on the chorus line, among post-academic conversations about literature and philosophy, as the bike couriers and costume rails from the fashion rooms passed by. And occasionally you would be summoned off stage by the editor, Miss Miller, to do something way out of your skill set. 'Charlotte, you play the cello, can you interview Segovia tomorrow?'"
Charlotte du Cann
Vogue

Despite its strident features, *Vogue* didn't lose its sense of who the core readership was, and who it needed to employ to understand that audience.

"Sometime in the mid 1990s I was called up to the personnel director Barbara Timms' office to find her roaring with laughter. She had unearthed a 1970s file showing that I was the first ever Vogue House intern. My father was always a great believer that one should experience one's chosen career before one launched into it and I'd been quite determined since I was six years of age that editing a glossy magazine was a perfectly reasonable idea. So, when I was sixteen, he was on the case. Luckily the then managing director of Condé Nast, John Perry, happened to be a good friend, so he invited him to dinner with Bea Miller, the then editor-in-chief of *Vogue*. Over dinner 'work experience' at Vogue House was created and a week in my Easter school holidays was suggested. The fashion editors were mystified, but fabulous – Sheila Wetton took me on a shoot with Barry Lategan; Grace Coddington taught me how to iron a shirt for photography; Liz Tilberis gave me an outfit from the fashion cupboard; and the American Melanie Miller took me for a manicure. Barney Wan showed me a hideaway in Vogue Studios so I could watch a closed David Bailey sitting. I was sold."
Jane Procter
Tatler, Vogue

"Bea always said that she was very good at spotting talented amateurs. I think she was right because many people that she took in went on to do great things."
Geoffrey Aquilina Ross
Vogue

"Crossing Hanover Square to start my first day as features editor, at *Vogue*, it struck me not only that I had no idea what I was doing there but, whatever it was, I was probably the last person

who should be taking up a post in a woman's magazine staffed largely by women dedicated to female fashion."
Adrian Hamilton
Vogue

Bailey described Miller as "The first British *Vogue* editor with any gumption. She hired art directors who weren't 'yes' men, who had an opinion." Wan shared Bailey's opinion of Miller in a Vogue.com obituary when he said that "She had a great vision... She understood fashion and built a great team. She checked every page herself... if someone was going over the top she'd say, 'It's just a magazine, don't cast it in marble.'"

"Beatrix Miller was a powerful presence. She led through questions rather than instructions. Seated around her in the weekly meetings in her office, most of the fashion and other editors cross-legged on the floor, she would keep pressing you to come up with ideas that were new or exciting, that reflected the mood and energy of the times far wider than just clothes. When I remarked that computers were now capable of writing poetry, she urged me to commission one, which I did from the University of California at Berkeley. Declaring that a very young academic, Roy Strong at the National Portrait Gallery, was the most exciting figure in museums and was doing a show of portraits by Cecil Beaton, she instantly chimed, 'Get Beaton to photograph him then.' Returning to Vogue House from interviewing Roy Strong, when I had suggested his museum showed portraits of ordinary people instead of the famous, I was met by an amused Beatrix, who said that he'd been on the phone to her, declaring I was 'clearly a communist and should be fired immediately'. When I argued that, instead of always profiling the well-known, we ought to do something on the figures of influence behind them, she said, 'Right, and who should we use to photograph them?' 'Cartier-Bresson,' I replied tentatively, naming the man I revered above all. 'Then we'll get

him,' said Beatrix. And so, we did, although he hadn't done anything like that for *Vogue* before."
Adrian Hamilton
Vogue

As gender roles were evolving, and women were becoming more independent and economically active, feminism was questioning the fashion world and its representation of beauty. As Warner noted, "In the features that I wrote there was a common thread of interest in how women were represented." Warner was replaced as features editor by Joan Juliet Buck, who continued Devlin and Warner's intellectual and cultural mission by featuring culture disrupters such as Andy Warhol, Conrad Brooks and Fran Lebowitz on the *Vogue* pages. In a 2017 interview for the website Fashionista, Buck commented on taking up the position, describing it as "the one job I ever really wanted" and noting the differences between herself and her predecessor Marina Warner, who was "brilliant, well-born and went to Oxford. I wasn't any of those things, but I loved it." She went on to describe that as features editor she "felt that I owed an allegiance to what was then called the counterculture." Buck was born in Los Angeles but grew up in France and London after her father, a film producer, relocated the family to Europe. After attending the Lycée Français de Londres, Buck returned to the United States to start college but swiftly dropped out, moving to New York City to write book and film reviews for *Glamour* magazine. She was made features editor at British *Vogue* aged just twenty-three.

Buck's career trajectory followed a familiar path, whereby a series of unexpected and unrelated consequences seemed to lead her to Vogue House. She had been in London in 1972 whilst her father made a film. As she retells in her book, *The Price of Illusion*, Buck was certainly not looking for a job in publishing, although she was enjoying the fashions of the time and went to lunch with Barney Wan: "Soon, Marit Allen called from *Vogue* to ask if she could photograph me [...] Then the call came [...] Beatrix Miller heard I'd interviewed Robert Redford and wanted to meet me. She found the interview 'a bit thin' but, lighting a cigarette from a gold box, told me that Marina Warner was leaving for

Vietnam, and *Vogue* needed a features editor. The pay was only £10 a week, but did I really need the money?"

Despite being from a different background to Warner, Buck's reflections of working under Miller were similar. "Working with Beatrix at British *Vogue* was like being back at school under a benevolent headmistress, but after seven weeks in the cork-floored halls at Hanover Square, I'd started doubting I'd done the right thing." Buck left to relocate for a brief period at the *Observer* before returning to the Condé Nast fold, where she stayed in a variety of positions until 2011.

In contrast to the features editor, the role of managing editor on a magazine is not an easy or glamorous one. It requires patience, firmness and empathy without weakness. Vogue House welcomed many fine managing editors through its doors who stayed with their titles despite the merry-go-round of staff, art directors and editors. The calm at the centre of the storm, the managing editor oversees production schedules, budgets, copy flow and staffing. Georgie Boosey provided exactly that sense of continuity on *Vogue* from 1978 to 1993. Boosey was the only child of Cecil and Donald Harden. Harden was an antiquities curator at the Ashmolean Museum in Oxford, and a close friend of Agatha Christie, who was Boosey's godmother. Whilst at school in Oxford, Boosey became determined to enter the world of magazine publishing on *Vogue* or *Queen* and in 1956, aged twenty, she got her wish and began working at Vogue House as an editorial assistant on the *Vogue* Pattern and Knitting books. Within a few years, and with an honourable mention in the *Vogue* talent contest, she became a sub-editor on *Vogue* where she was regularly promoted. Boosey's reputation was one of dependability, resourcefulness and diplomacy, key skills for any managing editor, and it is true to say that generations of 'Voguettes' regarded her as a surrogate mother, often repeating her reassuring words, "Don't worry, the fashion room spend more than that on their sandwiches."

"'Do you like shopping?' the editor had asked me in an interview after taking part in the *Vogue* talent contest that year. 'No,'

I said, 'not much.' 'Oh, you will be perfect,' she said. 'You will keep the advertising department at bay.'"
Charlotte du Cann
Vogue

Another important member of Miller's team was also given access to Vogue House thanks to the *Vogue* Talent Competition, a free-to-enter annual writing competition open to anyone that read the magazine. Georgina Howell was born in South Africa in 1942. An only child, her father was a Royal Air Force flying instructor who returned with his family to London in 1944. After attending several unsatisfactory convent schools, Howell was enrolled at Miss Ironside's 'Dame' School in Kensington, run by the great-aunt of the journalist Virginia Ironside. Persuaded by her mother, Howell entered the *Vogue* Talent Competition in 1960. She won, and gained a job at Vogue House assisting Peter Coats, the garden editor of *House & Garden*, a role she described as "watering the plants and taking messages" for Coats who had "a very demanding social round that permitted few visits to the office". She was soon moved to the *Vogue* editorial department at the suggestion of Miller, winning £5 in a staff competition by coming up with the slogan "Buy nothing until you buy *Vogue*." Miller promoted her to features editor. Howell was a calm, cool and modest presence; whilst on *Vogue* – and in subsequent positions as fashion editor on the *Observer* and as deputy editor of *Tatler* under Tina Brown – she was known for never raising her voice.

The Vogue Studios within Vogue House continued to be used but, as the 1970s progressed, more and more photographers began to establish their own studios across London. This saw the gradual decline of the Vogue Studios as the meeting place for photographers commissioned by the Condé Nast magazines. However, Vogue House was always a welcoming starting point for the connected photographer; many already knew each other through family and school connections. There was always a core within Vogue House of those who were unfairly but commonly described as 'gentlemen photographers'. These photographers all achieved broad commercial and critical success, but were born into positions of social standing in a way that outsiders such as Bailey, Donovan and Duffy were not. Let me give you some examples. Antony 'Tony' Armstrong-Jones (Lord Snowdon) was bought up in Belgravia and married the Queen's sister, Princess Margaret. Patrick Lichfield was the 5th Earl of Lichfield, whose mother was niece to the Queen Mother. Cecil Beaton studied at Harrow, as did the *Tatler* social photographer Hugo Burnand. Norman Parkinson was educated at the exclusive Westminster School. Willy Christie studied at Eton and his mother was Lady Jean Agatha Dundas. Interiors photographer Christopher Simon-Sykes was also educated at Eton. Beaton, Parkinson and Armstrong-Jones all had their early social photographs published in *Tatler* and *Bystander*. Editors and journalists employed within Vogue House were not the only ones to benefit from a form of connected nepotism. The work that they created certainly was no lesser than that of others from less illustrious backgrounds; I give these facts merely to illustrate that some doors are more easily opened when you know someone who has a key.

Fashion had reacted to the times by welcoming personal expression, emphasising possibilities rather than insisting on adherence to strict rules. The design of *Vogue* magazine's pages reflected this change, the soft-focus stylized art deco aesthetic of Biba sitting alongside Helmut Newton's intense colour images documenting high-life glamour whilst model and actress Lauren Hutton featured on the cover of the 1974 Christmas issue with no make-up, gap teeth and tousled hair. Vogue House was embracing a decade of contrasts but still remained a world within its own world where some traditional values held. In a 1970 summer issue *Vogue* stated that "the proportion begins and ends with your body, meaning a natural line, soft fluid fabrics and the bosom God gave you... Don't let them know you wear a bra."

"As one of the very few men on *Vogue's* editorial staff my friends thought I'd be in clover. What I learned instead is that there is nothing more a group of young women like to do than to tease a man, particularly one as innocent as I was. My suits and my taste in French cigarettes aroused endless derision. The fact that I coloured at the slightest embarrassment induced a competition as to how red to get me by changing clothes in front of me. 'I want to take you home,' said a powerfully built German female photographer, advancing towards me. It was only the quick action of a colleague that stopped me backing out of an open window behind."

Adrian Hamilton

Vogue

The greatest fashion challenge for Vogue in the 1970s was punk. Its influence could be seen on full display every Saturday afternoon on the King's Road, the epicentre of the 'Chelsea Set'. Vivienne Westwood's shop (named at different times Let it Rock, Too Fast to Live Too Young to Die, Sex and Seditionaries, before being reinvented as Worlds End in 1979, a title it still holds today) was at the World's End, then considered to be the downmarket end of the road. Those wearing her designs, as well as their own homemade and customised punk outfits, promenaded up and down the length of the road from Westwood's World's End, past the Safeway's supermarket, and on to upmarket Sloane Square. Demanding to be recognised by the established fashion bible, Westwood herself once stormed into Vogue House "with a bag full of bondage trousers and a ring through every orifice" and announced that her designs should feature on the magazine's cover, as Coddington revealed in her autobiography: "She had a very aggressive manner. Everyone in the office shrank from challenging her demeanour. But in the end, I stood my ground, talked her down, and eventually she left."

House & Garden remained largely unaffected by the changing tastes and turbulence of the 1970s. Under the stewardship of Robert Harling it continued to feature the latest trends in decoration and interiors; it was a decade that both embraced the image of the rural idyll and city living, with designer and retailer Laura Ashley's image of the 'Edwardian Country Lady', French countryside accessories and William Morris fabrics alongside the intense colours and moulded plastics created by experimental French, American and Italian furniture designers. The 1960s had evolved into the 1970s but little had changed in the way that the *House & Garden* reader chose to decorate their home.

An occasional contemporary piece added to a foundation of traditional design remained the go-to solution for interior designers employed to undertake complete renovations and those looking to update their homes themselves. Habitat founder Terence Conran described his store at the time as "packaged good taste" and it would not be inaccurate to use the same description of Harling's magazine.

Just as *House & Garden* remained a steady ship, *Brides* travelled a calm path throughout the turbulent seventies, continuing to deliver its monthly diet of wedding-based content for its readers planning their big days. Despite its longevity, it suffered from the perennial issue that all wedding magazines must grapple with – a transient readership. A wedding magazine cannot rely upon a committed reader willing to subscribe to it for any longer than it takes for them to plan and execute their wedding. Once married, the bride's need for the magazine no longer exists. This churn of readers presents issues from a circulation perspective, but also relieves the editorial team from the pressure of constantly producing innovative content. A successful wedding magazine has a format and formula that is based upon repeated articles and issues to cover, which the editorial team understand and accept. Consistency and stability are required to produce such a magazine and *Brides* had this down to a fine art. During this period the magazine's editor was Drusilla Beyfuss, then latterly Sandy Boler, and Anna Harvey was the fashion director; all of whom would go on to become mainstays within Vogue House over the following decades.

"I wanted *Brides* to have wonderful photography and it did, and seriously good writing, but I think I may have been the wrong editor for the magazine as it was difficult for me to get into the mind of a potential young bride. Condé Nast is a business and there is always pressure to be commercial and to sell magazines; there are no prizes for a beautiful magazine that doesn't sell. I put together a wonderful team, which I am very proud of, but my one regret is that it was not more commercially successful."
Drusilla Beyfus
Vogue, Brides

"Anna Harvey understood photographers. Editors would plan the shoots, get the girls dressed and oversee the accessories, shoes, hats and sometimes the look didn't work for the photographer, but Anna would pre-empt problems and suggest a solution. She knew when a photographer was struggling, whereas other editors would have their ideas set in stone."

John Swannell
Vogue, Tatler, Brides

"I did quite a lot for *Brides* but one of the nicest jobs I did came through a Princess Anne Wedding Special. I was commissioned to photograph the most expensive florist, caterer, suit hire etc. that was available should you wish to spend huge amounts of money on your wedding day. The element concerning car hire enabled me to organise five vintage Rolls Royce to photograph at Osterley House, Chiswick. I travelled in one of the cars with my assistant and a step ladder, but we had to leave the convoy and go via Vogue House to pick something up. As we arrived, just behind us a VW campervan pulled up. As I got out of my Rolls Royce, the side door of the van opened and out stepped the unmistakeable figure of the legendary Norman Parkinson complete with his fez-like hat. He looked at me and my car and saluted before getting back into the VW to be driven off."

Rod Shone
Vogue, Brides

Anna Harvey began her career at *Harper's & Queen* magazine where she worked alongside Anna Wintour as a junior fashion editor. On the recommendation of photographer Norman Parkinson, Harvey joined Condé Nast in 1970 as the fashion director of *Brides*. Subsequently, in her many years working within Vogue House, she was the deputy editor of *Tatler* and then fashion director of *Vogue*. Whilst at *Vogue* she became the personal style advisor to Diana, Princess of Wales and eventually became deputy editor under Alexandra Shulman, a role which was created specifically for her. Having met Diana at *Vogue* for the first time in 1980, when she was still Lady Diana Spencer, Harvey was chosen by Bea Miller to advise Diana on her choice of wardrobe, a role she continued throughout Diana's marriage to the Prince of Wales. Harvey is also recognised as having brought a number of well-known photographers, designers and fashion figures to *Vogue* and subsequently to the attention of the wider public, including photographers Steven Meisel and Bruce Weber, models Linda Evangelista and Naomi Campbell, fashion editor Isabella Blow, and fashion writer Plum Sykes. In 1986, *Harpers & Queen* named Harvey as the 23rd most influential person in Britain, with the Princess of Wales eight places behind her.

It is easy to think of magazines from the 1970s onwards as being filled with glossy colour pages. However, printing was still not a cheap process and magazines were balancing the cost of colour printing against the cheaper process of printing in black and white. Each issue had a set number of pages that had to be printed in black and white and only certain pages of the magazine would be reproduced in colour. This usually meant that the fashion images in the centre of the magazine, known as 'the well' were in colour and the pages either side of the fashion section were in black and white. This economic necessity affected the photography: most of the portrait photography was shot in black and white, as that was how it would be printed. Only specific fashion and beauty images could utilise colour. However, the following decade was to turn this established order of things on its head. A whole new generation of designers, photographers and stylists coming out of the UK art schools were keen to change this sense of tradition and produce magazines for themselves created by themselves that would express the cultural explosion of maximalism and colour. I will write about what this meant for the Vogue House magazines in the following chapter but suffice to say here that, despite this revolution, when I started at *Tatler* in 1991 the number of colour pages allowed in each issue was still limited.

Chapter 3: 1980–1990
Salads Were More
Popular than Pies

The 1980s were a decade of excess, of 'Loadsamoney', yuppies and Thatcherism, but they were also the decade of the miners' strikes, Greenham Common protests and the Red Wedge. Youth culture was fashion-led and tribal: goths, punks, mods, blitz kids, skinheads, New Wave, New Romantics, psychobilly's, break-dancers, buffalo girls and boys all staked their style claim on the streets. The 1980s also saw new magazines being launched on a regular basis: unisex style magazines *The Face, i-D.* and *Blitz* all published their first issues in 1980, weekly listing magazine *City Limits* launched in 1981 and British *Elle* was established in September 1985. All these new titles provided Vogue House with multiple publishing challenges, the most difficult of which was how to remain relevant in the decade of street culture.

"It was a decade that had begun with the New Romantics, with clown collars and pirate sleeves, with girls in tutus and ballet shoes flitting down the corridor, and ended with 'grown up' tailoring and the beginning of corporate style. When I returned to

71

Vogue House later in the decade I was dressed in Japanese black, like everyone else, my head wrapped in fabric (I don't think anyone saw my hair for a year). But the playfulness and iconoclasm of the street fashion years had not stopped in the writing. I was a beauty editor who never wore make-up and told 'Our Reader' that wrinkles were 'In', alongside a portrait of Edith Sitwell. I was now visiting another floor where *Tatler* was in its heyday, as celebrity culture began to infiltrate the global consciousness."

Charlotte du Cann

Vogue

The Condé Nast titles were the old kids on the block and in the 1980s this was a problem. The first issue of *Vogue* had been published in 1892 and the first issue of *House & Garden* had hit the newsstands in 1901. Despite their continual editorial evolution, both struggled to compete with the energy and the sense of irreverence of the new titles, which had been created by young journalists, photographers and designers inspired by a punk ethos to kick over the statues. Young graphic designers looked to hand-made zines, Russian Constructionism and the Bauhaus for design influence on pages that embraced a new young generation of fashion designers coming out of UK art schools and promoted their own community of new wave musicians, filmmakers and artists who all wanted to be seen in the cool new magazines rather than those of the cultural establishment.

Beatrix Miller remained as editor-in-chief at *Vogue* until 1984. Her tenure at the helm had been successful but just as Audrey Withers had found two decades to be enough, so Miller also saw her twenty-year anniversary as an appropriate point to step down. Her replacement was someone who was to become short-hand for the very essence of *Vogue*, and would become known by some within the building as 'Nuclear Wintour'. As the head of US *Vogue* in New York and Condé Nast internationally, Anna Wintour's name is synonymous with the *Vogue* brand, in print, online and on film, however her time in London at Vogue House was relatively short. Despite this, if I ask people who the editor of *Vogue* is today, it is incredible how many are convinced that it is Anna Wintour. This has happened so often that I now use it as a test with students looking to study fashion photography to see if they really do read *Vogue* or if they are saying they read it because they think they should.

Anna Wintour was born in Hampstead, London. Her father, Charles Wintour, was the editor of London's *Evening Standard* newspaper and he arranged his daughter's first job, at the influential Biba boutique in Church Street, Kensington, founded by fashion designer Barbara Hulanicki, when Wintour was just fifteen years old. She began to take fashion classes at a nearby school, further immersing herself in the world that would become the centre of her life and career, her ambition obvious even at such a young age. Wintour's first experience of magazine production came at the controversial 1960s underground newspaper *Oz* thanks to her then boyfriend, the Australian magazine co-owner, writer and journalist Richard Neville.

In 1970, when UK *Harper's Bazaar* merged with *Queen* to become *Harper's & Queen*, Wintour was hired as one of its first editorial assistants, telling her co-workers there that one day she wanted to edit *Vogue*. However, she left in 1975 after disagreements with Min Hogg, (who will reappear in the Vogue House story in a later chapter) who was the chief fashion editor, a position that Wintour felt she should have been given. Hogg was later quoted on the 8 Percent website as saying "She had a degree of ambition that must have eaten away at her heart. Fashion was her absolute world, and she did know more about it than me. So, she just didn't know how to deal with having someone like me over her."

Wintour moved to New York to become a junior fashion editor at *Harper's Bazaar*. Once again, her time on the magazine was fractious as her innovative but off-brief photography shoots led the editor to fire her after just nine months. A few months later, she secured the position of fashion editor at *Viva*, a women's adult magazine published by the soft porn publisher Bob Guccione. It was at *Viva* that Wintour was first able to hire a personal assistant, which began her reputation as a demanding and difficult boss. In late 1978, Guccione shut the unprofitable magazine down and Wintour was unemployed once more. She took a two-year break from the publishing world.

In 1980, she returned as the fashion editor for *Savvy*, a new women's magazine that sought to appeal to career-conscious professional women who spent their own money how they wished – exactly the readers Wintour would later target at *Vogue*. Once again, she was soon moving on and the following year she became the fashion editor of *New York* magazine, where she started to get noticed once again for the fashion shoots she was styling and directing. However, Wintour's ambition could not be concealed and when a former colleague arranged for her to have an interview with the US *Vogue* editor Grace Mirabella, Wintour told Mirabella that she wanted her job. The interview ended abruptly, but Wintour was not deterred: she was on a mission.

Legendary US *Vogue* art director Alexander Liberman had been promoted to editorial director and publisher of US *Vogue* and, recognising her obvious talent, in 1983 he talked to Wintour about a position on the title. After a self-created bidding war that doubled her salary, she finally accepted and became the magazine's first ever creative director, with vaguely defined responsibilities, under the editorship of Mirabella. Despite not being the editor, Wintour started to make changes to the magazine without Mirabella's knowledge, causing friction amongst the staff who were loyal to their editor. It was obvious that the situation was unsustainable and in 1985 Wintour left New York, crossed the Atlantic and took on her first editorship, as editor-in-chief of UK *Vogue*. She was tasked with a corporate mandate to Americanise the magazine that Bea Miller had nicknamed '*Brogue*' to differentiate it from its US counterpart. Wintour immediately made her presence known, replacing existing staff and adopting an extremely hands-on approach to running the magazine, whilst setting strict rules concerning office hours and the expected dress code, which included high heels, leggings, pearl chokers and bouclé jackets. Wintour also required her female staff to be slight of figure.

"While the 'big wigs' headed to Le Caprice or The Ivy for lunch, the lower orders could buy a sandwich at 'the hatch', a small kitchen on the same floor as the *Tatler* office, where salads were more popular than pies. In summer, Hanover Square was filled at lunchtime,

with Vogue House staff not eating much. Most people ate rice cakes and drank hot water. Though morning toast was a big hit."
Clare Gogerty
Tatler

"The third floor was the *Tatler* floor. I worked briefly on *Tatler,* and I ate my body weight in granary toast and honey from 'Tony's Hatch'."
Susannah Coe
Vogue, GQ, Tatler

Members of the editorial team who escaped the cull referred to this time as 'the Wintour of our discontent'. Her approach and changes to the magazine may have suited the aggressive fast pace of New York City but they certainly jarred with the more genteel approach of the incumbents of Vogue House. Alongside the staff changes informed by Wintour's editorship, and the insinuated dress code, the new editor-in-chief also made physical changes to the offices by implementing a new layout, more open-plan than previously, and moving the departments within it. However, it was the change she made to her predecessor's office that made the most direct statement as to the new direction of the magazine and expected work ethic of her staff, as the renovation was completed in just one weekend. Wintour had a wall knocked down to create a new entrance, the remaining walls were painted linen white, and her own Buchsbaum desk and Biedermeier sofa were installed. Bookshelves were erected to store bound copies of *Vogue* and a 'No Smoking' sign was placed on the shelves alongside Wintour's collection of colourful Clarice Cliff pottery. The carpets were removed, and the original wooden floor restored and polished to a deep glossy shine.

This was the end of Beatrix Miller's era and the new broom, in the shape of Wintour was determined to sweep clean. In her autobiography, Liz Tilberis recalls the Friday before the weekend makeover. "On her last day, I found Bea in her office at five o'clock and realized no one had organized a final goodbye, she was just going to walk out of there forever, alone, on a Friday night. I rushed down the street... for champagne and got everyone together for a proper send-off.

The decorators moved in over the weekend." It is a familiar tale; I have often seen an editor leave in a similar way. The new becomes the focus as the past is rapidly dismissed.

Wintour spoke of her time at British *Vogue* in 1997 at a talk given at a Women in Journalism event in London (later edited and published by the *Guardian*), taking little personal responsibility for the atmosphere she had created amongst her new staff, though she did clearly identify the issues the magazine was facing: "Replacing Bea Miller wasn't easy... there was a 'cosy' but mildly eccentric atmosphere at British *Vogue*... out of step with the fast developing social and political changes that were thundering through Britain in the eighties... So, I decided to infuse the magazine with a bit of American worldliness, even toughness." She continued by stating that, "I still thought of myself as totally English, to my surprise everyone thought I was some sort of American control freak... a wicked woman of steel... I remember letting only two or three people go... a number left of their own accords." Grace Coddington, Wintour's long-time colleague on British and US *Vogue,* has a more succinct view of Wintour's approach, "We, the editorial staff, were all used to hanging about together, being chummy and chitty-chatty, but she wasn't."

"The man who ran 'the hatch' used to come around the offices twice a day with his trolley and offer us cake and coffee for us to eat at our desks. There was something post-war in the way in which the building was run."
Isabella Kullman
Vogue

"I used to just wander in, go up to the fourth floor, and have a cup of tea with the retouchers in the *Vogue* art room."
John Swannell
Vogue, Tatler, Brides

In 1987 Wintour returned to New York to take over *House & Garden* before returning to US *Vogue* as its editor-in-chief. On her leaving it would be fair to say that the building and many of its staff let out a sigh of relief. Two turbulent years on *Vogue* had ended; the new editor would have to not only bring a sense of calm to the team at Vogue House but also change the wider perception of the title and the building as being past its prime.

At this time, I was still a student at art school but I had started working as an intern at British *Elle* on 6th January 1986, just three months after its launch. I did not leave for four years, and when I did, I held the position of design director. The editorial team I worked with at *Elle* came from *The Sunday Times* and the *Observer* magazines and *The Face*, a perfect combination of journalistic experience and style magazine hipness. British *Elle* re-wrote the rules for fashion magazines in the 1980s under its inspirational editor Sally Brampton, who had previously worked at both *Vogue* and the *Observer*. Its design was bold, graphic and unlike any magazine at the time, its features were challenging, intelligent and culturally aware. Twenty pages were devoted to the Mexican artist Frieda Kahlo in one issue, in another a similar number of pages were dedicated to Andy Warhol. Its fashion was directional, bold and creative thanks to the styling and direction of its fashion director Debbi Mason and fashion editors Lucinda Chambers, Anna Cockburn, Harriett Jagger and Debbie Barry. The reason I mention my time on *Elle* here is that, certainly within the *Elle* offices, *Vogue* was never seen as a rival title, and neither was *Harpers & Queen*. At that time within the magazine industry, the Vogue House titles were not seen by many as innovative or a threat. When the team later launched *Elle Decoration* it was intended to be something new, rather than a competitor to *House & Garden*. Vogue House may have been having its own dramas, but they were of little relevance outside its own four walls.

"I went to see Miss Timms in her office in Vogue House. Coming from *Elle* and still in my twenties I thought *Vogue* was a bit fusty and establishment, but I was aware that things were changing. Miss Timms was immaculately dressed in a tweed suit with a silver bob, she was witty and erudite in her wood-panelled office complete with secretary. I immediately felt at home. I'd spent a week getting my portfolio together, but she never asked to look at it, she was more interested in the gossip from *Elle*, and

I remember her regaling me with some internal strife currently taking up her time with *Tatler*. She said there might be positions coming up and would keep me informed."
Geoff Waring
Vogue, Tatler

An interesting aside to this, and further evidence of *Vogue*'s disconnect from what magazines such as *Elle* were doing, is revealed in Jerry Oppenheimer's Anna Wintour biography *Front Row*. According to Oppenheimer, the immediate success of US *Elle* led Si Newhouse and senior management to send a firm message to Grace Mirabella, the editor-in-chief of US *Vogue*, directing her to make her magazine more like *Elle*. She refused to do so, a decision that added momentum to the planning underway for her dismissal and replacement by Wintour.

Wintour's replacement at British *Vogue* was Liz Tilberis. Born in Bristol and expelled from Leicester Polytechnic where she was studying fashion for having a man in her room, in 1967, she was the runner-up in the *Vogue* writing contest. As part of her prize Tilberis gained an internship on the magazine, making tea, picking up dress-pins and ironing clothes for fashion shoots for a salary of £25 per week. Bea Miller noticed how pleasant and enthusiastic Tilberis was and promoted her to fashion assistant in 1970, which in turn led to her becoming an important fashion editor on the title. After twenty years at *Vogue*, and under Wintour's brief editorship, which proved to be an especially turbulent time for Tilberis as her approach to fashion styling and photography was directly opposite to Wintour's, she was offered a lucrative position in New York as part of the US fashion designer Ralph Lauren's design team. Tilberis sold her house and was about to leave for the United States when Wintour called her into her office and informed her that she was moving to New York to become the new editor of *House & Garden*. Wintour offered Tilberis the job of editor-in-chief of UK *Vogue*, and she accepted. Why and how Wintour was allowed to appoint her successor, rather than this key position being a management decision, is open to debate, but it is perhaps an indication of how she saw her role and position of power at the time.

> "When Anna left, management felt that they needed someone with a background in fashion to take over, so they appointed two editors in effect: Mark Boxer (who was the editorial director for the magazines in the building) and Liz Tilberis. Mark supervised the overall look of the magazine, the features etc. Liz was more of a figurehead so as not to lose the advertising. Mark moved up to the fifth floor and we would have these awkward editorial meetings when you didn't quite know who was in charge. Liz was lovely; she was warm and fun, but she didn't have the background that Mark had and everything he could bring to the magazine."
> **Isabella Kallman**
> **Vogue**

Tilberis was a very different *Vogue* editor to her predecessor. She was also a very different editor to Boxer, as she identified in her autobiography: "We clashed constantly, not even so much about substance as management style. I edit by encouragement and discussion. Mark was much more autonomous and brusque [...] He was a talented man, but the two of us had been locked in an impossible bloodless fray." Tilberis's aim was to bring about a sense of calm and create a magazine that sat stylistically between her mentor Miller's *Vogue* and Wintour's American take on what a magazine should be. She swiftly achieved this and, as the magazine began to adopt a new more relevant personality for the times in the UK, sales began to increase. This success was quickly noticed and in 1992 she moved to New York and took the helm of *Harper's Bazaar* alongside the highly considered art director Fabian Baron to completely re-invent the magazine for the 1990s. Sadly, in December 1993 she was diagnosed with ovarian cancer at just forty-six years old, and spent the next seven years at *Bazaar* balancing chemotherapy and editing the magazine. Tilberis died in 1999, a loss that was felt deeply by the staff who worked with and for her in London and New York.

"I've been trying to call the location van for over an hour. 'Don't go over budget!' screamed Liz Tilberis. I couldn't face explaining that Lauren Hutton had been on the phone to L.A. nonstop."
Sarajane Hoare
Vogue

Sarajane Hoare was perhaps the wildest card in the magazine's fashion pack in the late 1980s and very early 1990s. Hoare was bought to *Vogue* by Wintour, and as senior fashion editor under Tilberis she was given complete creative freedom. She had attended Cheltenham and Gloucester College before studying at the Chelsea School of Art, then working as a stylist for the portrait photographer Roger Phillips. The photographers Mario Testino and Herb Ritts both credit her with making their careers; it was her work with Ritts, reminiscent of the travel fashion photography pioneered by Norman Parkinson, that marked her out as a visionary fashion editor. In 2011 Hoare made a rare public statement concerning her work that was included in the book *Secrets of Stylists: An Insider's Guide to Styling the Stars*: "What I loved about Herb's approach to photography is that it was always organic... It was always extraordinary when we worked together, as something new and strange would evolve out of our stories... We were lucky to be able to explore and take risks in those days ... as magazines like British *Vogue* had not been over commercialised." Despite her own free-spirited nature, Hoare spoke positively about Wintour: "There's so much crap in the fashion business, and Anna sliced it all out... She cut out all the artsy, whimsy stuff and made it real: models in real attitudes, wearing clothes of flesh-and-blood women." Hoare's time at British *Vogue* was short but she set an expectation of creativity for other fashion editors to follow. In 2018 she was named as a contributing fashion editor at *Tatler*.

"Sarajane Hoare was really fabulous, Liz gave her a much freer rein than fashion editors had under Anna Wintour. She did some fantastic stories with photographer Herb Ritts, that were

quintessentially the beginning of how we began to think about supermodels. She was terrific."
Isabella Kullman
Vogue

I have already mentioned the *Vogue* Talent Contest several times in the pen portraits of those that began to work at the magazine, and I will be mentioning it again as it proved over the decades to be the one consistent method for an outsider to achieve a position working within Vogue House. It also achieved almost mythical status due to its uncanny knack of sourcing not only magazine writers, journalists and editors, but multi-talented polymaths capable of achieving considerable success across many creative fields. One of these was Patrick Kinmonth, who won the competition in 1981. Kinmonth studied English Language and Literature at Mansfield College, Oxford and enrolled as an associate student at the Ruskin School of Drawing and Fine Art at the same time. During his undergraduate years he participated in theatre productions and worked as a director, designer and actor. He also took on the role as the art director of *Isis,* the Oxford University magazine. After graduating in 1979, he moved to Venice and worked as a painter and lecturer on modern art and poetry. In 1981, Kinmonth returned to the UK and after winning the *Vogue* Talent Competition was subsequently appointed as assistant features editor of *Vogue.*

Kinmonth's role at the magazine included the creative direction for fashion and portraiture shoots and he collaborated with many renowned fashion and portrait photographers, including his future wife Tessa Traeger, who was creating beautiful and timeless images of food for the magazine to accompany Arabella Boxer's words. Towards the end of the 1980s, Kinmonth returned to painting, before moving on to working as an internationally respected opera director and designer, filmmaker, writer, interior designer, creative director and curator. In 2023 he became contributing editor at large of *World of Interiors.*

Another graduate of the *Vogue* Talent Contest was Sarah Mower, who became associate editor under Tilberis. Today, Mower is chief critic at vogue.com, writing regular columns for both US and Japanese

Vogue, however she started out in a home that had neither a telephone nor a television. Reading and creativity were encouraged, however, and at the age of twelve Mower's Aunt Dodo gave her a subscription to *Vogue*. She studied Art History and English at University Leeds, and it was during her final year that Mower was informed that she was a finalist in the contest. However, the finalist lunch held at Vogue House coincided with her final university exam. Mower arranged to travel to London for the lunch accompanied by a member of the university staff to allow her to both attend the final of the contest and sit her exam the following day. Unlike other future *Vogue* employees, Mower did not immediately use the contest as a stepping stone into Vogue House, choosing a career in journalism on a variety of different titles before finally entering the building and securing a position on *Vogue*.

So far, I have spoken at length about *Vogue* and *Tatler* magazines, their staff and their content but I have not spoken about how the fashion pages are produced. This process evolved over the decades, but it was in the 1980s that it adopted a schedule related to magazine publishing that remains today. Fashion is broken down into two seasons, Spring/Summer and Autumn/Winter, and fashion houses create collections for every season. These are shown to fashion editors and retailers in catwalk shows, usually held in the four 'fashion capitals', Milan, London, Paris and New York, during specific weeks of the year: The editor of each magazine takes their fashion director and a few select fashion editors to the collections, where they sit alongside the catwalk, make notes and return home. Back in the office, themes are identified that occur in more than one collection. These themes become fashion stories, such as 'military', 'block colour', or 'tailoring', for example, and everyone involved ensures that the main brand advertisers are included in each story alongside a smattering of high-street retail names to give further advertising coverage and a sense of affordability. These stories are then allotted to specific models and photographers chosen by the fashion editor, magazine editor, fashion director and art director. Locations are chosen, approaches discussed and finally the photographs are taken. In her book *Talking Fashion,* Sarajane Hoare brought to life the type of conversation that would surround such decision-making within Vogue

House in the 1980s: "'I'll do random edits and use up the heavies!' shouts one editor. 'I'd kill to do wild warrior-women in tweeds on a hilltop,' says another. 'I'd like to show it off, but oh, you know, on old but new,' adds another. 'What about those massive Bombers, should we blow them up?' 'You've got to show the 'Chunkies.'"

This may sound like an environment of chaos, but Hoare suggests that this was not the case, remarking that at *Vogue* these fashion meetings lasted just minutes but "themes were quickly translated into key trends, broken down to shooting assignments, and allocated to the editors most suited to styling them."

After the relative calm of the 1960s, and the settled environment within Vogue House in the 1970s, the 1980s had provided *Vogue* with three editors in just ten years and more than a little drama. Elsewhere in the building little changed. *House & Garden* kept doing what it had done for the past two decades under the editorship of Robert Harling and *Brides* did the same under its Australian editor Sandy Boler. Boler had taken over as editor of *Brides* in 1983. Another editor from the 'Miller School of Editing', Boler had begun as the underwear editor on *Vogue* under Ailsa Garland before becoming a qualified corsetiere, a position gained having "skipped" into Vogue House on impulse while crossing Hanover Square and asking for a job.

"The first time I walked into Vogue House was by accident. It was in May 1962. I was nineteen and had come to London for a party, having been given two days leave from my boss, Sheila Scotter, who worked in fashion couture promotion in Paris where I lived. I had never heard of Hanover Square but found it taking a short cut for Bond Street. The building immediately stood out and the words, so proud and simple, seemed to say it all: Vogue House, Hanover Square. I walked in and a few hours later found myself in the senior fashion editor Pat Cunningham's office, being interviewed for a job as a junior fashion editor of *Vogue* in London. After a while she made her excuses and left the room. Ten minutes passed and I was just about to get up and leave when she returned and offered me the job. It turned out that Sheila Scotter was also

in London, also in Vogue House, and was being offered the job of editor of Australian *Vogue* at that very moment. I felt like Alice in Wonderland. One hour, one building, had changed my life.
Sandy Boler
Vogue, Brides

Boler swiftly gained the respect of her colleagues and staff on *Brides*, embracing the bridal world and becoming an authority on all things wedding-related. The magazine became a reliable and confident title with some commercial success, despite the number of brides declining by 50% during her tenure as editor. In 1982 *Brides* sold 58,412, and in 2002, on her departure from the magazine, its circulation was 65,450. Boler was regularly asked to consult and comment on high profile and royal weddings and found her own husband within Vogue House when she married the *Vogue* features editor Adrian Hamilton.

"Four totally different looks were my aim for every issue. No more 'Dash than Cash' by name as that would have sounded too down-market, which would never do. No bride wanted to seem too frugal in those days. David Bailey, Terence Donovan, Julian Broad, Tony Armstrong-Jones, David Montgomery, Tony McGee and Paolo Roversi, Sandra Lousada and Sheila Rock were just a few of the photographers who photographed wonderful pages for us and one of the most successful features we did in every issue was 'Real Life Brides'. It was always difficult to choose who to feature and we were inundated with requests, letters with pictures, snaps of ideas and descriptions of what they wanted to look like. I think my favourite was a reader I met at a fashion show of wedding dresses we arranged for our readers, a small girl in the front row. There was something special about her. I realised that she was a victim of the Thalidomide scandal looking for ideas for her dress. We made wonderful pictures of her, and she was thrilled with the result. I remember Beatrix Miller telling me when I went to *Brides* that the readers shouldn't dictate the look. For once I disagreed and years later, she called

me, rather exhausted from shopping with her niece for her wedding dress. She apologised and said that I was right."
Sandy Boler
Vogue, Brides

One magazine that had openly recognised and ridiculed the launch of *Elle* magazine was *Tatler*, in one issue marking the arrival of the French magazine in the UK with a series of spoof fashion images aping the design, spirit and language of the new pretender. However, *Tatler* had undergone a series of seismic reinventions of its own over the many years it had been in existence. Founded in 1901 by the journalist Clement Shorter, previously the editor of *The Illustrated London News* and founder of *The Sketch*, the magazine's history goes even further back as Shorter chose the name *Tatler* based on a literary and society journal founded by the Anglo-Irish playwright and politician Richard Steele in 1709. A leather-bound copy of the journal used to exist in the Vogue House archives, and I hope it still does.

In 1940, the magazine absorbed the social events magazine *Bystander* and became *The Tatler and Bystander*, a history referenced in *Tatler* today with the party section still titled *Bystander* and including that magazine's black and red illustration of a figure. In 1961, Illustrated Newspapers, which published *The Tatler*, *The Sphere*, and *The Illustrated London News* was bought by businessman and publisher Roy Thomson, which led in 1965 to *The Tatler* being re-named *London Life*. However, Thomson soon sold the magazine and in 1968 it was bought by Guy Wayte's Illustrated County Magazine Group and the *Tatler* name was restored. Wayte's group had a number of county magazines in the style of *Tatler*, each of which mixed the same syndicated content with county-specific local stories. This may have seemed like the perfect publisher for the magazine, but in 1980 Wayte (described in the *Independent* newspaper in 2009 as "a moustachioed playboy of a conman") was convicted of fraud for inflating *Tatler*'s circulation figures from 15,000 to 49,000.

"When I first began working for *The Tatler* in 1981 it was owned by an interesting Australian entrepreneur called Gary Bogard. The

magazine was getting a lot of attention and Condé Nast bought it in 1982 for what we heard was a million pounds! We moved offices from Covent Garden to Vogue House and there was a welcome drinks for the staff in a boardroom, where I took a picture of Miles Chapman and Tina Brown with Bernie Leser, who was one of the suits at Condé Nast. It felt a bit like we were joining the grown-ups."
Dafydd Jones
Tatler

Prior to Wayte's fraud conviction he sold *Tatler* in 1977 to the Australian real estate millionaire Gary Bogard, who relaunched it as a monthly magazine, returning to its 1960s title of *Tatler & Bystander*. It retained this name until June 1982 when it was purchased by Condé Nast, moved into Vogue House and the title reduced to simply: *Tatler*. The *Tatler* story is a complicated one, with its owners, title and staff constantly changing, and it was not until 1989, seventy-eight years after its first issue, that it finally began to find a commercially sustainable identity thanks to its new editor Tina Brown. Brown's time at the magazine was brief but her impact was powerful and long-lasting.

"The first time we met Tina Brown I was surprised at her bluntness. She would speak her mind. She was always on the lookout for new talent. She gave the impression she'd drop you if she found someone whose work she preferred."
Dafydd Jones
Tatler

"Dafydd changed the face of parties. That was Tina Brown's influence. Tina said, 'Listen, we don't want Lord and So-and-so descending the staircase. We want someone being thrown into a swimming pool or debagged. We want outrageous photographs.'"
John Graham
Tatler

Tina Brown was born in Maidenhead, Berkshire in 1953. Her father was active in the British film industry as a producer, and her mother was an executive assistant to actor/director Laurence Olivier on his first two Shakespeare films in the 1940s. These influences may have informed many of her editorial decisions later in life, as she certainly recognised the power of celebrity and Hollywood. In an interview with the *Guardian* in 2010, Brown admitted that she was considered "an extremely subversive influence" as a child, resulting in her expulsion from three boarding schools. Despite this she entered Oxford University aged seventeen and graduated with a degree in English Literature. As an undergraduate she wrote for *Isis*, the university's literary magazine, and for the *New Statesman*, winning *The Sunday Times* National Student Drama Award. Brown was already a prodigious and ambitious talent at just twenty-six when she was asked to edit *Tatler*.

In a 2023 article in the *New Yorker* Brown described in blunt terms how she saw the magazine that she inherited, calling it "a threadbare shiny sheet with staples through it". Her opinion was that the front pages of "choleric colonels and plump-shouldered débutantes grimacing at each other over a glass of warm amontillado or milling with company directors in very new deerstalkers at country-race meets where you might get a whiff of the royals" were the only decent part. She identified that the Thatcher-era eighties hid beneath its harsh edges a "nostalgia for the *Brideshead Revisited* era of aristocratic whimsy and frolicky romance" and determined that *Tatler* needed to "reflect all these crosscurrents, the emerging social edge, the high-low social mix, the secret excesses that still existed behind the closed doors of the great houses of England, and it needed to be chronicled with a cleverly irreverent point of view."

Brown immediately turned the magazine into a modern glossy title with covers by celebrated photographers such as Norman Parkinson, Helmut Newton and David Bailey. Fashion was overseen by the brilliant Michael Roberts, known for his wit and sense of immaculate style. Party and social photography was led by Dafydd Jones, a photographer who brought an insider sense of documentation to his work, revealing a seldom seen side of aristocratic parties and events. Articles were written by Brown's contemporaries and those from her literary circle, including Julian Barnes, Dennis Potter, Auberon Waugh, Brian Sewell, Martin Amis and former *Vogue* employee Georgina Howell, whom Brown appointed as deputy editor. The *Tatler* office had two large rooms, a glass editor's office and six small three-person offices where gossiping, reading and smoking were the order of the day. It was only later in the decade that the offices were removed to create an open plan space under Mark Boxer's editorship. Brown wrote articles for every issue and was obviously on a mission to establish both herself and *Tatler* within the publishing sector as important players. *Tatler* increased its sales from 10,000 to 28,000 over just two years that she was editor.

Such a circulation increase made the magazine commercially attractive, and Condé Nast became the final publisher in its chequered history. However, despite the commercial success of the magazine and the profile Brown had created for herself, she resigned in order to become a full-time writer once more. Her sabbatical from magazines didn't last long and she was lured back to *Tatler* and Vogue House for just a few months before being given the editorship of US *Vanity Fair* in 1983, a title Condé Nast had resurrected earlier that year.

As well as bringing a formidable cast of contributors to the magazine Brown had built an editorial team of creative eclectics with strong personalities. Michael Roberts was certainly one, and his vision and humour infused the look and design of the magazine. Born in Aylesbury in 1947 Roberts' mother came from St Lucia in the West Indies. He studied graphic and fashion design at High Wycombe College of Art before working as a freelance fashion illustrator for publications including *The Sunday Times*, *Nova* and British *Vogue*. In 1972, he was appointed as the fashion editor at *The Sunday Times* and in 1981 he moved to *Tatler*, also as the fashion editor. In 1983 he moved to *Vanity Fair* in New York but swiftly returned to *Tatler* the following year as the fashion and art director, a rare combination of roles at the time and even today. In 1986, he was appointed design director of British *Vogue*. The combination of Roberts' graphic skills and ability to transcend the formal responsibilities of having to work within one area of creative practice saw *Tatler* develop a visual identity unlike any other magazine on the newsstand at the time. His cultural heritage also added some much-needed diversity to the building. However, his creative adventurism was not always met with a positive response.

> "Michael Roberts had the idea to commission the artist Damian Gascoigne to make drawings of my party photographs and to publish them rather than my photographs. When the terminally ill Mark Boxer heard of the plan from his hospital bed, he ordered the whole project to be scrapped."
> **Dafydd Jones**
> **Tatler**

When I became the art director of *Tatler* it was Roberts' wit and willingness to take risks that informed everything I did. I reached out to him when writing this book, and although his reply stated that he didn't want to share his memories, he wished me luck with the book. Just two weeks after I received his response Roberts died.

> "I'd been hired by Tina Brown on a flat fee including expenses which meant that if I worked hard, I lost money. When Libby Purves became the editor, she paid my expenses separately which doubled my pay. Of course, my expenses were nothing like Michael Roberts'. His expenses were legendary."
> **Dafydd Jones**
> **Tatler**

One of the most eccentric, loved, tragic, unique and – for some – exasperating personalities who ever worked at Vogue House began her time in the building as Roberts' assistant. Isabella Blow (the Hon. Isabella Delves Broughton) was the granddaughter of the wealthy businessman Jock Delves Broughton, who fatally shot the playboy lover of his much younger wife Lady Diana Broughton and upon whom the film *White Mischief*, set in Kenya in the 1940s, was based. She began working on Boxer's *Tatler* in 1986 and, as her husband Detmar Blow and Tom Sykes recount in *Blow by Blow*, she started as she intended to continue: "She was wearing a feather cocktail hat, a very short pouffe cocktail dress, and a pair of very worn-down Manolo's." Even in Vogue House this was an outfit that would mark her out as an original. However, such original thinking was not a solid foundation for the administrative duties required for the role of assistant so Blow was soon moved out of the fashion room by Boxer and given four pages in every issue to oversee and commission. As we will later discover, Blow's approach to commissioning paid little heed to editorial budgets. Famously she submitted perhaps the highest expenses claim in Vogue House history. As Detmar Blow revealed it was, in his wife's words, "Just £50,000 for a very small ruin which was really a must!" Unsurprisingly it was never paid.

Such an unconventional approach to magazine protocol was also present in her approach to commissioning photographers, as Dan Lepard revealed in conversation with Detmar Blow: "The night before I was to meet Issie, I was carried out of The Ritz completely drunk. I arrived to see her at Vogue House with a bad hangover and sick in my hair. Issie told me, 'On that basis alone I will work with you!'"

In 1989 Blow returned from her honeymoon and was fired from *Tatler*. Despite her upset at such a turn of events she immediately took the lift up to the fifth floor and introduced herself to Liz Tilberis. The next day she received a handwritten note from the Vogue editor stating that "I can find a job for you on *Vogue*." Blow was still in the building.

Part of my attempt to recapture some of *Tatler*'s irreverence when I was its art director was to reemploy the photographer Dafydd Jones after he returned to London from New York in the mid 1990s, to document the social events that featured in the 'Bystander' pages each month. Jones had been originally employed by Brown who described him as "a strikingly elfin presence, so young, so hesitant, so unassuming" in the *New Yorker* in 2023. She went on to note that "His own humble origins, including attending a state-run school in Oxford and making extra money as a campus cleaner, were the perfect townie vantage point from which to view the privileged antics of the Oxford jeunesse dorée." Jones had brought an informed sense of documentary narrative to the party pages, showing the aristocracy more often than not misbehaving and indulging in extreme decadence. As Brown commented, "Dafydd was never co-opted by the world he covered. There is no one better than Dafydd at capturing the moments of privileged pretension."

Despite Brown's departure the *Tatler* team largely remained intact, which is unusual when an editor leaves. The experienced and highly regarded cartoonist, art director and editor Mark Boxer (whose wife Arabella was the Food editor on *Vogue*), was Brown's successor. The magazine under Boxer continued Brown's ethos for the title, appealing to the young aristocracy and children of the 1960s 'Chelsea Set' – or 'Sloane Rangers' as they were named in 1975 by style commentator Peter York, leading to the wildly successful book *The Sloane Ranger's Handbook,* a bestseller in 1982. The magazine now had a young audience, but it was a limited and exclusive readership. This worked as long as the magazine was sharp, witty, intelligent and irreverent, and under Boxer it achieved these aims. This success resulted in Boxer being given the positions of editor-in-chief of *Tatler* and editorial director of Condé Nast. Tragically he developed a brain tumour and died in 1988 aged just fifty-seven. His loss was a great one to publishing, to *Tatler* and to all the magazines within Vogue House. As the decade ended and the economic state of the country declined, *Tatler* became increasingly detached and marginal.

"When Mark Boxer became editor *Tatler* had a golden period. It was the best magazine I've worked for, with fashion by Joe Mckenna, Isabella Blow and Michael Roberts. Spoofs by Craig Brown and brilliant writing and photography."
Dafydd Jones
Tatler

Much has been written about Tina Brown and there is no doubt that her time at *Tatler* was a launchpad for her stellar career but Boxer's time in Vogue House was longer, and although his name may not be as well known to those outside of publishing his impact on British journalism is worth recording at this point. Boxer was the son of a second-hand car dealer from Watford who was educated at the independent Berkhamsted School before attending Kings College, Cambridge, where in 1952 he became editor of the student magazine *Granta*. Upon leaving Cambridge, he became the editor of *Lilliput*, before being made art director of *Queen*. In 1962, Boxer was appointed as the founding editor of *The Sunday Times* magazine, but in 1965 he left to relaunch the ailing *Tatler* as *London Life*. However, never one to sit still for too long he soon returned to *The Sunday Times* in a reduced role, giving him time to develop his work as a cartoonist. After a brief period as a book publisher at Weidenfeld & Nicolson in 1983, he accepted the editorship of the revived *Tatler* now under the ownership of Condé Nast.

Drawing under the pen-name 'Marc', Boxer also came to prominence as a cartoonist with the regular cartoon 'Life and Times in NW1', which ran in *The Listener* from 1968 and satirised the lifestyles of North London trendies. He then began to be regularly commissioned by *The Times* and subsequently the *Guardian*, in collaboration with the humourist, 'jazzer' and Soho bon viveur George Melly. Boxer was rare in the world of publishing – not only was he well connected in literary and newspaper circles, but he was also multi-talented, bringing a similar professional but laid-back approach to all disciplines.

In an article for *The Oldie* magazine in 2018 writer Mary Killen spoke of her time working on *Tatler* when Boxer was editing the magazine: "Why did young journalists want to be on *Tatler* in 1984? My older friend Anne put it succinctly, 'In the sixties, it was pop stars; in the seventies, it was photographers; in the eighties, it's the upper classes. They are where it's at!'" To prove Killen's point, it was a parody in a 1987 issue of *Tatler* of a *Spectator* political column that led to her flatmate at the time, Craig Brown, who was then the editor of the *Bystander* pages, being asked by *The Times* to do four parliamentary sketches each week. At £250 pounds for every piece of writing, it was what he described as being his first real money and first regular employment.

"Marc Boxer took me to Lords for the day to watch the cricket. Someone in Vogue House had organised a Fortnum's hamper with all sorts of delicious sandwiches and a bottle of Chablis. Mark had lots of ideas to discuss with me, but he also had a problem. The journalist Vicky Woods had negotiated for herself a company car as part of her salary package. A white Mini Metro. But Vicky was leaving and returning the car. Mark didn't want it to be generally known in the office that a company car was possible for anyone, but he also didn't want to lose it. So, he asked would I have the car? That question led to my meeting Miss Timms who organised the handover of the car to me. I let my wife use it to do the school run."

Dafydd Jones
Tatler

Boxer was an anarchic figure who followed few rules, and he evolved an editorial team that was very much in his likeness. The writer and features editor Jonathan Meades certainly fitted this description. In one particularly infamous event a furious Meades grabbed Albert, a colleague's dachshund, and threatened to dangle the dog by its back legs from the third-floor window. Fortunately, the threat was never carried out, but it is a good illustration of the freewheeling office protocol under Boxer. Whilst at *Tatler*, Meades started writing short stories about rural lowlife, however they were considered to be too rich for *Tatler* pages, so they were published in *Harpers & Queen*, a rival publication. In due course they were collected and published in the book *Filthy English*. Meades left *Tatler* in 1986 and became the restaurant critic for *The Times,* a job he did for the next fifteen years. I reached out to Meades to contribute to this book and his wonderfully succinct response adds an interesting take on the writer's time on *Tatler*: "Thanks for the invitation but I'm afraid your project doesn't interest me. Good luck with it."

Alongside Meades, Craig Brown, the satirist, novelist, writer and critic, was another of the *Tatler* editorial team at the time. Brown was educated at Eton, where he wrote for the school magazine, and at the University of Bristol, where he studied drama before setting out as a freelance journalist. He reflected upon his time at *Tatler* "writing amusing captions and punning headlines for party photographs" in a 2022 column for the *Daily Mail*, "My job... took at most two hours a month, but I was employed for eight days a month... I found the comings and goings at the fashion department particularly diverting. Skinny models arrived clutching folders... people from the fashion and art departments flicked impassively through their photographs, brutal customs officers at the barriers to the world of glamour... men and women, with names familiar from their own designer labels, would pop their heads round the door from time to time, in order to schmooze and be schmoozed by the fashion editors."

You will have noticed reading this book how many people who worked within Vogue House attended Oxford University in particular, as well as various public schools including Eton. These educational similarities are particularly prevalent in the editorial teams. In a sense you could identify this sense of educational nepotism not only as a theme of this book but of Vogue House itself. Brown commented on the impact Eton had on his career in a 1994 interview with the *Independent*, and perhaps unintentionally gave some explanation as to why so many privately educated people have worked and continue to work at 1 Hanover Square. "The world is interested in Etonians [...] It's been said that Eton's greatest gift is arrogance, which you can choose whether to use or not."

The replacement for Boxer at *Tatler* was Emma Soames, the former features editor on *Vogue* under Anna Wintour. Soames was born in 1949, the granddaughter of Sir Winston Churchill, a self-confessed non-academic who skipped university and who studied at the Sorbonne in Paris. Her appointment came at a time when her marriage had broken up and she was drinking heavily, whilst the death of Boxer hung over the building. Soames, a self-confessed alcoholic at the time, could not fill Boxer's shoes and *Tatler's* circulation dropped rapidly. Just two years later she was very publicly sacked.

"The art director, Dorothy Ann Harrison, stalked the corridors wearing a zebra-patterned Philip Treacy hat (she had 'discovered' him at the RCA) on her way to talk to Isabella Blow about her next shoot. Michael Roberts made the occasional, shadowy appearance, delivering another clever, witty set of pictures (Vivienne Westwood as Margaret Thatcher, or the *Too Rich to Walk* cover shot about US heiress Barbara Hutton) then

vanishing. Mary Killen (now of *Gogglebox* fame) wrote a society advice page called 'Candid Counsel'."
Clare Gogerty
Tatler

"My first *Tatler* commission, in April 1989, was to write a feature about Boy George interviewing Mary Whitehouse. I couldn't believe my luck getting the idea into *Tatler*, but it was true to the anarchic spirit of the magazine"
Jessamy Calkin
Tatler

The 1989 *Tatler* cover featuring Vivienne Westwood dressed up as Margaret Thatcher is a classic example of the type of trouble-making the magazine became famous for. This trouble-making spirit was also possibly one of the reasons why the magazine's sales plummeted, as it was just too clever and self-referential to attract and retain a broad readership. The April 1989 cover shows the iconic designer (and previous Vogue House interloper) wearing a black suit and pearls, with an exact recreation of Thatcher's signature 'Iron Lady' hairstyle. The words "this woman was once a punk" are plastered across the cover in graphic designer Jamie Reid's iconic punk ransom-note typography. No other cover lines were included or reasons to buy the issue given. This was not a cover designed to sell magazines, but one based on self-gratification; this is not a criticism but merely the reality. In her diaries titled *Get A Life!* published in 2016, Westwood explains how she played the role of this divisive figure wearing a suit from Aquascutum that the prime minister had once ordered and then cancelled which provided her with motivation: "Margaret Thatcher was a hypocrite. That's what I put in my head. I thought there's the child in the hospital bed and there's the TV camera. I'm going to show the world how much I care." She goes on to note that when the controversial cover was blown up on billboards during London Fashion Week "even I had to look twice to believe it was me. One-week, later *Tatler's* editor Emma Soames got the sack. I've never asked Emma if there was any connection."

"Emma Soames became editor, but she had a difficult job following Mark. I wasn't sure how much she 'got' my pictures. The party coverage could be cruel if the pictures were used in the wrong way. Then there was a recession on the horizon. Someone mentioned introducing colour photography to Bystander and having more flattering pictures of smiling faces. At that point I decided to go to New York."
Dafydd Jones
Tatler

One of the *Tatler* members of staff at this time was Nicholas Coleridge, who in 1979 was made associate editor under Tina Brown, whilst his university debating friend Craig Brown was also contributing to the magazine. The son of David Coleridge, chairman of Lloyd's of London (the family is descended from a brother of the famous poet Samuel Taylor Coleridge) and educated at Eton and Trinity College, Cambridge, Coleridge began his career in journalism as a cub reporter on the *Falmouth Packet* newspaper in Cornwall before joining *Tatler*. From there he went on to becoming the editor-in-chief at *Harpers & Queen* before returning to Vogue House in 1989 as editorial director after the death of Mark Boxer, before being appointed as managing director Condé Nast Britain, and latterly as vice president Condé Nast International and then president Condé Nast International. Coleridge retired in 2017.

One contributor I have not mentioned so far is John Graham, the magazine's Bridge journalist. Yes! Bridge journalist! John was still contributing his monthly Bridge column when I started at *Tatler* in 1991. My memory of him was of being the type of man that could easily have been in the Guards: polite, well-spoken but not to be crossed. He was made of stern stuff: according to his obituary in the *Telegraph* "his indefatigable search for the perfect cocktail almost killed him when he was once served a drink containing a shard of glass that he mistook for ice. Since the operation that saved him also uncovered cancer for which he was treated, he regarded the incident as something of a blessing."

Graham's career began in Washington, where, after five years as a correspondent for the *Financial Times*, he became that newspaper's US editor in 1969, aged just twenty-nine. After Washington, he was then their correspondent in Belfast, Vietnam and the Middle East. In 1972 he was named the specialist writer of the year in the National Press Awards for his reports from both Northern Ireland and Vietnam. In 1986 Boxer took him on as a sub-editor at *Tatler*, at a time when Graham was short of funds, as he already wrote the bridge column. In his youth, he had attended Eton and St Paul's before attending Worcester College, Oxford, where he was a classical scholar. A gifted sportsman, he was named as one of Wisden's most promising schoolboy cricketers and continued to play the game into his fifties. However, he found himself increasing drawn to playing bridge and backgammon, on one occasion reaching the semi-finals of the world backgammon championships. The sub-editing didn't last but the *Tatler* bridge column did until Graham's death in 2011.

Tatler had come to Vogue House in 1982 but it was not the only magazine that Condé Nast brought to the building in the 1980s. *House & Garden* was well-established and professionally run but in 1983 a new lifestyle magazine was purchased by Condé Nast that covered similar ground and came with an editor who epitomised the magazine she led. *Interiors* magazine had been launched in November 1981 by the Irish publisher Kevin Kelly, with Georgina 'Min' Hogg as its editor. Beautifully photographed and elegantly designed, its individual approach to interiors and its literate approach to articles, informed by Hogg, set it apart from existing interiors titles. In fact, the magazine proved so successful that within six months of its launch in November 1981, Condé Nast had made an offer to purchase it. In June 1982 they acquired a half-interest, changing its name to *World of Interiors* as there was already an American magazine titled *Interiors*.

Hogg was born in 1938 and was the daughter of Sir James Cecil Hogg, an ear specialist whose patients included Queen Elizabeth II. She attended public school and went on to the Central School of Art to study graphic design with furniture designer and Habitat retailer Terence Conran. Conran's wife, Caroline, was working at *Queen* and asked Hogg to join the magazine as a typist. Hogg briefly left to write for the *Observer* on interior decoration and architecture, and worked as a photographer's agent, but in 1974 she returned to *Queen* (now rechristened *Harper's & Queen*) as a fashion editor, eventually progressing to chief fashion editor much to the frustration of Anna Wintour, who had wanted the role as I have previously mentioned. Hogg stayed on at *Harper's & Queen* until 1979 when she left to become the fashion editor at *Sheba*, an Arabic-language magazine aimed towards the wives of Middle Eastern oil barons before being appointed the launch editor of *Interiors* in 1981.

Condé Nast's official position was that *World of Interiors* offered an exclusive upmarket image which would appeal to those seeking escapism and fantasy, whilst *House & Garden* was more accessible, and wanted the titles to be complementary rather than rivals. Each editor would certainly be able to hold their ground, Hogg having had serious magazine experience by this time with the type of people who inhabited Vogue House and Harling well established in his editorship of *House & Garden*. However, it is hard to see *House & Garden* at the time as not being upmarket or being accessible to the majority of the British public. It is more likely in my opinion that Condé Nast took a business decision to purchase a potential rival to its existing title, to protect one and profit from the other. The success of *World of Interiors* would support this theory, as the December 1983 issue had a circulation of 52,000 issues per month, with 7,000 in the United States where they could not sell the UK *House & Garden*. It also boasted many notable subscribers, including Jacqueline Onassis, Paloma Picasso and US fashion designer Bill Blass. In 1983 alone, the advertising revenues on *World of Interiors* rose by 68 percent year-on-year.

"We all had these giant pinboards, and there was a sort of thing where if you started at the *World of Interiors*, you weren't really allowed to take off the other person's pictures, but you were allowed to add to it. They were a layer upon layer of images to show what your eye saw, and your aesthetic was. And so, you would add your layer on to this pinboard, but they became four inches thick with references."
Faye Toogood
World of Interiors

World of Interiors was Hogg's magazine and remained so until she retired as editor in 2000. It reflected her tastes and interests and as such remained consistent in its editorial tone and identity throughout her time, maintaining consistent sales with a large and important subscription base. It defied and ignored fashion, creating its own world within the interiors sector, a difficult feat to achieve but one which it did with ease and confidence. Hogg's approach followed no rulebook, as she revealed when she stated that: "I think we've got a knack for trapping what's in the air, and it's always far too soon for the mass-market." She also had no time for modern publishing's obsession with market research and finding out what the readers wanted. "You mean you actually care what they think?" was her opinion of such perceived folly. In Hogg's opinion, if readers failed to buy *World of Interiors*, then there were other magazines for them to purchase. That was not her problem. Hogg ran *World of Interiors* primarily to please herself, and according to her obituary in the *Guardian* in 2019, written by Veronica Horwell, she once threw a solid pottery ashtray at her publisher when they queried the financial returns her magazine was achieving.

> "Min Hogg gave me chances when I was just beginning in photography, and extraordinary opportunities. She was amazing to work with on shoots, giving me so much freedom and choice, whilst quietly steering here and there; I think I was always keeping an extra eye on what she was looking at, or where she was looking at the room from. I learnt a lot from her."
> **Simon Upton**
> **Homes & Gardens, World of Interiors, Tatler, Vogue, GQ**

> "I heard about a job at *World of Interiors*. So, I went to see Min Hogg and asked if I could apply. And she said yes – 'Can you sew, and can you tie bows?' I could tie a bow. I couldn't sew but I knew my sister could, so I thought that's fine, I will just lie about that. And then she said, 'I want to see your eye and how you see the world.' So, I took an old suitcase full of things that I had collected drawings, found objects, you know, stones

in their shells, postcards, scrapbooks – it was a massive suitcase. And I dumped it on her desk. And then two days later, she called me and said, "You've got the job". And that was it. That was the interview process. It was classic Condé Nast. Literally three weeks later I was working with a photographer photographing ten pages for the magazine not really knowing what I was doing at all. In my first week I dropped a seventeenth-century teapot that was worth £1,500!"

Faye Toogood
World of Interiors, House & Garden

Hogg described her approach as celebrating homes personalised by their residents, rather than interiors created by professional decorators, and stated that she wanted to promote eclecticism, vintage style and individualism, not modernism or minimalism, promoting interiors that used historical textiles and artefacts to create a romantic and rarefied effect. Although she also stated that she was simply doing whatever pleased her.

"Min had a daily stream of visitors who would perch beside her regaling her with their adventures. Nicky Haslam on his nights at Annabel's, James Mortimer on his Greek excursions and Simon Upton on his latest photo shoot. They gossiped and plotted their trips abroad in search of new houses to poke around in. I so loved being around the WOI team. They were all so brilliant and ahead of all the trends and fashions. Min and I co-existed harmoniously, most of the time, although disagreements were debated for hours. She loved the back and forth of an argument and would never hold back. Irrational, irrepressible and so compelling – always with a cigarette, pink lipstick and a loupe hanging from her neck, Min Hogg was a true great of Vogue House."

Ciara Hunt
World of Interiors

Whilst I mention *World of Interiors* at this point, as it seems to be the right time for it to enter the Vogue House story, it didn't actually move into the building for several years after the Condé Nast purchase. Instead they shared office space with the Condé Nast circulation department in another building across town.

The 1980s saw Vogue House welcome three new magazines through its revolving door – *Tatler*, *World of Interiors* and, in 1988, *GQ* – to join the three original magazines housed in the building. *House & Garden*, *World of Interiors* and *Brides* presented no controversy, only editorial stability. They seemed to understand their readerships, offering safe but professionally produced magazines each month. They were not setting the world alight, but they were doing what they did well. The staff on these magazines were employed through connections and referrals and seemed content to produce the magazines their experienced editors requested. Meanwhile, *GQ*, *Tatler* and *Vogue* had had a decade of change and challenge, as their sectors of publishing had become more competitive, diverse, inclusive and democratic, which they had struggled to respond to. Little did anyone know that the coming decade was to challenge them even further in ways that they could never have imagined.

Chapter 4: 1990–2000
Find It Yourself!

The 1990s were my decade in Vogue House. It was, if I am honest, a decade that I had given little credence to before starting to write. I had always had a nostalgic feeling that the 1960s were the fun years in fashion publishing, the decade when the most rules were broken and the best work was created. Now I think I was wrong, and I am not alone. In 2022, an announcement for a documentary television series to be called *In Vogue: The 1990s* stated that "the 90s was such an exciting and important decade for fashion. It was the period when fashion entered the mainstream – when it became inescapable, culturally relevant and full of iconoclasm and expression and difference." The 1990s were the decade when Vogue House became fully populated – perhaps overpopulated – and when *Vogue* magazine found itself challenged for relevance and importance by two new titles within its own building. This challenge came not in a fashion sense but instead for controversy and personality, and for newspaper headlines.

There is no doubt that the 90s was the decade when Vogue House caught fire – not literally, of course! There was even talk of the mailroom and loading-bay being the centre of an illegal drug-delivery service around London (and there were subsequent arrests) as this was the decade when everything was delivered to and from the building on the back of a motorbike or in a taxi.

"You heard stories from *GQ*, and you heard stories from *Tatler*. You didn't really hear stories from *Vogue*, you definitely didn't hear stories from *Brides* or *World of Interiors* or *House & Garden*. The bad boys in the operation were *GQ* and *Tatler*. They were just naughty!
Sarah Miller
Condé Nast Traveller

"Vogue House was the hallowed 'Temple of Style' where everyone was in equal parts incredibly chic and absolutely terrifying. Going there as a photographer was like being summoned to the headmaster's study, filling my stomach with butterflies and the nervous desire to hustle out of there as quickly as possible. On each departure I'd breath a deep sigh of both gratitude at being summoned and relief at being back out in Hanover Square's leafy calm."
Andrew Macpherson
Vogue

Having ridden the wave of 1980s style, culture and fashion, magazines entered the new decade as important vehicles for communication. They had become political, intellectual, stylish arbiters of what was cool. The magazine you read said a lot about the type of person you wanted to be, and maybe were. The 1990s was the decade of Cool Britannia, Tony Blair and the Spice Girls, Oasis and Blur, the YBAs (Young British Artists) and lad culture, and in Vogue House a decade of high-profile editors, controversy, elastic expense accounts and high salaries with associated perks for some. Meanwhile, entry into the building and access to working on the magazines was still as politically incorrect and as abstract as it had ever been. Jobs at Vogue House were never formally advertised, they were always discovered through word of mouth.

"I got my job there after a tip-off that someone had resigned on *Vogue*; little did I realise people barely left, so this information was gold. Full of naivety, I sat with the information for an hour or two, then decided to 'cold call' the publisher. I thought nothing ventured, what was the worst thing that could happen? On the call, his extremely efficient PA told me that the publisher was not available, I went to hang up, but was quickly chastised: 'One does not call the publisher's office and not leave your name!' Oh, okay I said, and much to my amazement I was requested to come in at 8.30 a.m. the following day to meet him. I was early – I always am – and sat in my borrowed trousers and smart new jacket and watched other 5'10" well-dressed women slowly (it was a bit early for Condé Nast employees) file into the building. Two things occurred to me: first, I had the wrong bag, a Stüssy mini backpack wasn't going to cut it; secondly, by the look of everyone else, I was the right height for the job. I made the then wise decision to leave my mini backpack with the two nice men at the front desk – 'The Peters' – and I was briskly escorted to the fifth floor, a monochrome rather chilly looking place, and was ushered into the publisher's office. During the interview, a bit of a blur for me, the publisher spent a lot of the time talking and looking out of his large corner office windows onto Hanover Square. I remembered him telling me, 'You know, some women wear the same outfit to work more than once in the same week, that would never happen here.'"

Rachel Reavely
Vogue

"I remember on my first day walking to Vogue House from Oxford Circus tube and seeing this fleet of Condé Nast women heading towards the building immaculately dressed in pashminas and kitten heels with designer handbags, all beautifully accessorised. I instantly thought that the one good pair of shoes I had, the one Mui Mui top and quirky bits I'd bought at Portobello Market weren't going to cut it! It was obvious that I was going into a rarefied world."

Samantha Scott-Jeffries
Tatler, GQ, House & Garden

"It was the autumn of 1993 when I arrived at *Vogue* to do two weeks' work experience. Those first few days entering Vogue House were intimidating to say the least, as women and seemingly confident girls my age and younger, filled the lift, all chicly attired in black opaque tights and Manolo kitten heels. The conundrum of dressing for 'a day at the office' initially induced daily anxiety until I worked out my own personal morning mantra: to nail a quirky cocktail-party look. This made life easier; I could almost throw on what I had worn the night before."

Laura Campbell

Vogue

"In those days job applications were so much simpler. There were no online applications. It was either the *Guardian* media jobs section every Monday or you heard via word of mouth. There were no 'filter bots' dumping applications because they didn't have enough 'keywords' or stressed out, overworked staff having to wade through hundreds of CVs in their lunch breaks. It was 'old school', literally. It was about handwritten letters and chemistry. It was human."

Geoff Waring

Vogue, Tatler

"I was employed by Fran Bentley at *Vogue*, straight out of university in 1998. I sat with her in her smoke-filled office as we went through my CV. I answered her final question and she then sat staring at me in silence; after a minute or two she said, 'No one with a degree in astrophysics has ever asked to work at *Vogue* before. So, I am going to give you a job.' And with that I was promptly deposited in the fashion features department under the watchful eyes of Lisa Armstrong and Luella Bartley. I wasn't exactly shown what to do in my prescribed role as an assistant, but I did find myself listening to an interview with actress Minnie Driver through my headphones and transcribing it to a computer. I was about halfway through when I suddenly became aware of shouting behind me; I spun around to see what was happening only to witness a cup of tea, a full cup of tea, flying through the air and smashing against the glass wall divide in our little section. Tea and broken china were everywhere. And no one was moving. I remember locking eyes with Luella and both of us silently agreeing to vacate the area. Laughing at fashion tantrums never goes down well."

Emma White Turle
Vogue, Tatler

"I left *Vogue* to work in New York, and then returned to work freelance in London when Alex [Alexandra Shulman] asked me to come back to *Vogue*. I said yes, but only for four days a week as I had three children by that point. She sweetly agreed, but I think she then regretted it as then everyone who had a child wanted to only work three or four days a week."

Isabella Kullman
Vogue

"There is a myth, that is not entirely without substance, that to work at *Tatler* – my first entry point to Vogue House – you have to know people. Somehow I slipped through the net, my double-barrelled surname being enough to cloak my suburban childhood and second-rate education with a semblance of poshness. That and desperation – Carmel Allen, the beauty director at *Tatler*, was leaving to work in New York at *NY-LON* and they hadn't found a replacement. 'Ask them for anything,' she said. 'They'll give it to you.' So, with a baby boy who was barely six months old, and a stack of experience and qualifications that more than proved I could do the job, including *Marie Claire* Australia, *Frank*, a stint at the *Telegraph*, a degree in Law and post-grad journalism NCTJ qualifications, I felt emboldened enough to ask for a three-day week, and I was the first journalist in the building, or so I was told, to have part-time status."

Kathleen Baird-Murray
Tatler, Vogue

"After an initial interview on the fifth floor, I went down to meet HR. Walking into a very bright office the formidable Barbara Timms barely looked up from her copy of the *Daily Telegraph* that lay open across her desk. She would soon retire, and her replacement sat next to me. A lot of questions were asked about who I knew in the building."
Susannah Coe
Vogue, GQ, Tatler

"The building was a hive of gossip. When an editor changed there would be a race amongst staffers to tip off Fleet Street newspapers, who would in those days pay generously for 'titbits'."
Dafydd Jones
Tatler

Tatler features writer Harriet Lane described her own interview with Miss Timms, "the elderly personnel director who favoured little black dresses and pearls", in a *Guardian* article in 1999, expressing an experience that was common to many: "She seemed far more interested in my father's profession than my degree result. Later I found out that several colleagues had managed to see what Miss Timms had written down in the margins of their application forms during these 'little chats'. Apparently, she pencilled comments such as 'nice smile', 'good accent' and 'clean fingernails'."

In the 1990s the Newhouse family, owners of Condé Nast, held an estimated personal fortune of $12 billion. The result was that some of the editors could expect six-figure salaries, company cars, chauffeur-driven transportation, daily restaurant lunches and regular luxury perks from advertisers and brands keen to feature within their magazines. Some of the editors' offices were redecorated at great expense, and the building underwent a refresh with a new boardroom built and the reception moved down to the ground floor. A new crescent-shaped desk was installed, 'The Peters' now hidden behind its distressed gold leaf expanse; it was definitely designed to intimidate. On either side of the reception area two upright, uncomfortable velvet banquettes were fitted;

the one on the right would become a regular seating spot at the end of the day for the diarist and playwright Alan Bennett, waiting to meet his partner who was employed on *World of Interiors*. The rest of the time these were where those waiting to be seen would be lined up; models, journalists, photographers and those hopeful of being employed within the building. The new boardroom, where advertisers were wined, dined and schmoozed was decorated with iconic black-and-white images from *Vogue's* illustrious history. It was also the venue for daily drinks, which often became an essential social starter for an evening of further drinking, dining and clubbing across the West End of London.

To those outside Vogue House, the 'Condé Nasties' could appear to be spoilt, privileged and over-paid, but for many the lifestyle was just on loan and it could be withdrawn just as quickly as it was offered.

"Stylish, busy people breezed through and disappeared into the building, and as a visitor you awaited your fate. As time went by, I got to know some of the reception committee, who would say hello and ask how I was. On occasion I would be told to 'go on up' before a call was made – a sort of familiarity had been established, as if a test had been passed. Of course, the lifts were only the first hurdle – the inner doors on some levels were locked and you could be stranded, trying to catch someone's attention to actually get into a magazine. Another hazard that grew with time was seeing someone from another title from that which you were visiting – 'What are you working on?' Of course you couldn't say, but how to not make it a faux pas 'working for the other side', whichever title rivalry was going on at the time."
Simon Upton
World of Interiors, House & Garden, Vogue, Tatler, GQ

An example of the disparity between those who were employed within Vogue House and the rest of the London magazine industry was given by James Brown, the controversial editor of *GQ* whose time there was short-lived. In his autobiography *Animal House* he outlined the package he was offered on joining the magazine. This included a £20,000 signing-on fee and a 120 per cent increase on his previous salary, plus a £10,000 bonus if he increased circulation by 10 per cent every six months, an end-of-year one-off payment of £10,000 if he stayed for twelve months and an additional £20,000 for every further year he completed as editor. His perks included a new Jeep Cherokee, private health insurance, an unlimited expense account and biannual trips to New York, Paris and Milan. These perks were not uncommon. On being made editor-in-chief of *Vogue* in January 1992, Alexandra Shulman was given £4,000 to spend on clothing. Those whose employment ended abruptly in a way that would not meet an employment lawyer's criteria could expect large one-off payments transferred into their bank accounts to ensure that they disappeared quickly and quietly.

"The 1990s had something in common with the 60s, but I think that in reality Condé Nast was still stultified by royalty, hierarchy, status and tradition. They were the establishment wing of magazine publishing. I think in the 90s there was a much younger spirit, there was more adventure, there was a lot more boldness."
Sarah Miller
Condé Nast Traveller

Where once Vogue House had the rather genteel atmosphere of a gentlemen's club, public school or even a ladies' finishing school, the 1990s saw it develop a far more cut-throat and business-like approach to both employment and expectation. In the US, Si Newhouse's firing style was legendary and brutal and there was a sense that a similar approach maybe starting to infiltrate the London HQ. The prevailing wisdom was that changes would be made if expected monthly circulations were not achieved. Despite this new cut-throat attitude to employment across the pond, important positions within Vogue House in London were still primarily filled through connections or direct contact head-hunting. Si Newhouse's cousin Jonathan was starting to be far more hands on when it came to hiring and told Brown that "At Condé Nast we want our editors to be bold, outrageous, passionate and talented." He did not suggest socially connected or public school educated.

"Si used to come over every May and host an editor's lunch at Wilton's, where he always had gull eggs, but the first time I met him was in our office above Turkish Airlines in Hanover Street before we moved into Vogue House. There was nobody there apart from myself and the publisher at the time. I offered him a cup of coffee and went to make it. Probably Nescafe, it must have been disgusting. When I got back to my desk – I swear to God! – he was behind the desk, checking out the pair of Manolo Blahnik's I had brought in to wear to a cocktail party that evening. He was behind my desk, looking at my computer and what I was working on. He then shuffled out in his little slippers, a Loro Piana sweater and his soft trousers, sat down and said, 'Very good.'"
Sarah Miller
Condé Nast Traveller

"There was a distinct air of hierarchy, power and purpose at Condé Nast HQ. You had to brush up on your masthead 'who's who' so you didn't make the grave error of barging in front of an editor in your haste to get into the lift. There were unspoken rules in the office that were adhered to. 'Know thy place' might sum it up well. It was only later that I picked up on the elevator politics: *Vogue* girls headed for the fifth floor glaring dismissively at *Tatler* blondes going to the third floor, who in turn cold-shouldered their own counterparts in the marketing department. Writers being sniffy towards sub-editors and silent disapproval returned if the sub-editor didn't agree with a writer's grasp of grammar – or lack thereof. Assistants were lowly unless working as a magazine editor's PA. Editors were regarded as the most important people, especially those with a capital E for Editor as a title. Deputy editors had more kudos than department editors yet were generally more approachable than the editor-in-chief. Features writers had a sense of being more highbrow than stylists and so on."
Laura Campbell
Vogue

American *GQ* was an established pillar in the US publishing landscape. *Gentlemen's Quarterly* was launched in 1931 as *Apparel Arts*, a magazine for the clothing trade read primarily by wholesale buyers and retail sellers of men's fashion. Initially it had a very limited print run and was aimed solely at industry insiders to enable them to give advice to their customers. Its popularity amongst retail customers led to the creation of *Esquire* magazine in 1933 to capitalise on the growing interest amongst the public. *Apparel Arts* continued monthly until 1957 when it was transformed into a quarterly magazine for men, published for many years by Esquire Inc. In 1958 the name was dropped in favour of *Gentlemen's Quarterly*, which was rebranded as *GQ* in 1967. The rate of publication was increased from quarterly to monthly in 1970, and in 1979 Condé Nast bought the title, meaning it went into direct competition with *Esquire.*

The UK version of *GQ* was launched in 1988, just three years before *Esquire* also launched its UK edition in 1991. (I remember 1991 well, as I was in discussion with *Esquire's* US editor-in-chief Lee Eisenberg to be the launch art director of UK *Esquire*, before accepting the art director a job at *Tatler*) With such a head-start, *GQ* should have established itself as the premier men's magazine in the UK, but its launch had not gone well. The editor, Paul Keers, struggled to create an identity for the title that connected with an audience and after just one year he was replaced. The launch issue had featured Tory grandee politician Michael Heseltine on the cover, as it attempted to distance itself from 'cool' magazines such as *The Face*, which had unisex appeal, the men's magazine *Arena* and the soft porn top-shelf magazines such as *Playboy* and *Mayfair*. Stephen Quinn, publisher for the launch edition, admitted in *Campaign* in 1998 that "I wasn't happy with Heseltine on the cover, but I can understand why he was there, because we were playing it incredibly safe." Safe was not the right approach for the 90s – the second issue sold 30,000 copies and the third just 15,000.

In 1990 a new editor was put in place who brought to the title considerable journalistic experience and Condé Nast pedigree. Alexandra Shulman was born in 1957, daughter of the newspaper critic Milton Shulman and the writer Drusilla Beyfus, who was a former contributor to *Vogue*, and editor of *Brides*. Shulman began working as a fashion journalist at *Tatler* in 1982, under the editorship of Tina Brown and then Boxer. She subsequently went on to work at the *Sunday Telegraph* and *Vogue* before becoming editor of GQ. But once again the editor's chair was only briefly filled at the men's magazine – when Liz Tilberis moved to New York, Shulman swiftly moved upstairs in the building to her vacant office and took on the editorship of *Vogue*.

Shulman's replacement at GQ had been patiently waiting for his opportunity to edit the title, having been part of the original launch team. Michael VerMeulen was a larger-than-life figure in all senses, like a character from a Dashiell Hammet novel. VerMeulen was warm, informed, spirited, connected and confident, and completely out of place in the corridors of Vogue House.

Born in Illinois, VerMeulen had a more literary background than other staff members on the men's magazines, having come into contact during his late adolescence with the playwright David Mamet and the circle of actors surrounding him in Chicago at the Steppenwolf Theatre, including actor Willem Da Foe. VerMeulen contributed as a journalist to a number of US magazines, including *Vanity Fair*, before coming to London, where he initially worked for a financial publication before joining British GQ in 1988 as its features editor. He was promoted within GQ in 1990, becoming deputy editor when Shulman became editor and made editor himself in 1992 on her departure from the title. VerMeulen bought an energy and intellectual confidence to the magazine, with an American sensibility that combined news-based features with articles on fashion, culture and leisure. Strong editorial content was complemented by confident photography and sophisticated design, thanks to art director Paul Bowden, who had previously art directed *Tatler* when Michael Roberts was the creative director. VerMeulen and Bowden together helped to build British GQ into a viable publishing proposition. As a result, the circulation of the magazine climbed by 40 per cent to approximately 100,000 issues each month.

Whilst researching this book I came across a blog post that gives an insight into VerMeulen's approach to work and his lifestyle. Richard

Walker, a content strategy consultant and journalist, recalled his experiences of being commissioned by VerMeulen: "I phoned him out of the blue and pitched a couple of feature ideas, which he turned down flat. But he added, 'Come on over, we'll have a drink and see if we can make sense of you... In fact, we had a number of drinks... he became that rarest of things, a mentor. There were irregular alcoholic sessions (the Groucho Club, Korean restaurants, and the Hanover Square dive), and he commissioned a string of features from me... and all of which he paid for, generously."

Walker's experience was echoed by writer Douglas Kennedy, as he outlined in an *Independent* obituary after VerMeulen's death in 1995. "'You drink martinis?' were his first words to me. When I nodded, he said, 'Great – maybe I'll be your friend. Waiter! Two very dry martinis, straight up, heavy on the olives. So, you gonna write for the magazine? You want to know what *GQ* is all about? It's a real simple formula. A men's magazine with an IQ. In other words, great journalism in between neat shit to buy.'"

My own memory of VerMeulen is equally informed by alcohol. We had both attended a lunch at the Dorchester Hotel at which the filmmaker David Putnam was due to speak. Unfortunately, it was not one of his best speeches. VerMeulen and I exchanged a look that suggested we both thought it was time to leave, quite a little time before we were meant to. We had both had a few glasses of wine and he hailed a taxi to take us both back to Vogue House. He filled the width of the taxi, and I crouched on the small fold-down seat. I can remember him giving me wise words of wisdom concerning the world of magazine publishing, or at least they seemed so at the time. Sadly, today I can recall none of them.

Eventually, VerMeulen's all-or-nothing approach to life caught up with him and in 1995 he died of a drug overdose at his home in Islington. A coroner's inquest found that he had over two and a half times the lethal dose of cocaine in his system and concluded that his death was an unfortunate case of 'wild misadventure'. In his obituary, Kennedy mused that, "I often felt that VerMeulen erected a cordon sanitaire around that dark room we all have within ourselves, wherein lie our vulnerabilities, our doubts... he indulged his enormous appetites. His weight skyrocketed, he had a cigarette permanently embedded between his teeth, he could drink just about everyone under the table… he kept on indulging." Along with many others, I attended his memorial service, at which a lone piper played, and actor Willem Da Foe remembered his friend.

"My third commission for *GQ* was a cover story with the actor Robbie Coltrane. During the shoot I made a portrait of Coltrane from the back, and I showed the finished prints to Michael VerMeulen in his office. He said that we should use the back portrait as the back cover but it would never be agreed 'upstairs' as the back cover generated too much income from advertisers. Then he offered me some wisdom that I've never forgotten: 'The front cover sells the magazine … the commissioned work inside sells the photographer.' I liked the bluntness and sharpness of VerMeulen but I'm unsure how his creative wisdom would be treated today."
David Eustace
Vogue, GQ and Tatler

Once again *GQ* was without an editor, having lost its third in just seven years. The next off the rank was Angus MacKinnon, an appointment that raised some eyebrows within the building. Nicholas Coleridge, then managing director of Condé Nast, said that he chose MacKinnon because he came up with "the best, most interesting and well-argued job pitch: he appeared in my office every day with some new suggestion or intrigue." In contrast to VerMeulen's exuberance, MacKinnon was a reflective, rather serious character. He had started his career as a writer on the music paper *Sounds* in 1975, progressed through the *New Musical Express*, then to the *Times Educational Supplement* as a sub-editor. He joined *Time Out* magazine as sub-editor, became deputy editor, then went to the literary magazine *Granta* as its managing editor, before arriving at *GQ* in 1990 as deputy editor. In VerMeulen's years *GQ* had become a reflection of its editor and MacKinnon could not offer the same; within a year he had been replaced by an editor who also had a music press background, but one who was going to bring more controversy to Vogue House and the magazine than it had ever experienced or has experienced since.

"Michael passed away and then Angus (MacKinnon) became editor … personally I was never convinced Angus was right for the role, but I liked him and respected him, he moved on quickly, another editor came into play, and I felt the magazine was moving more towards a 'lads-trend-mag'."
David Eustace
Vogue, GQ and Tatler

James Brown was part of the 1990s Vogue House invasion of experienced magazine professionals who had been trained outside of Condé Nast and were successful elsewhere. The 1960s had seen the titles accept the working class as photographers and models, occasionally a journalist or stylist, but for many years the staff were still predominantly educated at private school or connected with the aristocracy. Now the company was having to accept those from more diverse backgrounds into the building in lead positions in order to make its magazines commercially successful.

Brown was born in Leeds in 1965 and attended a local school before beginning his career in journalism by contributing to a local alternative newspaper. In 1986 he was hired as a freelance features writer for the music newspaper *Sounds* before moving to the *New Musical Express,* and then onto writing features for the *Sunday Times Magazine*. In 1994 he launched *Loaded* magazine and won the Editors' Editor of the Year awarded by the British Society of Magazine Editors. Those are the facts, but the detail is far more interesting. *Loaded* was the perfect vehicle for Brown and the decade; it was the bible for 'Lad Culture' and Brown was its figurehead. The 1990s had seen a new form of men's magazine emerge. Loud, brash, sexy and often sexist, magazines such as *Maxim*, *Nuts*, *FHM* and *Loaded* dealt with similar subject matters as *Arena*, *Esquire* and *GQ* – cars, alcohol, sport and women – but they did it with wild abandon and little if any nuance, focusing on unapologetic self-centred pleasure-seeking, with a sense of humour that was more *Viz* than *Private Eye*.

The time was right for such an approach and Brown rode the wave with his magazine and in his personal life. He was high-profile and mixing with a new generation of musicians, writers, artists and sports stars, drinking, drugging and generally misbehaving whilst also creating a zeitgeist magazine. He was not shy of talking of his achievements. In a 1997 interview with the *Independent* newspaper, Brown said: "The facts are there. I started the most influential magazine in Britain in the last ten years and made my last company millions and millions and millions of pounds after an outlay of virtually nothing, and I've got something like six or seven major publishing awards." Not surprisingly, he came to the attention of Jonathan Newhouse.

Brown started at *GQ* in 1997 and immediately brought to the title his high-energy lifestyle, partying friends and passion for magazines. He has since confessed that he had no interest in the title but, "At Vogue House there are 460 employees, 50 of them men, many gay or ancient. The rest are great-looking posh girls." I was there at the time, in my early thirties, and I am heterosexual, so by Brown's maths definitely in the minority. Brown was certainly correct about the gender breakdown in the building: 86 per cent of the Vogue House staff were female, with only a few male art directors and publishers, the remaining male incumbents working in production, the mail room and IT services. On Brown's appointment some staff left *GQ*, as always happens when a new editor arrives, and others were brought in; the media outside of the building documented and reported every twist and turn of Brown's editorship whether true, false or somewhere-in-between. One report was that he had allegedly encouraged a member of the editorial team to leave by repeatedly leaving buckets of sick near their desk until they got the message. And then there is the story, which I have been told by numerous sources, that the personnel director would have to undertake regular sweeps of the *GQ* men's toilet for signs of cocaine usage. This was a particular problem for management as these were the toilets closest to the boardroom, where all of the magazines would hold lunches and events for influential advertisers and celebrity guests. I can confirm that not only was this story true, but it was not only the personnel director who found themselves having to clean up lines of dubious white powder. Brown was unrepentant in a 2022 interview in the *Guardian*: "There was not much fun in media before we came along...

We said, 'It's OK to f**k around a bit and be as you *really* are.' Older editors said we did things they wish they could have done... but anyone could have done it." Brown's editorship was certainly a rollercoaster ride; the atmosphere in the building at the time of his arrival was one of excitement, nervousness and incredulity. Many adventures were had during Brown's short tenure but, as he has openly confessed, his life was unravelling due to excessive drink and drugs, and he is not the only member of his staff who has since been through rehab.

> "A chatty, warm, big-hearted, little woman from Kilkenny, Bridget catered events, conferences, posh lunches, and leaving 'dos' in the boardroom. No matter what drama was going on in the magazines, Vogue House support staff were always there with a smile or an eyeroll as a healthy reminder to keep things in perspective."
> **Fiona Hayes**
> **House & Garden**

There are many apocryphal tales surrounding the life and times of those working within Vogue House, and it can be hard to discern the truth. A certain sense of *omertà*, the Mafia code of silence, remains amongst some people towards revealing the true cut and thrust of working within the building. Even those stories that are mentioned are often difficult to confirm. Whilst researching this book I was told of a time when the photographer John Deakin fell through a ceiling window trying to get the perfect shot of a model, but I could not confirm it to be true or false, or date it. Another concerned the actress Elizabeth Taylor finishing a shoot in the Vogue Studios and deciding that she would take home all of the clothes she had been photographed wearing. The photographer and fashion editor told her no, but Bea Miller placated Taylor by saying that she could. True or false? I don't know. Brown has had no such concern in telling the truth about two of the most infamous stories that led to his leaving GQ. The first can be best described as the 'champagne incident' or the 'window incident'. It happened on a sunny Monday afternoon as I was standing by the window in *Tatler* editors office, which was directly above where it occurred. Brown, his publisher

Peter Stuart and two journalist friends had started drinking early in the day and returned after lunch to Vogue House for more drinks. The party continued in the *GQ* first floor office and a fight broke out between the two journalists over a £10 note. A heavy glass ashtray was thrown and hit one of the large office windows, but luckily it did no damage. Brown then picked up an empty bottle of champagne and threw it through the main windowpane saying, "This is how you break a window." The bottle smashed, covering the pavement slabs and parked cars with shards of glass. I heard the crash as many of the people in the building must have done. Fortunately, no one was hurt, and Brown was sent to HR who suggested that he may need professional help.

"I worked on *GQ* for a long time and would go down to their first-floor offices for meetings. When I arrived, Peter Stuart was still the publisher, so I was part of the era when socialising was an integral part of the *GQ* culture, and I often popped down for Friday evening drinks. Peter would get his PA to fill up the fridge with beer at about 4pm and drinks started promptly at 5.30."

Susannah Coe
Vogue, GQ and Tatler

Despite this sense of unprofessionalism, the magazine gained a new confidence in its refreshed identity, although it was one that did not fit the Vogue House profile or the promise that Brown reportedly gave to management to not take *GQ* downmarket. Condé Nast had financially supported the magazine with a considerable marketing budget, and the majority of issues featured free CDs, CD-ROMs, books and magazine supplements, all standard but expensive promotions to raise sales. The tactics did not have the expected results; the last six months of 1998 saw only modest sales with an average of 132,000 copies a month. Condé Nast would have had an eye on the lads' magazines such as *FHM* and Brown's former title *Loaded* selling more than 500,000 copies a month, and although they would not have wanted to replicate the editorial approach and look of these magazines, they had employed the editor of one and some of those sales would have been very enticing.

It was obvious to any reader that GQ had increased its female 'nipple count' (despite Brown's later protestations that all the models were well clothed), changed its writers and introduced more lists and short pieces of writing, all aspects that 'lads mags' featured, and saw as positive competitive elements. In a 1999 article in the *Independent* Brown's editorial approach was described as a double-edged sword: "He is [...] acknowledged as a promoter of innovative talent. Those who have worked with him call him a charming tyrant." The same article also suggested that: "At the very least, Condé Nast wanted him to bring the title up to 250,000 or 300,000 a month." It is important to record that Brown's own reporting of sales figures for GQ differ from those I have given here, which are taken from the Audit Bureau Circulation and are therefore as formal a source as we have for magazine sales in the UK as I will discuss later in this book. Understandably, for most editors it is important for them to stress an increase in sales to prove their success over their predecessor; sales are the only true indicator of a positive impact being made. I have spoken with many editors over the years and it is a common theme. It is also in the publisher's interest to demonstrate that their new choice of editor was a good appointment, so self-reporting cannot be relied upon for accuracy. Inconsistency in the figures often varies greatly between sources and can rarely be definitively supported by facts.

Despite working to get clean and sober Brown was still playing a high-risk game with GQ, and his time at the magazine came to an end when he played the wrong hand and included the Nazis and Field Marshal Erwin Rommel in an article listing the best-dressed men throughout history with an introduction describing those in the list as 'cool' and 'movers and shakers'. Never a good idea, but certainly not when you are working for a Jewish family-owned company. Brown's replacement, Tom Haines, proved to be a short-term fix lasting just one year before once again another journalist with a music magazine background came to Vogue House and GQ. Dylan Jones was to bring some sanity and stability to a magazine that had experienced five editors in just ten years.

Whilst all of this was happening on the first floor of the building, things were no less controversial on the third floor, where *Tatler* magazine was under the editorship of Jane Procter. In 1990 Procter was brought in to save the title, replacing Emma Soames at a point when the circulation had dipped below 30,000 and losses had reached £3 million a year. Proctor's task was not an easy one; *Tatler* was completely out of time with the new decade and required a complete reinvention. Procter remembers receiving a good luck card from Stephen Quinn, a director at Condé Nast, which told her not to worry if she couldn't turn it around, describing it as "an impossible job". Her idea was to create a satirical hybrid magazine that recognised the rise of celebrity culture whilst retaining the magazine's traditional readership, concentrating on high-brow content with a mass-market approach and appeal. Hollywood celebrities featured on the cover, as did Princess Diana which always guaranteed a high-selling issue as her relationship with the future King unravelled dramatically throughout the decade. Images by photographers such as Jane Bown, Richard Avedon, David Bailey, Don McCullin, Sylvia Plachy, David Eustace, William Klein, Abbas, Steve Pyke, Jean Loup Sieff and Corrine Day, amongst many other established and young photographers, graced its pages. Its dual personality is perhaps summed up in one infamous issue from 1998, in which the popular television personality Anthea Turner appeared on the cover, naked and wrapped in a live snake whilst inside legendary photographer William Klein documented riots in Paris with graphic black-and-white images over six pages. In art directing the cover, I was inspired by the portrait of the German actress Nastassja Kinski, who was photographed naked wrapped in a snake by Richard Avedon, and the inclusion of Klein's photo journalism was my pay-off response to the choice of Turner as cover star. It was a creative, exciting place to work, but not without its eccentricities amongst the staff and dogs in particular remained a permanent fixture within the *Tatler* offices.

"Editorial meetings at *Tatler* were always a bit unconventional, made up of a fabulous cast of eccentric characters, swapping barking-mad features ideas – all to a soundtrack of actual barking from the office dogs, Steptoe and Bubble. One particular meeting proved more memorable than most. I was pontificating and slowly became aware that the journalists sitting around my corner office were giving each other pointed glances, the corners of their mouths twitching as they tried not to laugh. Annoyed by their lack of concentration, I carried on talking, raising my voice slightly to try to drown out a strange rhythmic noise that had begun to reverberate around the office. It was only after the meeting ended that I discovered that Steptoe and Bubble had been enjoying a magnificent coupling – right under my desk. Kenzo, my Cairn terrier, only accompanied me to work on rare occasions. However, a nanny crisis meant that I had to bring him into work for a week. The most entertaining dog was certainly Studley, who had the run of Vogue House in the early nineties. At one point I was called to the managing director's office to explain why I allowed such a dangerous creature into our offices. My pleas for mercy and second chances were to no avail – all the dogs had to go. I told him bluntly that we weren't paying the staff enough for them to be able to afford dog sitters. If he wanted the dogs to go, he'd have to give the staff a pay rise to compensate. The result? The dogs could stay. Studley's reprieve was short-lived as he died a few months later, to be replaced by Steptoe, who was a brilliant tipster. Every morning, the names of the horses racing that day would be laid out on the floor and, using a variety of chicken treats placed on each horse's colours, Steptoe would be asked to choose which horse he fancied. His tips were then published in a national newspaper."

Jane Procter
Tatler, Vogue

"I think my dog Amos, a pretty Jack Russell, was the first dog in Vogue House. I just turned up with him one day in 1966. Then everyone bought their dogs. The fashion editor Mandy Clapperton always had three or four dachshunds with her that barked and bit."

Geoffrey Aquilina Ross
Vogue

Procter was ambitious for the title and recognised the importance of compiling an editorial consultant team of talented and well-connected individuals – 'TTPs' or 'Tatler Type People' as they were referred to in the offices – to provide the latest society news, gossip, trends and issues of interest. Procter had previously worked at the fashion magazine *W*, *Country Life*, the *Express* newspaper and the *Sunday Times* and was used to constantly re-inventing editorial content to maintain interest for her readers by commissioning contributors with a broad range of connections from the advertising world to the theatre, from the aristocracy to politics. Her time on the magazine was controversial due to her high expectations but she was also outstanding in giving responsibility to extremely young, keen staff and inexperienced journalists looking for a break. It is perhaps worth noting just how many people were given their first or early opportunities in the publishing world by Procter at *Tatler*. Journalists employed by her on the editorial team included Giles Coren, AA Gill, Tamsin Day-Lewis, Emilie McMeekan, Sarah Vine, Tina Gaudoin and future Secretary of State Michael Gove, as well as the novelists Wendy Holden, Harriet Lane and Kate Karko. Interns included television personalities Ben Fogle and Claudia Winkleman, and Nathalie Massenet who would go on to launch Net-a-Porter; and Nails Inc London founder Thea Callen was a fashion assistant. Many who worked at *Tatler* under Procter went on to become magazine editors, including Samantha Scott-Jeffries, Kate Reardon, Clare Gogerty, Melinda Stevens, Catherine Ostler, Lucy Yeomans and Jeremy Langmead. All magazines should act as training grounds for future journalists and editors but the sheer volume and quality of talent that came out of *Tatler* in the 1990s is particularly impressive and a testament to Procter's editorship.

> "During the latter half of the 90s I worked for *Tatler*, a world unto itself in terms of diversity. Folk from very different types of estates came together to produce that magazine. As for memories of the magazine … laughs, encouragement, editorial freedom and a dark corner of the editor's office to crash in whenever I had migraines."
> **David Eustace**
> **Vogue, Tatler, GQ**

"For what was my second piece for *Tatler*, I was sent out to interview the ex-boyfriend of a royal and ended up in bed with him. In SW6! I'd arrived."
Christa D'Souza
Tatler, Vogue

"Tory grandee Charles Powell came to one of our parties, leading in his wife Carla, who was clad in couture, accessorised with handcuffs. Very *Tatler*."
Emilie McMeekan
Tatler

"I moved downstairs to *Tatler* after a year at *Vogue*. *Tatler* was full of incredible people and some remarkable characters. A lot of the memories of this time will go with me to the grave; I am still friends with these people after all! But as a tribe of assistants, Emilie McMeekan, Imogen Lloyd Webber, Ben Fogle, Ana Urena, and myself, would help fund our lives by attending every single launch party that any one of us was invited to. It is amazing how long you can actually live on canapés. By attending these events we could then use taxis to get around London as technically it was "work" – the petty cash was a godsend. It is only at a *Tatler* party that you will find yourself standing in between Joan Collins and Billy Zane discussing the latest restaurant launch and if Le Caprice mint chocolate-chip ice-cream is the best in London."
Emma White-Turle
Vogue, Tatler

The life of an intern on *Tatler* could launch someone with no prior experience in magazines into a media career, and two of perhaps the best-known examples are Claudia Winkleman and Ben Fogle, who both started at Vogue House on the same day and have both gone on to be incredibly successful broadcasters. A third intern who started at the same time, Tobyn Andreae, (brother of successful cartoonist Giles Andreae) has also established a career from *Tatler* building blocks.

He was placed into the features department and today is the head of communications and the spokesperson for HM King Charles III and HM Queen Camilla.

Claudia Winkleman had been given an internship thanks to her mother, the newspaper and magazine editor and television personality Eve Pollard, who contacted Procter asking for her daughter to be given some time in the magazine's office. Procter complied and offered a placement within the fashion department. On the day of Winkleman's arrival the fashion assistant resigned; on the spot, the fashion director Kate Reardon employed Winkleman as the replacement. In the space of just one day, and with absolutely no experience of what she had been employed to do, Winkleman had joined the staff. This was not an unusual experience within Vogue House.

Ben Fogle began an internship at the same time as Winkleman and was placed with the long-standing and ever patient *Tatler* managing editor Harriett Wilson, before coming to me in the art department. In an era before answering machines or mobile phones, Fogle's job with me was to answer my phone and note down in a small book who had rung when I was not available. He was a pleasant and popular intern so when my picture editor left, I gave him that job. He was not very organised or knowledgeable on photography or photographers, but I liked having him as part of the team. One day he asked if we could have lunch, I said of course and he told me that he had two opportunities to appear on television, one to be a contestant on Cilla Black's Saturday night entertainment show *Blind Date,* the other to go to a Scottish island for a year to take part in a new reality programme, *Castaway 2000*. I said that *Blind Date* did not sound like a good idea, so if he wanted to spend a year on a farm, I would keep his job open for him. He left for Taransay in January 2000 and the rest is history: he never returned to work at Vogue House.

"I remember a bomb scare and the whole of Vogue House being evacuated (this was around the time of the IRA Bishopsgate bomb in April 1993.) The *Tatler* fashion department decamped to Claridge's and spent the day working from there. Having Vogue House as my first ever office was mind-blowing to me. I'd

spent my teenage years obsessively buying, reading and collecting *Vogue*. To be working there was just bonkers to me, and I had to pinch myself every morning I walked through the door."
Tomo Delaney
Tatler

"At *Tatler*, my first office was across the corridor from the main editorial room and was perfectly placed for 'the hatch', as well as being a refuge for anyone in need of a cool-down moment after meetings or hoping to scrounge a freebie mascara. I can still see the features intern and future *Tatler* editor Catherine Ostler under one of the desks in tears, upset when the editor rejected a piece, and Claudia Winkleman, fresh from a few weeks in below-freezing Canada on an internship with CNN, entertaining us with stories of her singed eyebrows, burnt off with the cold. The beauty office was a haven at times with my team, Fleur Clackson and Nicola Formby (aka 'the Blonde' as she was sometimes referred to in print by her partner AA Gill), sharing the space. People endlessly popped in, from Isabella Blow sharing some risqué personal details to managing director Nicholas Coleridge with advertisers' comments, writer Adrian (AA) Gill to entertain and bitch and sometimes even Jane Proctor, a rare editor in that she enjoyed and encouraged beauty ephemera, escaping from her all too public glass office on the other side of the corridor."
Kathy Phillips
Vogue, Tatler

Procter's office was a wooden framed glass box in the corner of the building, the same office that Brown, Boxer and Soames had previously used, with windows that looked out upon Hanover Square. Procter plastered the walls (well, I say she did, but I actually put them up!) with the covers of past issues and the faces that *Tatler* had made into icons under her editorship in the 1990s, including Elizabeth Hurley (who won the Estée Lauder contract at Procter's suggestion), Jemima Khan and the 'It girls' Tara Palmer-Tomkinson and Normandie Keith.

Just as 'lad culture' had become a phenomenon in the 1990s so did the re-imagined 'It girl'. Much has been written about the 90s 'It girls', focusing on four well-connected Chelsea girls, Tara Palmer-Tomkinson, Normandie Keith, Tamara Beckwith and Lady Victoria Hervey. Many have claimed ownership of the moment that they were promoted as such, but the truth is slightly different to every version I have read – I know this because I came up with the concept in Procter's office. This is what happened and why. The photographer John Swannell had taken a series of photographs of Tara Palmer-Tomkinson styled by her friend, the *Tatler* fashion director, Kate Reardon. Although it was not unusual for the fashion director to style a shoot, the styling was always overseen by Procter and commissioned by me, and on this occasion we knew nothing about these pictures. Budgets were tight, money had been spent and so they had to be used. But they had come as a surprise, and we needed to come up with a reason for them to exist – we needed a story that explained why we had included them in the magazine. Jane and I closed her office doors and started to brainstorm, as we often did. I had recently bought a copy of the photographer John D. Green's 1967 book *Birds of Britain* that featured portraits of young society women, including members of the sixties 'Chelsea Set', some of whom were described as 'It girls'. I suggested that we should bring the It girl back, and that we could use Swannell's photographs to do so. I went to my desk and designed a layout with the headline 'The IT Girl', showed it to Procter, who approved, and the 1990s It Girl was born. You may hear other versions of this story, but this one is true.

I don't think any of us knew what a cultural phenomenon the reimagined It girl would become for the 1990s; the tabloid newspapers hooked on to the idea as a form of short-hand for upper-class partying and poor behaviour. I never knew Tamara, Victoria or Normandie, despite Normandie once storming the building with Tara Palmer-Tomkinson in a state of extreme excitement to thank me for designing the cover of *Tatler* on which they both featured. Their thanks came in the form of physically sandwiching me by my desk and placing their respective tongues into my ears from either side. I did photograph Tara after I left *Tatler*, though, and gave her a lift afterwards along the Fulham Road in my car. A hysterical and crazy journey, Tara was in full voice, as pedestrians were alerted to her presence and alarmed by her behaviour. Her fame led to a weekly column for the *Sunday Times* where she documented her activities from the preceding week. It was ghostwritten by *Tatler* deputy editor and latter-day author Wendy Holden, who would speak to Tara on the phone about what she had done. There is no way of knowing if the pressure to live up to her 'It girl' label contributed to Tara's growing addiction to cocaine or the mental health issues she dealt with, but I do often wonder about the power of the media to place the unsuspecting into a spotlight that can be so seductive, yet so destructive. I often think back to that time in the office, designing a cover with her face on it. In 2017, Tara was found dead in her London flat. According to the coroner's report, she had developed peritonitis due to a perforated ulcer which developed in her stomach. She died in her sleep aged forty-five.

One of the most famous regular visitors to the building throughout the nineties was HRH Diana, Princess of Wales. The paparazzi were often outside Vogue House hoping to catch a 'snap' of her either entering or leaving the building, where she would visit Anna Harvey for fashion advice or counsel. She would arrive and leave without any security detail, just as any member of staff would do. I'm sure that many had unexpected meetings in Vogue House with the then wife of the future King of England but here is mine. *Tatler* was on the third floor of the building and one afternoon, as normal, I pressed the button for the lift to go down to the ground floor. The doors opened and there, standing in the right-hand corner on her own, was Diana. She looked shyly at me from under her fringe, as she was famous for doing, and we nodded at each other in recognition as I entered the tiny lift. I pressed the button to descend. We both looked at our feet in silence as the lift passed the second and first floors, and then continued past the ground floor, the lift doors opening on to the basement staff car park. I instantly panicked as I realized that I had pressed the wrong button in my nervousness. I smiled at her, embarrassed by the situation, and she smiled back at me. No words were spoken as I pressed the correct button and we ascended to the ground-floor reception. As the doors opened once more, I motioned for her to leave the lift first and again she smiled and nodded her head in thanks and left the building. The expression on the faces of 'The Peters' on the reception desk when I walked out behind her from the lift were ones of disbelief. They had been told that Diana was coming down and had been filled with panic when they had seen the lift continue on to the basement, fearing a major incident was taking place. My emergence was not what they were expecting, and their relief was obvious.

Princess Diana was not the only celebrity visitor to Vogue House, and one could expect to see the unexpected when coming to work there. There must have been many unexpected encounters in the Vogue House lifts over the years; Liz Tilberis remembers an occasion in 1971 when "I bumped into Bianca Jagger in the elevator, not long after she'd married Mick, looking like a fictional dandy in a Saint Laurent white tuxedo with a hat and cane."

Just a couple of years after I'd shared a lift with Diana she was killed in a car crash in Paris in 1997, an event that shocked the world and began a period of unprecedented mourning across the nation. Within Vogue House her death was deeply felt, but it also had a practical impact on some of the magazines, including *Tatler*. I had myself returned from Paris late on the Saturday evening and heard the news on the radio in the early hours of Sunday morning. That month's issue had already been printed and was ready to bind. Unfortunately it contained references to Diana that could be construed as being negative. I was contacted by Procter and a decision was made to physically remove the offending pages. The printer was in Devon and local women were employed to perform this task and the magazine went on sale without the pages mentioning Diana. *Tatler* was not the only magazine affected.

"I was on holiday in Martha's Vineyard staying with Doris Saatchi when the phone rang in the middle of the night. It was the *Daily Mail* asking for Alex Shulman's phone number. They told me that Diana had died. I got quite a few more calls from other people trying to reach her and I suddenly remembered that in our very first issue, the back page included a photograph taken from the hotel in Portofino where the yacht was that Diana

and Dodi were on. And I suddenly thought, Holy hell! I'm going to have to pull this because I don't really know what's going on. We had to drop the entire section, which was a scramble as it was due on sale a week later. It was a baptism of fire."
Sarah Miller
Condé Nast traveller

Tatler in the nineties under Procter was a hotbed of young talent but perhaps its most interesting employee was also its oldest, and also its most eccentric and secretive. Peter Townend was born in 1921 the son of Florence Lily and Claude William Townend, a farmer and Army riding instructor. As a child, Townend had suffered from meningitis, which meant that he had spent a lot of time at home and received little formal education. However, perhaps this would prove to be the foundation of his future career. His mother keenly followed the activities of the Royal Family and aristocracy, and he was surrounded by society magazines from an early age. Townend served in the Royal Navy during the Second World War as a writer/clerk, and afterwards joined *Burke's Peerage*, the book devoted to the ancestry and heraldry of the peers, baronets, knights and landed gentry of Great Britain and Ireland, as an archivist. He became editor of *Burke's* in 1960 until he was replaced in 1972, by which time he was also the Social editor on *Tatler*. It was here that he became the central figure in organising and maintaining the annual debutante season, in which young ladies from well-connected families were introduced to London society.

Townend's time at *Tatler* meant that he was a guest at every party over three decades, and this, combined with his time at Burke's, resulted in him gaining an encyclopaedic knowledge of titles, connections and relationships within the British aristocracy. He was therefore invaluable to a magazine like *Tatler*, which was reliant in demonstrating such knowledge, particularly in its 'Bystander' party pages. He also kept a list of the names of young men whom he thought 'suitable', which he would provide to the mothers of debutantes, that he named his 'Debs' Delights'. In his tired suits and with his shuffling gait, Townend was a relic from a different time, but he was a discrete storyteller with a gentle demeanour. All of his correspondence was handwritten in turquoise ink, and he survived largely on canapés at evening events, and on lunches with his debutante-season alumni. Each afternoon Townend would come into the office to check the page proofs for mistakes from his seat at the end of the subeditors' desk in a chair near to mine. He would often drift into sleep after his lunch and occasionally need to be gently woken after a reasonable period of rest by one of the subeditors ringing his desk telephone. Despite little of his checking work being completed he would then announce that it was time for him to leave. We would all say goodbye and he would head off to his Chelsea apartment on the bus, a solitary figure out of time with the changing world of publishing.

In his later years, Townend's role at *Tatler* was reduced even further, but his debs activities continued unchecked. In 2001 he suffered a severe heart attack in a restaurant near Vogue House over lunch with Geordie Greig, then the editor of *Tatler*. When the paramedics asked him who his next of kin was he pointed to Greig. Subsequently, Greig visited Townend frequently in hospital, often taking the latest copy of *Tatler*, upon which Townend would comment, up to a few hours before his death. Townend, a confirmed bachelor with no surviving family, left his Chelsea apartment to Ben Fogle in his last will and testament. Whilst I was aware that Ben would occasionally drop off page proofs to be checked by Peter at home, no close friendship was evident between the two when Ben worked for me, and Peter sat next to my desk. He remained an enigma to the last.

"At one leaving drinks, the art editor opened a bottle of champagne and the cork hit his eye. As he headed to A&E, someone remarked that anyone who couldn't open a bottle of champagne shouldn't work at *Tatler*."
Clare Gogerty
Tatler

Vogue House was party central in the 1990s and *Tatler* was a leader in coming up with reasons to celebrate. There were parties to launch new restaurants, most notably the 'Ego' party at Nobu in the Metropolitan

Hotel, and one for Marco Pierre White's re-opening of the Mirabelle in Mayfair, an evening when the leather floor was ruined by a multitude of stiletto heels. Travel guides were launched at The Ritz, and the Little Black Book, a singles' dating event that saw numerous members of staff find their future partners, was launched at Michael Chow's in Knightsbridge. Each Friday somebody seemed to be leaving and the editor's assistant would be sent to the local Marks & Spencer to buy party platters of sandwiches, whilst copious amounts of white wine seemed to just appear from nowhere. To mark Thanksgiving a cooked turkey and all of the trimmings would be delivered from a restaurant in Notting Hill, and myself and Procter would carve and serve the staff a Thanksgiving lunch from her office. During one particular Friday late-afternoon party two or three unknown men came into the open plan office to remove some of the computers. As is polite they were offered wine and food, but they declined. It was only on the Monday morning that we discovered that they had in fact stolen the equipment we had seen them remove.

However, all parties must come to an end and after nine years, and despite having raised the magazine's circulation to over 90,000, Procter's editorship ended abruptly in 1999. I left shortly after she did. It is hard for me to comment on this as I was so closely involved in what happened, but suffice to say that it can be dangerous when an editor becomes bigger than their magazine and the publishers feel their grip on the title slipping away. Procter's success with and on the magazine had fulfilled all of the commercial requirements a publisher could have, but sometimes the publisher wants to be the star. At the end of the day, there are few people without an ego in magazine publishing. Procter took *Tatler* seriously but has stated that she felt that her ambitions for the title were never fully supported within the building. *Tatler* was certainly the only magazine in the building not to have a penny spent on its office space or redecoration when I was there. Perhaps the end of the decade, the century and the end of Princess Diana's life all pointed to a change. A new editor was waiting in the wings and *Tatler*'s 'Diana Days' were over. Procter stated in a 2014 article for the *Daily Mail*: "As I left the building for the last time, I felt a huge weight being lifted from my shoulders."

"Once I got into the lift with a willowy girl from *Vogue* who looked at my jacket (a charity shop bargain) and asked, 'Whose jacket is that?' 'Mine,' I said. The ladies' toilets were often occupied by a sobbing girl who had fallen foul of the editor, or at the end of the day by rows of young women in a fog of perfume and hairspray, wriggling into little black dresses, getting ready for a PR event."
Clare Gogerty
Tatler

Vogue may have remained the elder statesman of the building but that didn't stop it from creating its own controversies during the 1990s. With Alexandra Shulman's time as editor came a new approach to what the magazine should be, with an instruction from management that she had to cut costs and lose staff. Making her presence known, she brought in her own bespoke curved desk, painted the walls turquoise and installed a Matthew Hilton leather sofa. Shulman had not come from a fashion background like her immediate predecessors Anna Wintour and Liz Tilberis and initially this caused some confusion and discontent. Within both Vogue House and the quick-to-gossip fashion industry, many had believed that Anna Harvey would and should be the new editor. Perhaps because of this lack of fashion background, Shulman recognised the importance of employing people on her team who had come from the magazines that had defined the previous decade. Creative director Robin Derrick had come from *The Face* and *Arena;* features editor Lesley White had also come from *The Face;* fashion editor Lucinda Chambers had been at *Elle,* as had art director Geoff Waring and features editor Lisa Armstrong. Importantly, the magazine maintained its link with its historic past with the hugely respected Anna Harvey professionally remaining as Shulman's deputy editor.

"My years on British *Vogue* were creatively very free. Both Robin (Derrick) and I came from a comprehensive school education and were something of a novelty in the building. I remember Robin very early on saying how he couldn't believe how everyone would just say 'yes' to all of his ideas and then make them happen.

There was a lot of trust, especially between him and Alex, and that makes for a great environment to work in. I don't think we ever did any of those dreadful focus groups where you sat behind a two-way mirror to watch members of the public rip your work apart for a free glass of wine and a stale sandwich. They employed you for what you were not what they wanted you to be."
Geoff Waring
Vogue, Tatler

"Watching the upcoming month's issue take shape on the walls of the art room in the form of printed pages displayed vertically for the editor to approve, move, crop and/or reject was always inspiring, even if being summoned to Robin Derrick's office for layout meetings could be nerve-wracking."
Kathy Phillips
Vogue, Tatler

Robin Derrick, art director from 1994 to 2011, was a considerable factor in Shulman's *Vogue* appearing so confident and graphically appealing. Born in 1962, Derrick attended Filton Technical College just outside Bristol and was first inspired by magazine photography when he walked into a lecture and found an October 1976 issue of *Vogue* with a cut-glass logo and plain red cover, which had been art directed by Terry Jones and photographed by James Mortimer. The issue contained photographs by David Bailey and Guy Bourdin, which Derrick cut out and put on his bedroom wall. Derrick studied graphic design at St Martin's School of Art (one year above me on the same course, although at that time we met only once). Whilst a student he began working at *i.D* magazine with previous *Vogue* art director Terry Jones and at *The Face* with legendary art director Neville Brody, before going to *Arena* magazine with future *GQ* editor Dylan Jones. With such a pedigree it is no surprise that his design of *Vogue* was both confident and informed. The addition of my former art department colleague at *Elle* Geoff Waring as design director in 1994 further strengthened the team.

"Perhaps the strangest and most rewarding story from my time at *Vogue* was when Robin Derrick and I helped catch a murderer. It was 1995 and a woman's body had been found in a ditch on a remote road in rural Lincolnshire. There was nothing to identify her, no clothes and only one piece of jewellery. She didn't match the description of any missing persons in the local area and had been missing for several days when a dog walker stumbled across her body. The detective in charge wanted to release pictures but knew that those he had were inappropriate to share. However, he remembered seeing a television programme in which it was explained how magazines retouched covers. He didn't remember the name of the magazine, but his wife did so he phoned Vogue House and got through to Robin who said "yes" we can help. The detective immediately drove down to London, and we spent the evening scanning and working in Photoshop on the disturbingly sad images he had brought with him. He returned home with several Photoshopped print-outs and drawings I did from our scans. These then appeared in the local and national press within days, and incredibly the girl was recognised by someone from the closed religious community she came from. Once they had her identity, they found that she had been given a lift by a man she had just met. He took her in his car from Cornwall to Lincolnshire where he strangled her and left her body. He was caught soon after and received a sentence of life imprisonment."
Geoff Waring
Vogue, Tatler

Not all of the staff were as supportive of the new *Vogue* image of professionalism, as Shulman revealed in a 2023 article for the *Mail Online* when she recalled a staff member who was discovered to be stealing from the fashion room rails and "hoarding the booty [...] in the ceiling above his desk. Unfortunately for him, one day the ceiling tile gave way, and it all came tumbling down." It was also not an environment for the shrinking violet, as features editor Lisa Armstrong explained in a 2022 article in the *Telegraph*. After being on features at

Vogue for a year, she was moved to the fashion department and after only three weeks sent to cover Milan, Paris and New York. "On day one I was so naive I didn't even fret about what to wear. Why would I? 'NO ONE WILL BE LOOKING AT YOU!' Sarajane Hoare, *Vogue's* prodigiously talented and forthright then fashion director, had yelled at me across the 'Great Divide' (the corridor that protected the Chanel-clad stylists from the Phase Eight lot in features)."

Shulman inherited a magazine with a monthly circulation of approximately 150,000 issues a month and created a template for what she considered to be a successful magazine. Covers in the 1990s were invariably similar headshots against white backgrounds, the model's hair blowing gently thanks to the photographers' wind machine. Kate Moss, one of the few British supermodels of the time, featured on eight covers in the 90s alone, ensuring sales for the title in the same way that Diana did for *Tatler*. Nigella Lawson became the magazine's food writer before she was known as a television cook and Shulman built a professional team of talented and experienced contributors and editors, including journalists and writers Liz Jobey, Polly Samson, Bronwyn Cosgrove and Eve MacSweeney amongst many others. The editorial team worked alongside a powerhouse fashion department, including Lucinda Chambers, Kate Phelan, Cathy Kasterine, Izzy Blow, Jayne Pickering and, of course, Anna Harvey.

> "If I hadn't been offered a job by Hilary Alexander at the *Daily Telegraph*, I would have stayed on at *Vogue*. Anna Harvey, *Vogue's* deputy editor at the time unwittingly encouraged me to jump ship. 'You either stay here in comfort, get married and have children or you further your career working at a newspaper.' It was time for change and a very different pace."
> **Laura Campbell**
> **Vogue**

Kate Phelan and Cathy Kasterine were important factors in *Vogue's* fashion success through the 90s, alongside Chambers, Blow and Harvey. Phelan was the epitome of class when it came to fashion styling and stayed on the magazine until 2011. Born in Exeter in 1964, she grew up in Devon and, after seeing a shoot by photographer Bruce Weber styled by Grace Coddington, she became obsessed with *Vogue*. Phelan told topshop.com in 2012 that "I begged my mum to let me have the pictures from her *Vogue* to stick on my wall." In 1984, she moved to London to study fashion communication and promotion at Central St Martins. Whilst there she undertook a university work placement at *Vogue* and didn't return to complete her degree. After the initial three-month placement she was soon offered the role of fashion assistant. After three years she left to become junior fashion editor at *Marie Claire*, before returning to *Vogue* in 1993 thanks to Shulman, to work as a co-fashion director alongside Chambers.

Kasterine's journey to British *Vogue* was somewhat different to that of Chambers' and Phelan's. After leaving school, she moved to New York and began assisting on advertising campaigns and editorials with photographers Richard Avedon, Bruce Weber and Horst P. Horst, whilst assisting her father, photographer Dmitri Kasterine. On returning to London, Kasterine was employed by Liz Tilberis as a fashion assistant at British *Vogue*, bringing a sense of the young creative energy in London at the time thanks to her collaborations with photographers such as Glen Luchford and Corrine Day.

As we have seen, those who found themselves working within Vogue House were either lucky enough to know someone who suggested that the door may be slightly open or, more frequently, from a very well-connected background. Shulman herself was part of an aristocratic publishing dynasty. Her sister Nicola, who became the Marchioness of Normanby after marrying Constantine Phipps, the fifth Marquess, in 1990, has written several books. Her brother, Jason Shulman, is an artist and the former *Harper's & Queen*, Harvey Nichols' magazine and *Sunday Telegraph* magazine art director, who is married to the writer and author Susan Irvine, the former *Tatler* beauty editor. Shulman's editorship of the magazine in the 1990s saw the circulation grow and the magazine develop a new relevance to both fashion and the glossy magazine market that it had not previously had commercially. However, the same staffing issue remained and just like other titles within Vogue

House it was accused of nepotism when it came to employing staff. It would be hard to argue with this fact: for most members of staff their connections to the establishment and media hierarchy are clear to see. Historically, all applicants for jobs that came through the Condé Nast HR department had to complete a form asking which school they had attended and disclose the exact sum of any monthly allowance they may have had awarded to them by a trust or supportive relative and it was only in 1992 that this practice was stopped. Questions concerning family connections continued to be asked in interviews, however.

> "A call was made, and I was whisked to HR on the terrifying fourth floor, to meet with the personnel director. I was memorably asked 'What does your father do?' I found it so funny I couldn't resist replying 'Why, has he applied for the job too?' As it turned out luckily not, but with no subsidised trust-fund I could see I was going to have to negotiate hard and it was declared that I would make a 'wonderful *Vogue* girl'."
> **Rachel Reavley**
> **Vogue**

> "'Work experience' were runners for everyone; you scuttled up and down the back stairs on endless errands to the post-room and made tea for whomever requested it."
> **Laura Campbell**
> **Vogue**

Throughout the decade, both internally and externally, the magazines at Vogue House had controversies as they adapted to the changing times. *Tatler* was covering the life and times of Princess Diana and the public dramas of the Royal Family, *GQ* grappled with the world of 'lad culture' and suffered the sad loss of one editor and the very public dismissal of another. At *Vogue*, the fashion world was faced with 'grunge'.

Just as the punk movement had burst out of London and New York in the late 1970s and redefined what music, fashion, writing, art, publishing and photography could be, so 'grunge' was to become short-hand for a cultural aesthetic that embraced all forms of creativity and rejected the glossy, supermodel world that magazines such as *Vogue* had been promoting for the previous decade. Coming out of Seattle in the US, with bands such as Nirvana, Pearl Jam, Mudhoney, Alice in Chains and Dinosaur Junior, grunge was more than just a group of loud musicians with little if any interest in fashion. As with all youth cultures in the UK, grunge took hold amongst young photographers and fashion stylists who were looking to document the present moment; to show their friends how they looked and felt in the images they made.

The *Vogue* fashion editors were keen to ensure that they worked with new young British talent, including designers such as Alexander McQueen and Stella McCartney, as well as those who had made their names in the 1970s and 1980s but who were taking over the fashion establishment, such as John Galliano and Vivienne Westwood. They also sought to showcase up and coming photographers. David Sims, Glen Luchford, the brothers Mario and Davide Sorrenti, Elaine Constantine and, most controversially, Corinne Day and her muse Kate Moss, all of whom had been looking at documentary photography of the 1970s by Larry Clark and Nan Goldin. This style pulled no punches in showing the darker side of life in all its grim glory and this was the approach they wanted to bring to their fashion images. Nick Knight, Steve Pyke, Jurgen Teller and Kevin Davies were also photographers working at the time who had made their name on the Austrian magazine *Tempo* as well as *The Face*. Together, the two groups were an outstanding set of photographic talent all experimenting with the medium in and for magazines. Working for *Vogue* was a mark of acceptance and attainment, as well as the key to lucrative advertising campaigns. But this did not mean they were willing to easily bend to direction. I'd commissioned four of the five photographers I've mentioned prior to their *Vogue* callings, and without doubt the one who was least likely to compromise her vision was Corinne Day.

To give you an insight into how Day worked I will relive for you a shoot we did together photographing the actress Patsy Kensit. We started the shoot in a large, attic photography studio on Scrutton

Street, just off Old Street in London. Corinne's two male assistants had erected a vast white stretched scrim on a frame and surrounded it with banks of lights: a clear statement that Day was a professional photographer. There was no stylist, just a rail of clothes to consider working with. The atmosphere and approach were low key. Corinne began working with a Polaroid camera and Patsy stood in front of the scrim. Corinne had bought some handmade bracelets with her, which she gave to Patsy, encouraging her to bite and chew them, but the studio lacked personality and wasn't giving Corinne anything to work with, so a decision was made to relocate. We needed more of a Corinne kind of location. The old hotel that sat on top of Paddington station had certainly seen better days in the 90s and we had no trouble getting a room to shoot in. Cheap fake wood panel walls, broken furniture, stained carpets, thin blankets, nylon sheets on the beds and deserted, cavernous hotel corridors all delighted Corinne and her mood noticeably lifted. It was grim but Corinne was alive, and Patsy was happy to go along for the ride.

The clothes moved from a simple white shirt to a sexed-up evening dress falling off one shoulder and spike heels carried not worn. The premise was simple: it was the early hours of the morning, Patsy was coming back to her hotel room from a traumatic, dramatic night out. Corinne wanted her to storm down the corridors, kicking the walls, furious with the man who had wronged her. "It's two in the morning," she told Patsy. "He's left you; show me how you feel." Again and again, Patsy stormed down the corridor until Corinne was content that she had the pictures she wanted. That one set-up was the shoot. The pictures that had been taken in the morning were dismissed. Patsy and I laid across a narrow, stained single bed back in the room, leaning on our elbows, watching *Top of the Pops* on a static-filled screen as Corinne and her assistants packed up the minimal kit they had brought with them. "It's all about freedom," Day once said, "and being proud of the holes in your jumper." Those two comments sum up perfectly my experience of working with her on that day, when I was expected to shoot a magazine cover and a series of portraits, and ended up with images that were neither. Despite this they were used. Budgets were too tight to ever waste a shoot on *Tatler*.

Shulman's lack of fashion experience had been commented on within and without the building on the announcement of her ascendance to *Vogue* editor-in-chief, but her relatively down-to-earth approach to interviews, in which she was self-depreciating and honest, provided her with positive press coverage. It was obvious that she was a professional journalist and editor who had a clear plan as to how to make the magazine approachable and commercially successful. One fashion story in particular, however, was to catapult her and the magazine into a maelstrom of controversy with the tabloid newspapers, and Corrine Day was at its centre.

Just as punk had turned dark due to the deaths of Sid Vicious and Nancy Spungen, so grunge found itself dragged towards a similar darkness with the suicide of Kurt Cobain. The two movements shared the growing use of heroin as a touchpoint. The hero of young photographers in the 1970s was the photographer Larry Clark, best known for his book *Tulsa* that documented the drug life of his friends. Day's approach in the 1990s mirrored Clark's: anti-glamour and based on realistic documentation of a life lived. She made a series of images of Kate Moss for the 1993 issue of *Vogue*, for a story titled *Under-Exposure*. The photographs were based in the flat that Moss, Luchford and photographer Mario Sorrenti, Moss's boyfriend, shared in Notting Hill at the time. It was a typically scruffy rented flat with cracked walls and mismatched furniture in the same London square as the apartment used for the 1970 film *Performance* featuring Mick Jagger. (Coincidentally, the first time I met Sorrenti was when he came to show me his portfolio whilst I was still at *Elle*. The portfolio contained photographs of his girlfriend naked in various parts of the same apartment, images that subsequently appeared in the book *Kate* in 1995.) The clothes in Day's shoot looked thrown together, grabbed from what was lying on the floor, but were deliberately mismatched by Cathy Kasterine, the fashion editor on the shoot. Moss was beautiful but thin, for many too thin. The images were instantly seized upon for being inappropriate for a magazine such as *Vogue* to publish, and labelled 'heroin chic'. It was a fashion look born out of reaction against the healthy and vibrant look of leading 1980s supermodels such as Cindy Crawford, Elle Macpherson and Claudia

Schiffer, but pale skin, dark circles under the eyes, emaciated features and lank hair were all traits associated with heroin abuse. Day and the team seemed to many as if they didn't care that this was controversial, and therefore were not paying *Vogue* the respect that many believed it was due.

"I had to handle an overwhelming number of irate phone calls from mothers complaining and questioning why 'this skinny new model' was portrayed so extensively throughout the magazine. Comments were made such as 'She looks anorexic and like a drug addict' or 'Surely, this is not the message we want to give to our daughters.' It was part of the controversy that arose during the early days of Kate Moss's modelling career, referring in particular to a set of images in which she is shown in underwear with fairy lights decorating a bedroom with an unmade bed. Her images were a marked difference to the retouched and enhanced images we had become used to featuring. Kate's hair was unmade. It seemed as though she had just woken up, her expression a bit blank and she slouched… unusual in the super-stylised *Vogue*. It provoked astonishment and a reaction amongst many *Vogue* aficionados. It was the beginning of a new era of fashion photography, and I was there to witness it, right at the forefront, ensconced at Condé Nast in Vogue House."

Julia Fullerton-Batten

Vogue

Shulman was accused of propagating the 'heroin chic' look, whilst contributing to a national increase in eating disorders and promoting unrealistic expectations for women. She hit back by stating that she was bored of discussing her editorial decisions and, in a BBC Radio 2 interview with the pop star and actor Lily Allen, insisted that *Vogue* readers did not want to see 'real' women representing fashion. Whilst the debate on fashion models' bodies and representation in magazines has continued to evolve and develop, the 1990s ended with *Vogue* once again at the centre of the fashion conversation and more attractive to a broader audience than it had ever been. It was not to be until the end of Shulman's twenty-five-year editorship that controversy would once again visit its doors.

After her departure from the magazine in 2017, in an article on the *Fashion Network* website in 2018, Shulman and Fiona Golfar, *Vogue* features editor, were said to be working on a television drama based upon a British monthly fashion magazine in the 1990s, and its group of staff including photographers, stylists, journalists, PRs and designers. With a working title of *Gold Dust Nation*, the drama proposed to draw on Shulman's and Golfar's experiences at a time when London re-emerged as a major fashion hub, touching on topics such as the rise of 'heroin chic' and celebrity culture. Golfar suggested that the series would be "a show about love and loyalty, treachery and creativity, beauty and body image. Can these co-exist when there is so much at stake in the highly charged world of fashion magazines? Between us Alexandra and I have seen it all, from the boardroom to the bedroom, there is never a dull moment in the world of fashion." At the time of writing, it has yet to be broadcast.

Brides and *House & Garden* are the two magazines based within Vogue House that, so far, I have spoken little about across any of the decades. There is good reason for this, as both had been oases of calm ever since they arrived in the building in 1958. The editors on *Brides* had changed across the years but the format of the magazine had not; incredibly the editor on *House & Garden* had not changed once. The position of editor on a magazine can be precarious at best. It is not unusual for editors to leave or be asked to leave if they either cannot or have not met their publisher's expectations, however realistic or unrealistic those expectations may be. If you had little knowledge of how magazines operate before you started reading, then be aware that Vogue House has been home to some of the longest-lasting editors within magazine publishing over the last six decades, with some remaining in position for twenty years and more. Robert Harling surpassed them all with twenty-eight years at *House & Garden*.

Harling was an editor from the old school who would lunch every day, often with his deputy, at Claridge's, which is just a short walk from Vogue House. I have previously mentioned how Harling was recommended to the position of editor by the novelist Ian Fleming, pointing to the high level of his connections in both the literary world and within the secret service, because, just like Audrey Withers, Barbara Timms and Bea Miller, Robert Harling was involved with the secret service as an intelligence officer prior to his move into publishing. In addition to his time as the editor of *House & Garden* Harling was a typographic adviser for almost forty years to *The Sunday Times* newspaper. He was also the author of eighteen books, including novels, and his non-fiction ranged from the works of typographer and sculptor Eric Gill and artist Edward Bawden to modern furniture and interior decoration.

His obituary in the *Sunday Times* described him as "a handsome man of energy, kindness, a certain 'raffishness' and great talents; typographer, graphic designer, advertising executive, novelist, editor and intelligence operator." The *Observer* called him a "brilliant typographer and editor whose imagination helped transform domestic taste in Britain" and "a key-figure in mid-20th century graphic design." For *The Times* he was "perhaps the most innovative and distinguished typographical designer of the last century," his work leading to "a range of typographical journals and books which were visionary at the time and unequalled today.

Perhaps one of Harling's great achievements on *House & Garden* was to bring people into interiors photography, a revolution at the time, making the images less sterile and more believable and relatable. It was an approach that became known as the 'lifestyle feature' and one that interiors magazines still employ today. Despite this desire to show people living in their homes, Harling remained a seriously secret man who never featured his own houses in his magazine, neither his Gothic pile in Surrey nor his holiday home in Majorca. He edited *House & Garden* until he was well into his eighties with unflagging ebullience and legendary style, often dressed in leather trousers and wearing a broad fedora, but he finally left the magazine and building in 1993. After his death in 2008 his obituaries repeated Harling's own version of his early life, which as he had told it was that, following the death of both his parents, he had been taken from London to Brighton as a three-year-old and raised by a relative and her dairyman husband.

In his 2015 *Guardian* obituary of Harling, Ian Jack noted that research had revealed that this was a complete invention. In truth, Harling had made his own biography. He had grown up in Islington, North London with his brother, mother and father, a London taxi driver. He had also been previously married. All of this came as a revelation to his middle-aged children. The personal secrecy that had been his hallmark had concealed that Vogue House's longest surviving editor had, in effect, never truly been quite the person he claimed he was.

Harling's replacement at *House & Garden* was Sue Crewe, who at her interview for the position was able to correctly answer a question concerning the correct fabric choice and size of a bed headboard to confirm her appropriateness as editor. Crewe was born and raised in Cumbria where she learned to farm, gaining an academic qualification in dairy farming in 1970 and looking after her own herd. During this period she began to write and contribute a long-running column to *Vogue* called 'Country Matters'. In 1986 she moved to London and began working as the shopping editor on *Harper's & Queen*, before being promoted to the position of social editor, with the task of modernising the magazine's social events and diary column, 'Jennifer's Diary'. She continued to freelance as a writer for other magazines and newspapers whilst working at *Harper's* and prior to her arrival at Vogue House.

> "I graduated from Bristol University in 1997 and I went straight to Condé Nast. I had a work experience placement at *House & Garden* for six months making cups of tea and 'doing' the filing cabinets, and it was it was a total shock to me. It was a world that I had never seen before. The editor was Sue Crewe and she was very formidable, running the place with an iron rod. It was very much a group of ladies. I think there may have been one guy working on the magazine at the time."
> **Faye Toogood**
> **World of Interiors, House & Garden**

There was some discussion within the building as to how someone with no experience of the interiors market could take on a magazine with such a pedigree and reputation, let alone replace an editor of such long standing and character as Harling. Crewe addressed these whispers by immediately having her office completely renovated, giving it the look and feel of a contemporary, lightly waxed wood take on a traditional club library. Polite yet firm, Crewe had inherited a well-connected professional team and changed little of the editorial content, allowing her staff to provide the experience she initially lacked. In an interview in the *Independent* in 2007, Crewe outlined her responsibility to the "enjoyment and engagement of the people I work with and the perception of the magazine in the broader world" and noted that whilst "*House & Garden* doesn't break stories, so I don't really have to be plugged in to the news" she none the less would read a paper every day if she was having lunch at her desk, "a different one each day, because you have to fight being a creature of habit all the time. It depends whether I'm feeling frivolous and frisky or serious." Such an approach proved successful and the transition from Harling to Crewe was seamless.

An interesting addition to the *House & Garden* team at this time was the art director Fred Ingrams, who was the son of Richard Ingrams, co-founder and editor of the satirical magazine *Private Eye* as well as the founding editor of *The Oldie* magazine. Fred Ingrams was born in 1964 and studied at Camberwell School of Art before being later expelled from St Martins School of Art, after which he spent ten years painting in a room above the infamous Coach & Horses pub in Soho whilst exhibiting his work in various central London galleries. Ingrams then worked as a freelance magazine designer before finally arriving at *House & Garden*. For some, the journey to being employed within Vogue House was less straightforward than for others. Today Ingrams works once again as a painter in the Scottish Highlands.

"It all started when Fred Ingrams, then art director of *House & Garden*, called me in to discuss a project. He sounded quite excited about it, and those were the days when you actually used to go and see people. So, I popped into Vogue House, gained access via the reception committee in the lobby and up the familiar lifts to the relevant floor. After the typical chat and

146

hellos to everyone we passed, we went in to Sue's office – this was evidently an 'interesting project'. The concept was to do a special bath and shower shoot, including commissioning a glass bath, with someone pictured in it, which was intended for the cover! Having a person on the *House & Garden* cover was almost unheard of, and I think it safe to say that the magazine had not before entertained in its wildest dreams a 'nude' cover. Needless to say, it was all done with great taste and style, and I think it made a great cover. Sue was very much on board and part of the concept and planning, and even offered up the 'model', who was a relative of hers. These were expansive and experimental days for magazines, all magazines. Condé Nast was at the heart of it. There was time to work on ideas and be creative. There was a sense of 'let's try it out', which often lead to something special or interesting, and sometimes was just fun."

Simon Upton

Vogue, Tatler, GQ, House & Garden, World of Interiors

"When I was on *House & Garden* my day started every day with getting a banana and a cappuccino from 'the hatch' for the editor I was working for."

Samantha Scott-Jeffries

Tatler, GQ, House & Garden

As the decade came to an end, a new magazine joined the titles already based in Vogue House. *Condé Nast Traveller* UK was launched in 1997 under the editorship of another former British *Elle* alumni. Sarah Miller already had an impressive CV before she arrived in the building, starting out as an intern at *Cosmopolitan* before moving on to *Blueprint*, the leading architecture and design magazine, before editing the *Insight* arts and design pages for *Elle*. From there she went on to become assistant editor on *The Sunday Times*, launching their *Style* magazine, before moving on again to become associate editor and arts editor of the *Daily Telegraph*. It was almost an inauspicious start at Vogue House, however – she later admitted to arriving an hour late for her *Traveller* breakfast interview at which she was offered the position as her car had been towed away the previous night and she had spent the morning negotiating to get it back.

"You went through those revolving doors, past that lavish sort of gold-not-gold lacquered desk, up in the lift to the fourth floor and you felt at the centre of the universe. And very quickly, once you had started, you realised you really were at the centre of the universe. One was invited to boardroom lunches with people like Sebastian Coe and William Hague. I didn't ever go to a 'Diana lunch', but we knew they went on. However, when I first arrived, having experienced this kind of incredible glamour, *Traveller* was put in an office that was above Turkish Airlines on Hanover Street, next to Vogue House. All I can tell you is that there was a kitchenette and an old blue carpet with a telephone plunked in the middle of the floor. It was like, you've got three months to launch a magazine, get on with it. Those were the days when you did, and so we got on with it."
Sarah Miller
Condé Nast Traveller

Condé Nast Traveller had been launched in 1987 in the US by legendary newspaper editor-in-chief Harold Evans, husband of Tina Brown, with a focus on literary journalism and hard news reporting. Evans' motto was "Truth in Travel", which declared as its central credo that travel industry freebies would not be accepted. Miller continued with Evans' template and created a beautiful magazine that featured many distinguished writers, and which existed without controversy during Miller's fifteen years as editor. Her replacement would be Melinda Stephens, another one of Jane Procter's team on *Tatler* to become editor of a Vogue House magazine.

The building was now full and the future looked bright for magazine publishing, but there were clouds forming on the publishing horizon. A new decade and a new century would present the publishing industry, including those within Vogue House, with changes outside of their control. How they would respond to the challenges of a new millennium would affect the very existence of many magazines, and the employment of their staffs. It would not be an exaggeration to say that working in Vogue House would never be the same again.

Chapter 5: 2000–2010
We Don't Call it HR

A new decade and a new century in Vogue House meant new editors on two of the titles, GQ and *Tatler*, and challenges that magazine publishing had never faced before. The first of these began with the 'dot-com boom', when the unstoppable rise of the internet was touted by many to be the future for publishing and to sound the inevitable death knell of the traditional magazine. Such proclamations have in many ways proved to be correct, but such seismic change was a little premature. The analogue doomsayers and digital evangelists were both right and wrong. The late 1990s and early 2000s coincided with a massive growth in internet adoption, a proliferation of available venture capital and capitalists and the rapid growth of valuations in the new dot-com start-ups. Between 1995 and the peak of the dot-com boom in March 2000, the Nasdaq Composite stock market index rose by 400%; but as every bubble grows, the threat of it bursting is inevitably just around the corner. Venture capitalists, or 'VCs' as they were known, with money to burn invaded the publishing industry looking for clever ideas to create money-making platforms, primarily through potential retail tie-ups. With unrealistic expectations on return of investment, and no clear concept of what was required to create photographic and written content that would encourage an audience to engage with a platform, alongside a lack of talent capable of building the online infrastructure required, many lost all of their money when slow internet dial-up and download speeds hampered growth. Potential good ideas disappeared. One start-up asked me to be its art director. First impressions were impressive; they had spent considerable amounts of money on expensive office chairs. My first question to them was concerning the available budget for photography, only to be told that there was none, as all of the images would be taken from the BBC website. No thought or concern had been given to copyright issues or image ownership. That start-up, like many others, staggered to an unpleasant ending sooner than intended.

Venture capitalists were not the only ones exploring the idea of online publishing, however. Newspapers and broadcasters were connecting with retail brands to sell their products direct from the page via hot-links and click-through buttons online. Nobody really seemed to understand exactly how this would work commercially but the thought that it could do seemed to be proof enough for many to invest in projects that never saw the light of day. In Vogue House, this was an unprecedented challenge. Condé Nast had always been a risk-averse company, but also one that had often made the wrong decisions concerning technology. I remember arriving at Vogue House in 1991 only to be told that Condé Nast did not use the latest industry-adopted Apple Macintosh/ QuarkXpress double-act for designing magazines. Instead, they had chosen and invested in PageMaker, a system used by newspapers that did not show images, only type. This was an interesting decision for the production of magazines based on photography. Suffice to say that this system was soon replaced by Apple Mackintosh/QuarkXpress. A consultant from a fast-moving internet-based company was brought in during the during the 1990s to advise on technological advances who suggested that the building should adopt the latest popular 'hot-desking' system of the time, only to find that the computers were all too old for this to happen and that the company were unwilling to invest in updated machines. Their consultancy soon ended, and nothing changed.

On the subject of Vogue House and new technology, I am reminded of perhaps one of the strangest short-lived uses of one of the rooms on the fourth floor. Where once it had been home to Miss Timms, the personnel manager, an elegant stalwart of the building and the magazines within it, by the early 1990s it housed a multitude of mobile phones. At that time, Condé Nast supplied editors, art directors and the chosen few with a company phone. Each was numbered with a printed sticker and was collected in the morning and returned at the end of the day, so that the person employed with charging the phones could plug them into the sockets now lining the walls. The result was a queue two times a day of the building's great and good extending along the corridor. Well, it should have been; of course those who could sent their assistants to do this for them.

Condé Nast's lack of ability to move with or get ahead of the times was clearly illustrated in a 2017 interview in *In Publishing* with Hetty Byng, the *House & Garden* editor and publisher at the time, who was discussing the progress of their magazine's website. It had only been launched in 2014 and, despite its success, three years later there was still no mobile-friendly version of the site. That the magazine was waiting in a queue of other Condé Nast titles for this to happen tells its own story of digital awareness, investment and business priorities. Despite this the editor remained upbeat: "As soon as we've got the go-ahead for that, we will put new energy into what it looks like. Google prioritises mobile-friendly websites, so at the moment we are at a slight disadvantage but doing pretty well considering."

Stories like this do not come as a shock to me and it is therefore no surprise when I hear others say that Condé Nast is the company that missed the internet; at the beginning of this century they were definitely looking at the present without an eye on the future. Magazine sales and advertising revenues were still climbing, and Condé Nast were launching new magazines including *LOVE*, *Traveller*, *Easy Living* and *Glamour*, causing staff numbers to grow from 250 to 925. There was no space left in Vogue House and new offices were populated on Bond Street. The new titles launched at this time of digital infancy demonstrate the management's belief in the magazine format as a publishing vehicle for the future. Condé Nast was beginning to spread out from Grosvenor Square but, despite a spoof memo being circulated that claimed that it would be renamed 'Tatler House' for tax and legal reasons, Vogue House remained the mothership for the operation.

> "*Je ne regrette rien* my whole time at Vogue House, quite the opposite, except perhaps not printing out all the hilarious internal staff memos, such as, 'As the Manolo Blahnik sale is taking place tomorrow afternoon, the April in *Vogue* meeting has been postponed until Monday at 3.30pm.'"
> **Rachel Reavley**
> **Vogue**

In 2007 Apple launched its ground-breaking mobile phone, the iPhone, followed swiftly by the iPad in 2010. Social media platforms were on the rise: Facebook launched in 2004, Twitter launched in 2006 and Instagram launched in 2010. These new, free, easy-to-access platforms saw the magazine industry lose its monopoly on curating what had previously been magazine editorial and advertising content. It provided a conundrum for publishers with business models based on recompense on investment for the creation and dissemination of content. Magazines were understandably – although short-sightedly – unwilling to post content online for free and give reasons for people not to buy their printed material each month. A website requires content, yet despite all of the Vogue House magazines having decades of archive material these were not stored in any way that could be easily digitized. The photographic archive of prints and negatives was muddled at best. Text did not exist at all outside of the leather-bound volumes in the basement. Therefore, any online content would require a whole new team of scanners, curators and editors, alongside a considerable financial investment in equipment to complete the task. No direct financial return could be quantified at the time so the investment was never made. The issue of the need for websites to accompany the print editions was mostly avoided. *Vogue* launched vogue.co.uk in 1992 but when measured against print revenue it was not considered of any value and therefore sat moribund due to a lack of obvious financial return. Instead, the answer that was settled upon during the early years of the new millennium was the concept of a digital issue. Readers would pay to subscribe for twelve issues or pay for one issue only, and be permitted to download them onto a personal device. There was discussion about digital issues having links to retail outlets and offering multifunctional interaction, but in reality the majority of these products were created as standard PDFs without additional functionality, again due to lack of investment, staff and time. Initially the digital editions were popular, but the novelty soon wore off and sales either dropped dramatically or stagnated, with reports that *GQ*'s American iPad app sold just 365 copies. Despite these figures, UK *GQ* continued backing the concept and launched their own digital offering in late 2010 with Jones stating that: "It's a fantastically exciting part of our future business ... It's exciting from a creative point of view but it's more exciting from a commercial point of view." Unfortunately, the digital edition did not live up to its promise; it was not the secure financial or creative platform that many believed it would be. A digital edition is now often bundled together with a free gift as an enhancement to those taking out a print magazine subscription, rather than as a standalone product in its own right.

Despite proclamations to the contrary, the printed page was still seen as the bedrock of magazine publishing. Publishers like Condé Nast stuck with what they knew, hoping to survive, many believing that the 'good old days' would return. Of course, they did not, and they would not. The first ten years of the new decade saw dropping circulations and diminishing advertising revenues, as the economic crash of 2008–9 saw the luxury goods market dramatically affected with a 9 per cent drop in its value. In this difficult environment Vogue House was steadying itself.

"*GQ* felt very different to *Tatler*, less 'buzzy', James Brown had just left, and Dylan Jones was the editor. It was very male, and there was a very calm atmosphere, a business-like atmosphere."
Samantha Scott-Jeffries
Tatler, GQ, House & Garden

Dylan Jones had taken over the editorship of *GQ* in 1999. Born in Ely, Cambridgeshire he attended Chelsea School of Art before studying graphic design, film and photography at St Martin's School of Art in London, where both Robert Derrick and I, amongst others, had also studied on the same course. For Vogue House employees, St Martin's was the art equivalent of Oxford or Cambridge. Jones's career in journalism had begun at *i-D* magazine in 1983, where he became editor in 1984 before moving to edit *Arena,* an off-shoot of *The Face* in 1987. At the same time, Jones was also a contributing editor at *The Face.* When the *Observer* magazine was relaunched in 1992 he worked on it as an associate editor, and then went on to *The Sunday Times,* where he held various positions. In 1999, he moved to Condé Nast and Vogue House, bringing with him a roster of high-quality writers, including politician Dominic Lawson (father of Nigella Lawson), writer Will Self and Self's literary agent Ed Victor, and American writer Tom Wolfe. In an interview with the *Evening Standard* in 2019 Jones remembered his first day as an editor in Vogue House: "I remember being given a tour of the office by the publishing director at the time, who became a very dear friend of mine, a man called Peter Stuart. And I casually said to him, 'Oh, how many people work here?' And he said, 'Oh about half.'"

Jones had serious journalistic and style magazine chops and began to establish *GQ* as a serious brand more in tune with the Vogue House spirit than James Brown's iteration, as well as taking the magazine in a more political direction. In 2014 Jones told the *Press Gazette* that "If *GQ* was renowned for anything, it was renowned for being a sort of yuppy bible. But what it really wasn't renowned for was its journalism. And I thought, let's go out and get the best journalists we can."

Not content with just introducing serious journalists to the title, Jones also sought out politicians. He even hired future Prime Minister Boris Johnson as the magazine's car correspondent. This decision proved to be somewhat of an expensive one, as Jones admitted in a 2017 article in *The Sunday Times,* recounting that the managing editor suddenly started to be sent "rather a lot" of parking tickets: "And when I say a lot, I mean a lot. In Boris's own words, they started accumulating 'like drifting snow on a windshield'. Jones added: "I once worked out that, over the decade he worked for *GQ*, Boris had cost us about £4,000 in parking tickets. But then he'd also written more than a hundred incredibly funny motoring columns, so I figured it was worth it."

Jones's editorship reflected his personal interest in politics and included articles that made the newspaper headlines, including the revelation in 2000 that Conservative MP William Hague once drank fourteen pints of beer before lunchtime, and that Liberal Democrat MP Nick Clegg had slept with "no more than thirty" women. *GQ* and Jones also put their support behind Conservative MP and future Prime Minister David Cameron long before he was adopted by Rupert Murdoch's newspapers.

The jewel in the *GQ* crown, however, became its annual 'Man of the Year' awards'. Originally established in 1996 under James Brown's editorship, under Jones the awards became a major event for both the newspapers and television news to cover, as prominent national and international figures and Hollywood stars were chosen to receive a trophy.

On the first floor of the building *GQ* in the early 2000s was recovering from its turbulent recent past, and it was a similar story on the third floor at *Tatler*. Having documented the 1990s with such panache and success, Jane Procter's departure in 1999 had been acrimonious and left the magazine in a state of some disrepair. Its next editor was an establishment figure from the old guard, and very much in the tradition of the pre-Procter version of the magazine. George Carron Greig, known as 'Geordie', was born in 1960 in Lambeth, London and was the son of Sir Carron Greig and Monica Stourton, granddaughter of the 24th Lord Mowbray, Segrave and Stourton. Members of his father's family had been royal courtiers for three generations, including his twin sister Laura, who was lady-in-waiting to Diana, Princess of Wales. Greig had attended Eton and St Peter's College, Oxford and began his career as a reporter for the *South East London and Kentish Mercury* newspaper, before joining the *Daily Mail* and the short-lived *Sunday Today*. In 1987 he moved to *The Sunday Times*, progressing to arts correspondent in 1989 and then as its American correspondent, based in New York, in 1991. He returned to London in 1995 to become *The Sunday Times* literary editor before being appointed editor of *Tatler* in 1999. Greig certainly had the journalistic experience and society connections appropriate to leading the magazine into the new millennium, but it was to be seen if he truly understood a magazine such as *Tatler*.

"It was a wonderful time to work there. Full of larger-than-life characters, like the late Isabella Blow, who would perch on my desk and tell me lurid stories of lovers in Venice and then hit me up for a bottle of Fracas perfume. People would have full-on, no-holds-barred arguments, with shouting and tears in the Ladies, but mostly it was all good-natured, funny, and always very polite."
Kathleen Baird Murray
Tatler, Vogue

The 2000s in London were the decade of the oligarch, of Russian money and conspicuous shows of incredible wealth. The Royal Borough of Kensington and Chelsea had long been the epicentre of the Vogue House world and *Tatler* was its bible. In this decade it became the area targeted by rich Russians eager to buy up property in London and be accepted amongst the established occupants. Despite never being employed on any of the Vogue House magazines in the UK, there is one interior designer to the rich and famous who nevertheless featured constantly in its story. Nicky Haslam was regularly profiled in *Vogue, Tatler* and *House & Gardens* over the preceding four decades, and having worked for US Vogue in the 1960s there was a strong link between him and the magazines. Therefore, when the Russians wanted their houses decorated it is no surprise that they wanted Haslam to do it, and that it was often Grieg who introduced him to them. Haslam said in a *Daily Mail* article in 2022 that "they paid very handsomely and regularly, never quibbling over the bills. Some just took a little extra time because, perhaps, the money required laundering" but recognised with hindsight that "by associating with such powerful men, I was dancing along the edge of a volcano. Looking back, though, I could have been in poisoned underpants territory."

Tatler under Grieg seriously embraced this new echelon of high society, with the pages and covers of the magazine reflecting the parties, homes and spending of those whose sources of income were often mysterious but spending more than conspicuous. Such editorial content raised negative comments from its traditional readership, but the magazine used this new audience to create a new identity for a new decade. Dylan Jones had restored a sense of calmness on the first floor of the building and Geordie Greig attempted to do the same on the third, introducing contributors such as artists David Hockney and Lucien Freud alongside well-connected writers such as Tom and Emma Parker Bowles, the children of Queen Camilla from her first marriage, who were the food and motoring correspondents respectively. Greig also welcomed Sir Elton John's husband David Furnish to the *Tatler* team as a contributing editor, a decision that was not to end well. Furnish resigned from the magazine in 2005 after an article appeared in its pages concerning his friends Victoria and David Beckham, which featured the footballer's alleged former mistress Rebecca Loos offering advice. Despite Greig's desire to make the magazine more erudite it was clear that *Tatler* was still fully embedded in the world of celebrity and that it retained its essential party-based DNA.

"We used to get spray tans in there (the boardroom) before parties. I vividly remember standing in my knickers ... overlooking Hanover Square, as a 'celebrity' spray-tanner tried to give me abs before my first ever *Little Black Book*, the magazine's annual singles party. I'd only just recently arrived from the *Mail*; it was quite a different environment."
Sophia-Money Coutts
Tatler

"The boardrooms of Vogue House were lined with black-and-white photographs which were chic and timeless. Visitors who came to Vogue House for our '*Vogue* trend' presentations, breakfasts, cocktails and leaving dos must have imagined that the rest of the building was as slick, but the reality was slightly different."
Susannah Coe
Vogue, GQ, Tatler

"I never felt that I was posh enough. And that was fine by me. You'd see letters in neat piles destined for the mailroom addressed to titled people, and they were usually relatives of those who worked there (although quite why they'd be writing letters to their family, I do not know). A relatively common surname like 'Churchill' would have you questioning whether that colleague was actually a direct descendant of *that* Churchill. They usually were. In meetings I would suggest we cover people that perhaps didn't live in Chelsea and ask if anyone had been to Notting Hill (where I lived at the time) because, you know ... there were some cool people there. But back then Notting Hill was just a postcode too far – even though Geordie also lived there, my people were just a little too fringe, or too fashion. My ideas were politely ignored. Chelsea still ruled the day."

Kathleen Baird-Murray
Tatler, Vogue

Calmness was anathema to the mercurial, fragile and eccentric Isabella 'Issie' Blow, the new Fashion Director appointed by Greig in 2002. By the time of her return to *Tatler* Blow was a global fashion figure and close friend and patron of the milliner Philip Treacy and fashion designer Alexander McQueen. There is no doubt that Blow was a fashion genius, but she was also impulsive, fearless and prone to bouts of severe depression. Despite her by now extensive magazine experience she still had no interest in editorial budgets or protocol, deadlines or schedules. The stories about her behaviour in and outside of Vogue House are a book in themselves. She kept a rack of her own clothes in the *Tatler* fashion room, and it is even alleged that she once had a moment of passion with her lover, a Venetian gondolier, on the back stairs of the building between the second and third floors. She was always complaining about a lack of enough money to support the lifestyle she wished to lead, a situation that led to her requesting a 100% pay increase. However, by 2006 Blow had attempted suicide on three occasions and her moods and behaviour led to Greig offering her the position of Editor at Large.

Sadly, her previous and subsequent frequent attempts at ending her life prematurely came to an inevitable conclusion when she succeeded by consuming the weedkiller Paraquat in 2007. This was not the only self-inflicted death from within the building in the 00s. John Morgan the impeccably dressed aesthete Style Editor on *GQ* had also succumbed to internal demons and ended his life in 2000.

"I was briefly introduced to fashion editor Isabella Blow at *Vogue* and given a chair and desk beside her. I wasn't aware how massive her reputation already was in the world of fashion. Blow's larger than life personality and abrupt way of communicating was initially difficult for me to handle. Typical of my experience with her was when, immediately after my arrival, she asked me to take something to the art room. I asked her where it was. She swung her chair round and looked exasperated at me 'Don't give me more work! You are here to help. Find it yourself!' That set the tone for our relationship during my month's stay at *Vogue*, although she did show me occasional flashes of her acerbic sense of humour. In hindsight, that episode was a Eureka moment for me as I decided there and then to just get on with it, be independent and work things out by myself."
Julia Fullerton-Batten
Vogue

"You didn't really go to other people's floors or go in their offices, but Isabella Blow would come into *World of Interiors*. Depending what mood she was in that day, we'd start dressing her in silks in our fabric room and then she'd start crying. She would have split up with her boyfriend. I think she felt a kinship with the magazine and with the people who worked on it. But I'm sure everybody else in the building just sort of looked at us in a very strange way with our strange outfits. We sort of saw ourselves potentially arrogantly more intellectual than anybody else. And, you know, slightly more cultured."
Faye Toogood
House & Garden, World of Interiors

"The photocopier was next to my desk in the art department and Issie was always coming in to use it. One day Robin waved at me to look round and there was Issie with the back of her skirt tucked up into her knickers! To this day I'm sure she did it as a joke to give the art boys a giggle. She was more aware than anyone that fashion could be and should be fun. One of the biggest shoots of the year was an Issie Blow one with the stylist Joe McKenna. Steven Meisel was the photographer and the story featured 'English Roses' defining the 'London Look'. It was all in black-and-white, very 'punk', shot over a few days across London. There was a huge buzz in the office as it was Issie's base during the shoot and clothes were coming in and out on an hourly basis. Issie was like a tornado on a big story, with everyone and everything being pulled into the vortex. There was a mix of models, including Stella Tennant and Honor Fraser, with non-models such as the journalist Plum Sykes and fashion designer Bella Freud. I remember Issie having to explain to the managing editor, Georgie Boosey, why she needed to book a helicopter to bring Lady Louise Campbell from her holiday in the south of France and back the same day, as she could never possibly find another English Rose closer to home. Issy was never aware of budgets."

Geoff Waring
Vogue, Tatler, Glamour, Easy Living

Greig's closeness to the new Russian money, co-hosting parties under the *Tatler* banner and promoting his friend Evgeny Lebedev, the controversial oligarch, within the magazine (naming him the third most eligible bachelor in the UK) was to lead to the end of his time as the editor of a glossy magazine. Greig was instrumental in introducing Lebedev to the owner of the London daily newspaper the *Evening Standard*, and when Lebdev Holdings Ltd went on to form a new company to buy the paper, Grieg was given shares in the business and the editorship in 2009. Before the decade had ended, *Tatler* needed another editor.

"Min Hogg sat legs akimbo smoking a Gauloises. She was a vision in an emerald green smock dress and matching turban. 'So, you're Irish... I went to a Guinness wedding. Come have a look.' After a quick hunt through the (meticulously kept) archives, she brought forth a set of negatives of her fun-filled trip. She never actually asked me anything about my life as our conversation meandered from places, to people, to interiors shot by some of her favourite photographers and friends."

Ciara Hunt
World of Interiors

The third new editor to the building in the 2000s was at *World of Interiors*. Min Hogg had retired from the title in 2000; as its launch editor, she had become so closely associated with the magazine over her twenty-nine years in charge that any replacement would have to be a careful appointment.

"We felt so lucky to be there. I just couldn't believe that I was there. I couldn't believe that Min had chosen me to work at her magazine. And that magazine was one that I had become aware of at university – you felt so lucky to work there. I think we all adored her. She treated us like children, actually, in an endearing way but also in a kind of neglectful or abusive way. She could say anything. You'd walk into the office, and she'd talk about everything that you were wearing. You know, whether she liked it or didn't like it. There would be a full commentary, saying things that would not be acceptable now. I distinctly remember a shoot that I did. It was a really horrific moment. When you'd completed a shoot, you'd bring back all of the film, and it would be laid out on the big lightbox. Everybody was like, 'Oh, it looks great' 'That's great'. Min came over – and she'd smoke constantly, her Gauloises. We were always in a fog of cigarettes, all of us. And she came over with her bright pink lips and took one drag of her cigarette and then dropped ash on top of the transparencies and walked away. And I was like, 'Oh, God!

She hates it' and I had to reshoot. But she said nothing. She just dropped her ash on it. But there was wonderful freedom, huge creativity, anything went on shoots, you could do anything. And as long as you came back with a good shoot, it was okay. So, it came with wonderful creativity, but at the same time probably it was deeply inappropriate. A huge number of people that worked at that magazine went on to do incredible things. It gave you drive, it gave you ambition, it toughened you up, and gave you resilience. It really opened your eyes."

Faye Toogood
House & Garden, World of Interiors

"My desk was directly opposite Min's, as she shunned the big corporate offices that other editors had. She loved the daily banter and ideas bubbling from her top trio Rupert Thomas, Jessica Hayns and Lindsay Milne. She never failed to jump in with her creative flare, infuriating them as she followed them into the workroom where they were creating magic. There was a gorgeous bonhomie among this trio. They were the new guard, trying to bring slicker lines, cooler hues and starker interiors into the magazine, which was in total contrast to Min's chintz, flounce and colour. She reluctantly understood the need for this new direction but never delighted in it as much as her own flamboyant finds."

Ciara Hunt
World of Interiors

Rupert Thomas was Hogg's protégé, an old-school magazine person and therefore the obvious choice as her replacement. He was a calm, erudite, stylish and measured presence. Unlike the majority of Vogue House editors, Thomas grew up in a council house in North London with his mother, a costumier. He joined *World of Interiors* in 1992 having worked at the art book publishers Thames & Hudson, and then for Dorling Kindersley. He had no magazine experience prior to joining the title and working with Hogg; he was therefore a blank sheet on which the veteran editor could impress her beliefs and taste.

"Rupert was much more methodical. He's very much a thinking person, whereas Min was perhaps more instinctual. He was very much in his head and so the magazine was sort of run like that. It was less ad hoc, less chaotic. You know, the creativity was still really strong, but perhaps it didn't rule the roost in quite the same way. Rupert was much more academic in the way that he approached the magazine and he put much more weight on writing, not just the pictures. He was an art historian and so he was coming at things with a much more historical perspective whereas Min was from a fashion background, so she had that wonderful sort of frivolity about things, and she didn't care whether things were made of sticky tape. We were always cutting things up and making things out of nothing. That was her. She was just fantastic at that – get a paintbrush out, you know, make it look wonderful."

Faye Toogood
House & Garden, World of Interiors

The magazine's readership had always been small, with a circulation of approximately 55,000 including subscriptions, but it was influential and therefore Thomas's task was to maintain the quality of the magazine without losing its way. Under his control it remained the same as it ever was: no celebrities on the cover and rarely any inside, no obviously influenced editorial pandering to advertisers or publicists, a classic low-key design without gimmicky typefaces or colours. No articles encouraging its readers to 'get the look' or selling aspirational dreams. Thomas even maintained the magazine's requirement that all photographers should use analogue photography when commissioned, even in the developing digital age. *World of Interiors* had always had a small team and dedicated staff chosen by Hogg, and they remained to work with Thomas, a credit to their belief in him and in the magazine. Examples of this loyalty include the creative director Jessica Hayns, who oversaw the fabric and furniture shoots, who is a twenty-six-year-plus veteran, and Carol Prisant, the New York editor, who had been with the magazine since 1989. Vogue House may have been facing a digital revolution, but Thomas knew what worked for his readership and he had no intention of changing that.

"I was a fully trained Fleet Street journalist, but I learnt everything at *Vogue*. I learnt about visuals at *The Face* and *Frank*, but I learnt everything about magazine journalism from Alex Shulman. She gave people chances, and you had to perform, but she was a really good, rigorous editor. She knew how to edit copy."
Bronwyn Cosgrove
Vogue

Meanwhile, upstairs, *Vogue* in the 2000s continued under Schulman's steady editorship. As the most internationally recognised brand within the building, Condé Nast began to accelerate its franchise potential. International editions of *Vogue* had been established throughout the twentieth century, but the new decade saw rapid expansion of the programme in an attempt to increase global influence and revenue, open in new markets and respond to the pressures that the internet was applying to magazine publishing's profitability.

British *Vogue* was the first of the international editions, launched in 1916, followed by *Vogue Paris* in 1920, *Vogue New Zealand* in 1957, *Vogue Australia* in 1959, *Vogue Italia* in 1964, *Vogue Brasil* in 1975, *Vogue Mexico* in 1980, *Vogue Korea* in 1996, *Vogue Taiwan* in 1996, *Vogue Greece* in 2000, *Vogue Portugal* in 2002, *Vogue China* in 2005, *Vogue India* in 2007, and *Vogue Turkey* in 2010. The 2000s had seen five new international franchises launched, more than in any prior decade, and the following years would see even more on newsstands across the world.

What this meant for the existing *Vogue* magazines, and particularly for the US and UK titles, was that the editorial content they were producing could be used as potential syndication material for the new titles. This model for recouping initial investment is common amongst magazines with international versions but to work well it requires maximum efficiency and organisation, alongside transparency of sales and usage for those who create the photographs and words.

This is understood by syndication agencies, for whom this is their business, but rarely by publishing companies or the staff they employ, who see such work as disconnected from the roles they are paid to fulfil in producing a single title. In short it rarely works smoothly, if at all.

UK *Vogue* was producing strong, accessible and commercial content that could be syndicated if the structures to do so were in place, which is a credit to Shulman's direction in a difficult climate. When she had taken over the editorship, she had had very little hands-on fashion experience, but her knowledge had grown over the past decade to ensure that the magazine delivered on its fashion expectations.

"Thanks to Ryan the carpenter (Vogue House had its own full-time carpenter to make furniture for the offices, who had a fully equipped workshop in the basement) and Alex Shulman, in the 2000s I was designated a big space, a window overlooking Hanover Square and lockable CUPBOARDS! With products of all sorts from all over the world arriving, having cupboards was the ultimate luxury. And yet again, although I was slightly removed from the main fashion and features floor, there was a stream of visitors. It's amazing how many requests a day we had for perfume, mascara, lipstick and lip balm, not to mention SPF for holidays, fake tan, shampoos, conditioners and body lotions.

Bernadette Rendall from Chanel graced us with a visit one day and was shocked to see how many competitors' products were strewn around and piled into cupboards in a room where she had imagined only Chanel products would be on display. Sadly, I don't have photographic evidence of Kate Moss trying (and then taking) a fluorescent lipstick at my desk. When the TV cameras attempted to make a reality film of life at *Vogue*, they would have loved that shot. What they really wanted to film was us 'beauty girls' sitting painting our nails with our feet on the desks or being collected by huge black cars and taken to glamourous locations for press launches. They were very disappointed with the reality, although there was glamour in the shape of beautiful girls arriving for castings and endless bouquets of flowers. Not just for me. Many editors were sent exotic bouquets and Jordana Reuben, one of my last amazing assistants, would often get flowers from a boyfriend, more lavish and more extravagant than any of them. Indeed, I think I am remembered for asking, during the refurb, for bigger sinks in the loos in order to fill and re-fill the many vases we always needed. A bit of a first-world problem."

Kathy Phillips
Vogue, Tatler

"*Vogue* was definitely like a finishing school. A lot of the women had aspired to work there from childhood. They'd grown up reading it."

Bronwyn Cosgrove
Vogue

It was not until the following decade, at the end of her time as editor, that the fashion world would loudly exclaim their dissatisfaction with Shulman's *Vogue*. The expectations placed on the editor of a high-profile magazine have never been purely based on the pages of the magazine itself, but this was heightened in the early years of the new millennium. With the bestselling 2003 novel *The Devil Wears Prada*, a fictionalised account of life on a fashion title allegedly based on US *Vogue* and its editor Anna Wintour, which was made into a film in 2006, and documentaries such as *The September Issue* (2009), the editor had become as much a celebrity as the people the magazine featured. In this respect, Shulman did not fit the expected fashion profile. As the fashion publishing world evolved, with the arrival of bloggers, forums, chatrooms and social media, new voices were starting to be taken seriously by the very fashion brands *Vogue* needed to placate, please and feature in their pages. To stand up to this chatter and inspection required a strong figurehead who could not only produce a strong magazine but who also looked and acted the part. Little did Shulman know that her time as editor was about to come under intense scrutiny.

"The fourth floor was the grown-up floor, it seemed to me during my first years in Vogue House; it was the executive floor, but it was also the place to collect cash expenses at the end of the week, which was always useful for the weekend. Once I was more established, confident and senior I would sometimes wander down to talk to the *House & Garden* publisher, who had the most exquisite office more like a smart drawing room than an office, full of flowers and ambient lighting."

Susannah Coe
Vogue, GQ, Tatler

At *House & Garden*, Sue Crewe's editorship had seen the magazine settle into a defined space within the interiors magazine market. Confident and sure of its readership, the title continued to work on such an organised basis that they were commissioning content a year ahead of when it was required to be published. I was working for them at this point as a photographer, so I know this to be true. Compared to the other titles in Vogue House during the early 2000s, little if any excitement was occurring. I did find one reference in the *Evening Standard's* 'Londoners Diary' column, a regular recorder of Vogue House news, in which it was suggested that Crewe had employed an actor to perform as a hopeless waiter to play a prank on her PA Emily Pugh during her farewell lunch. The 'waiter' spilled food and joined in conversations inappropriately, horrifying the staff and guests. Whilst not quite the rock and roll excess of James Brown's *GQ*, for *House & Garden* it would have been quite an event.

As elsewhere in the magazine industry, however, sales and advertising revenue were under attack as retailers began to utilise the internet and their own dedicated websites to sell directly to their customers. Fortunately for *House & Garden*, the interiors sector, and particularly the luxury end of the marketplace, is a traditional and cautious beast, and brands had been slow to see the benefits of taking control of their own marketing, preferring to leave that to the safe hands of a Condé Nast title. For now, both *House & Garden* and *World of Interiors* were untroubled by the digital revolution but in the near future at least one of the titles would have to address the internet and everything that meant.

"Many of the Condé Nast staff were well-heeled, and the company was notorious for hiring people who could afford to work for tiny wages because they didn't need the money. I was once telephoned by the head of personnel – 'We don't call it HR' – to ask me to give work experience to someone 'who reminds me of my daughter, she's a St Paul's girl.' What, I wondered silently, was a St Paul's girl? But the staff of *House & Garden* were a whole other order of 'Old Order'. The locations editor and managing ed were both 'Honourables' (daughters of barons), the gardens editor was a 'Lady' (daughter of an earl), and the editor was the granddaughter of the Duke of Devonshire. Not that anyone ever mentioned any of that."

Fiona Hayes
House & Garden

"I was a state-school girl, and I definitely didn't feel like I fitted the mould. I remember seeing handwritten on CVs that I was given phrases like 'beautiful blonde daughter of such and such' and these CVs would come in as genuine recommendations. And that was quite shocking. People were being hired based on where they were in society and there was a sort of divide between those that were part of that and those that were not."

Faye Toogood
House & Garden, World of Interiors

The magazine publishing world in the 2000s was either embracing everything digital or in complete denial. There was little middle ground. The luxury magazine market was in more denial than most: when editors and publishers were asked about the rapid rise of online content in interviews, the standard reply was that people wanted a printed artefact, something to be seen with, and that they always would. In a 2017 article for the *Business of Fashion* website,

Shulman commented that although "the digital curveball thrown at print is powerful" that "doesn't mean that magazine brands don't require editors who actually edit" and warned of the risks of "chasing clickbait that is mirrored in a zillion websites and cravenly following a small pool of short-term celebrity names." Shulman dedicated much of the article to defending the importance and value of print magazines over digital, describing them as "not only information and entertainment but also image-defining accessories, endowing the buyer with membership of a certain tribe when carried or even placed on a coffee table or kitchen counter."

The idea that luxury cannot exist online was a common belief in the industry amongst publishers and those brands that advertised in magazines, but this was not the case with one of *Vogue's* most influential and creative photographers. Nick Knight was looking to the future in 2000, when he established his platform for fashion-related creativity SHOWstudio.com. Knight saw the impact that the internet could have on global fashion communication and the potential of the moving image, showing short fashion films with the same sense of energetic creative experimentation of 1980s music videos. He recognised the democratic nature of sharing for free that the internet offered, showing the workings of fashion shoots and catwalk shows, and the power that could be harnessed by fashion brands if they were willing to move with the times. Initially slow download speeds hampered the site but gradually as speeds improved so did the viewer experience. SHOWstudio brought the catwalk to the masses, streaming live shows via their digital devices, and soon began to accept advertising, firmly placing it into competition with the fashion magazine's market. Fashion films became the new fashion shoots, and not surprisingly many of the *Vogue* fashion photographers began to create personal work for SHOWstudio, using it as a platform to demonstrate their creativity to the brands they wanted to work for. Yet, despite this happening almost on their doorstep and with their own contributors, there was no appetite in the 00s within Vogue House or Condé Nast more widely to adopt such a model for their own titles. That would come later, by which time they were too late to the market.

Brides magazine was perhaps the first magazine to be most negatively affected by the online revolution. The bridal industry had been quick to move online, and editor Sandy Boler oversaw the magazine's early move into the field of e-commerce, but in 2002 Boler left the magazine. *Brides* had little if any constant audience, as what was an essential purchase post-engagement and during the planning leading up to a wedding had little interest to the same reader after their big day. This fickle readership soon moved online, where they found the information and aspirational content they were looking for, and the magazine post-Boler began to struggle to compete. It remained within the building but in 2019 it was sold and today exists only as a website.

The decade had begun with a dot com boom and ended with dot com bust and confusion. Publishing was struggling with what digital had delivered and what it had failed to deliver. Snake oil salesmen were talking of instant fixes and neigh-sayers were preaching a gospel of doom and despondency. The truth was somewhere in between but it was evident that the next decade would require informed, confident, brave and ambitious thinking for magazine publishing to survive. The big question was did those people exist within Vogue House?

Chapter 6: 2010–2020
Alan Passed Away
in a Tragic Accident

Ten years into the twenty-first century the world had already endured a global economic crisis and a digital revolution in global communication. The key word here, for the magazine industry in particular, was global. Although Vogue House titles had been slow to embrace the new world of websites, social media and emerging digital broadcasters, the 2010s was the decade that would see them fully embrace what was going on outside of the building's solid brick walls, whilst still attempting to hold onto their heritage. It was to become the decade in which the intent of its publisher to globalise content was clear for all to see.

Once again, *Tatler* had a new editor to start a new decade. Within a week of Geordie Greig's resignation in 2009, Condé Nast had drawn up a shortlist of seven names, whittled down from thirty-six applications. It was a swift response that suggested that they were following his work relationship with Alexander Lebedev closely, or at least had been expecting his resignation. The chosen replacement was announced a week later: Catherine Ostler, editor of *ES Magazine*, who had spent the 1990s working in the features department of *Tatler* under the editorship of Jane Procter. Ostler was a graduate of Oxford University, where she read English Language and Literature, with a specialisation in eighteenth-century literature. She had started at *Tatler* as an unpaid intern before being appointed features editor in 1994, but left to join the *Mail on Sunday*, where she stayed until 2000 before reuniting with Procter, who had launched the venture capital supported *People News* online. (Remember the short-lived start-up I was involved in? This was it.) Ostler then worked on a freelance basis at the *Daily Mail* before becoming editor of London's *Evening Standard ES Magazine* in 2002.

In an interview with the *Independent* conducted on her arrival at Vogue House in 2009, Ostler stated that her intentions for the magazine were to introduce more politics to its pages and seek inspiration from its 1711 founders (who went on to establish the *Spectator*): "I think *Tatler* has been and should be the journalist's magazine," she boldly stated. This was a strange opening salvo, as it could certainly be argued that not many journalists buy magazines and that, in a difficult economic climate, a focus on the actual existing readership, and growing that, might have been a wise idea. As for using the sixteenth century as a font of inspiration in a rapidly moving digital decade, well, *Tatler* has never been a straightforward title, but sales are important to a magazine's continued existence and a narrowly focused audience will never provide these or the associated advertising revenue.

Ostler's time on *Tatler* as editor was brief, just two years in fact, one of the shortest periods any editor had stayed on the title. The Condé Nast official press release statement on her departure made her position clear: "I feel it is time for me to move on and find the next big challenge. I am very proud of the magazine that I leave behind. *Tatler* at its best is a full blast of glamour and excitement. It's a privilege to have been captain of the rocket." Ostler returned to the *Daily Mail*, and later married Albert Read, the Condé Nast UK deputy managing director and future managing director.

Kate Reardon took over from Ostler in 2011. Describing herself as a "honking great Sloane!" (in 2014 she gave the following succinct advice concerning the do's and don'ts of being posh: "Never complain, be self-deprecating, don't be picky about food"), like Ostler she was not new to the building or to *Tatler*, having also been on the magazine under Jane Procter in the 1990s as its fashion director. Reardon began her career on US *Vogue* and was made fashion director of *Tatler* in 1990 when she was just twenty-one years of age. She remained on the magazine for the following nine years, before being offered the position of contributing editor on *Vanity Fair* in 1999, the year Procter left *Tatler*. Reardon was with *Vanity Fair* for the following eleven years, whilst also contributing to a number of UK national newspapers. In 2007 she launched her own website called TopTips.com, giving "real tips for real women". Reardon, educated at Cheltenham Ladies College and at Stowe, was announced in December 2010 as the seventeenth editor of *Tatler* since the magazine's relaunch in 1901.

There was much written and spoken about *Tatler* during the 1990s and particularly about its editor Jane Procter and her style of management. Much of this was negative and yet two of her protégé had been chosen to edit the title in the years since her departure. Procter's approach may have been challenging for some of her staff but the subsequent success of those who had worked under her cannot be understated. (I was once asked how I dealt with Procter during my years working closely with her producing the magazine, and I answered truthfully that in nine years we had argued only twice. Once was my fault, and the other time was, in my opinion, Procter's. I don't think that is a bad record over a nine-year-period within the high-pressure environment of a monthly magazine like *Tatler*.) Under Reardon's editorship, things were much less turbulent. *Tatler* reached a position of stasis; the magazine was non-controversial and safe, appealing to its traditional readership, with little ambition to reinvent itself or provoke controversy. It didn't want to upset anybody and settled into a comfortable world, typified by figures such as Samantha Cameron and Kate Middleton. Rather than a criticism of *Tatler* or Reardon, this is merely an observation that could be made about many magazines at this time. The 2010s were a decade of survival rather than experimentation, with previously successful titles closing regularly. For Condé Nast, these included titles launched in the previous decade such as *Easy Living*, which was closed in 2013, and UK *Glamour* and *Love*, which both were withdrawn in 2017.

CHAPTER 6: 2010–2020

Perhaps the biggest story associated with *Tatler* at this time concerned a dog called Alan (or, to give him his full name, Alan TBH Plumptre). He belonged to Jennifer George, Reardon's assistant. The Vogue House revolving door is one of the most recognisable features of the building, and one that has frequently been used as a metaphor for the careers of many returning members of staff over the decades. In my time at *Tatler* it was not uncommon for dogs to be seen around the offices; this was part of a tradition of canine acceptance within Vogue House. As you will by now have realized, Vogue House had always set and followed its own employment laws, creating its own unique office environments.

Alan (full name Alan TBH Plumptre) had 2,500 followers on his own Twitter account, so he was Vogue House's resident canine celebrity. On the day of the tragic event, Alan had been taken out for a walk during office hours by a member of staff. On their return, when they approached the Vogue House revolving door, Alan saw a man walking through and bolted towards him, rushing through the revolving doors. Unfortunately Alan got his neck caught. His walker also became stuck. Two fire engines rushed to the building, where onlookers crowded around the accident scene and a team of ten firefighters freed the *Tatler* employee. However, they could not save Alan, who was pronounced dead at the scene. George tweeted: "Yesterday my tiny much loved man Alan passed away in a tragic accident. Thank you to all that were there to help, all the kind wishes and all who followed @TatlerAlan."

Dogs had always been part of the *Tatler* offices but the instigation of a monthly 'animal takeover' for the magazine's website took the staff's love for animals to a level rarely if ever seen in any office workplace. Each month, for one day only, the editorial team would work alongside various four-legged friends. The former digital editor Annabelle Spranklen Moore told the *Independent* in 2023: "We would fill Vogue House reception with puppies, lambs, kittens, and giant aggressive rabbits that would pee all over the red leather sofa ... Then we'd have to get them into the lift and up to the third floor *Tatler* office. I used to dread this day every month."

The death of a dog wasn't the only moment in the spotlight for *Tatler* staff under Reardon's editorship. In 2014 a camera crew were allowed into the Vogue House inner sanctum to create a fly-on-the-wall BBC2 documentary titled *Posh People: Inside Tatler*. The documentary series gave a rare insight into Vogue House but with a very tongue-in-cheek approach to the frivolities and absurdities of the lives lived both by those who featured in the magazine and who worked for it. How much the documentary and its title did to change people's perception of *Tatler* or to reinforce their preconceptions can perhaps be most clearly seen in an interview Reardon gave to the *Guardian* at the time, in which she said, "I have virtually no interest... in where they went to school, or frankly their qualifications. I'm much more interested in their emotional intelligence and talent... the people working here can't be a bunch of moronic 'Sloane's' killing time before they get married." Despite this, Reardon ensured that all new and existing members of staff were given their own copy of *Debrett's New Guide to Etiquette and Modern Manners* written by John Morgan, the former *GQ* style writer who had taken his own life.

In December 2017, Reardon was announced as the new editor-in-Chief of *The Times* luxury quarterly magazine, *Luxx* and she left *Tatler* at the beginning of 2018. Despite rumours being rife at the time that *Tatler* was set to be sold-off or to become an online-only publication, a Condé Nast spokesperson said that it was business as usual, and the printed magazine continued. Reardon's replacement was Richard Dennen, the great-grandson of Field Marshal Douglas Haig, 1st Earl of Bemersyde and the son of Lyle Dennen, an Archdeacon of the Anglican Communion. Dennen had attended Charterhouse before studying French Civilisation at the Paris-Sorbonne University as a gap year. He completed his education at the University of St Andrews and graduated with a degree in the History of Art. Dennen began his publishing career at *Tatler* as a young assistant before being made features editor. He then moved onto *The Sunday Times* and the *Mail on Sunday* before returning to *Tatler* as editor in February 2018. It may have been the second decade of the twenty-first century but the qualifications required for editing the social glossy remained unchanged and were clear for all to see. However, Dennen's vision for the magazine seemed to misunderstand the very nature of *Tatler* over the years.

In an interview with *WWD,* shortly after his first issue as editor was published, he said: "I feel strongly that you can get wit across in a really sophisticated way, and I think visual wit is really important. I didn't want it to be puerile, or silly but rather something beautiful that both a grandmother and granddaughter can pick up. So, nothing rude." I don't think any previous *Tatler* editor had been concerned about being rude with their editorial content, and basic retail wisdom dictates that such a proposed broad age range of reader would inevitably and repeatedly fail to connect with aspects of such an undefined reader demographic.

Dennen's appointment was not to be the only evidence in the 2010s of the traditional Vogue House approach to appointing an editor. In 2014 Sue Crewe stepped down from *House & Garden* to be replaced by Henrietta Rose Byng, better known as 'Hatta' Byng, the daughter of Timothy Byng, the 11th Viscount Torrington. In 2021 Rupert Thomas left *World of Interiors* and was replaced by Hamish Bowles, the son of David Victor Bowles, vice-provost of University College, London. However, this is not to say that these editors were not the right people for the jobs. Byng studied History of Art and Architecture before working in interior design for three years, followed by two years at the South African edition of *House & Garden,* before returning to the UK as features editor on the UK title in 2006. In 2013 she became the deputy editor and in 2014 she was made editor. Bowles is a highly experienced journalist whose passion for interiors and fashion had been with him since childhood. He worked at *Harper's Bazaar* from 1984 until 1992, first as a fashion editor, then as fashion director and, from 1989, as style director. In 1992, he joined Anna Wintour in New York and the staff of US *Vogue.*

Whilst both Byng and Bowles evidence extensive magazine experience in their CVs, it could be argued that so do many others, perhaps with more expertise in the specific areas of interest these magazines cover. However, the truth is that Vogue House has always been a home to the people who know people who know people, and that has always been their unofficial and unpublicised recruitment policy. This was known by all within the magazine publishing industry; resented by some and accepted as an unfair reality by others. Staff on a magazine are employed to reflect the readership of the magazine, and some facts and figures may be useful at this point to support this belief. In a 2017 article for *In Publishing*, *House & Garden*'s editor Hetty Byng described the readership as "incredibly affluent, with an average household income of £141,379 and a home worth of an average £930,897."

An interesting aspect to Bowles' career success, alongside his devotion to fashion and his close friendship with Wintour, is the way in which he has embraced the multiple ways that publishers now see as being essential components to a magazine's brand. In addition to his editorial roles, Bowles has hosted the podcasts *In Vogue: The 1990s* and *In Vogue: The 2000s*, he narrates *Vogue*'s YouTube series *Everything You Need to Know* and has featured in a video series titled *Vintage Bowles,* where cameras followed him around the world as he shopped for clothes. He also co-hosted the prestigious New York Met Gala in 2022. In my opinion, this willingness to engage with alternate broadcast platforms is essential to grow magazines as brands in the digital age. Bowles himself said in a 2014 interview with *The Cut* website: "We're obviously in a strange environment where practically anyone can set themselves up as a pundit of sorts. It's all about sorting the wheat from the chaff, and I'm very interested in reading different points of view, and certainly different generations than my own that have such a very different world view."

The second decade of the new century had seen a high rate of change of editorships within Vogue House, and there was to be a fourth editor anointed in the 2010s who would be publicly proclaimed as a more socially aware, inclusive and diverse choice for the times, an appointment which would also prove to be both divisive and controversial.

2016 was *Vogue's* centenary year and the magazine commenced a year-long birthday celebration. It was such a momentous year for Shulman as editor that she maintained a diary, which was published as a book titled *Inside Vogue: My Diary of Vogue's 100th Year*. The Duchess of Cambridge featured on the cover of the 100th issue and in true Vogue House style a star-studded *Vogue 100 Gala* was staged. Shulman's book is an honest and revelatory diary of the reality of attempting to keep a magazine such as *Vogue* together, whilst dealing with the day-to-day chores of being a wife and mother, but it also acts as the final chapter in her story as editor. The magazine's year of celebration ended and in January 2017 an announcement was made that Shulman would be leaving by the summer of that year. Similar to *GQ* under Dylan Jones, *Vogue* had become a professional ocean-going liner under her editorship, both smooth-running operations that moved at a sedate pace, but *Vogue* was about to hit an iceberg and for some it was time to man the lifeboats.

"*Vogue* couldn't have been more different than *Tatler*. It was less haphazard, more like *Tatler*'s big sister, ruled with the iron rod of Fran Bentley, who was Alex's managing editor. It was like being in a very expensive girls' boarding school, very polite, quiet, efficient, always professional but at times a little cold. If I didn't feel posh enough at *Tatler*, well then, I didn't feel cool enough at *Vogue*. But I was fine with that. Alex was a writer's editor, and I loved writing, so it was great to be commissioned to write a story about summer sun, and then be told, 'But don't mention any beauty products.' A free rein! Glorious! Beauty was not her thing at all, I suspect fashion wasn't either, so our meetings were short, as I sped through ideas hoping to get them signed off quickly so I could get on with them. If, on the other hand, I changed the subject and chatted about a mutual colleague we both liked, and how I'd just seen her new baby, she would instantly soften and be happy to chat. People, friends, places, culture – these were the things that mattered to her."

Kathleen Baird-Murray
Tatler, Vogue

"US Condé Nast had hot- and cold-running assistants, there were so many people working there; that wasn't the case at Vogue House, so it was much harder work. I was always working, whether I was in the building or not. I never went out for lunch and Alex pulled me into her office and she said, 'Why are you always here? You need to go out for lunch!' So, I started going out for lunch to the Sotheby's Café. I was always there or

Claridge's or of course at my desk; they were my three centres of gravitation."
Bronwyn Cosgrove
Vogue

Change in the magazine world always comes with casualties and Shulman's departure certainly caused controversy and more than a small amount of vicious criticism, despite her advertising and circulation success with the magazine. Her tenure at *Vogue* was the longest of any editor in the London office and her time in charge had seen a revolution in magazine publishing, plus dramatic economic and social behavioural change. After she had left, her editorship was criticised not only for its lack of racial diversity but also for its continuation of Vogue House nepotism. Whilst the nepotism charge is indeed true, it was by no means restricted to Shulman's *Vogue* and had been the currency of employment in the building on all of its magazines over the previous decades, as I have shown.

As with any governance that remains in power for a considerable time, there was a growing desire for change amongst some within the company. *Vogue* saw dramatic changes after Shulman's departure. As always happens when an editor leaves a magazine, it instigated a series of fallings-out and firings. There was a mass exodus of Shulman's team, including experienced and well-respected fashion figures such as fashion director Lucinda Chambers, whilst a corresponding mass influx of celebrities began to appear on the magazine's masthead under the new editor's reign. In a 2017 *Business of Fashion* article, Shulman is quoted as saying: "It has been interesting and educative to see over the years which of the more dilettante or famous contributors really put some effort into their contributions and which liked the idea of an association to the magazine without the tedious business of actually doing any work."

"While meetings with Alex would be about getting through it as quickly as possible without boring her, the upside was her decisions were quick, firm, and usually right. You might not agree with everything, but you always knew where you stood. Once, in a meeting in the art room that was more stressful than usual, I made the mistake of saying I'd been too busy to finish a task that was due that day. 'Too busy?' queried Alex. The room fell silent. I never used that as an excuse again. Nor the word 'icon', which was banned along with its over-used friend 'iconic'."

Kathleen Baird Murray
Tatler, Vogue

"I learnt how to work with young people whilst I was there. The work experience people were near where I sat when I was features editor on *Vogue*. Owen Sheers, the Welsh poet, won the Vogue Talent Contest so he sat next to me, and I would take him out, and we are still friends. James Chow, a journalist out of Hong Kong, was there as work experience, I think thanks to Lord Snowdon, and he went on to work at CCTV in China; he's still a great friend. Charlotte Sinclair had also won the Talent Contest and she was there, now she's a *Vogue* contributing editor."

Bronwyn Cosgrove
Vogue

Nepotism and the lack of diversity on both *Vogue*'s staff and its pages were not the only controversial issues to be raised concerning the magazine in the early twenty-first century. Fashion photography was under the spotlight. A group of photographers and fashion insiders were accused of inappropriate sexual behaviour over the previous years at this time, all of whom had worked repeatedly for the title since the 1990s and been regular visitors to Vogue House. The Peruvian fashion photographer Mario Testino, who was awarded an OBE, had been a mainstay of British *Vogue*'s fashion pages and covers for two decades by 2018, when he was accused of sexually exploiting models. He was not alone, as fellow *Vogue* photographer Bruce Weber was also named. Both were immediately suspended from working for the magazine. Testino was accused by thirteen male assistants and models of subjecting them to sexual advances, allegations that went back to the mid 1990s. Weber was accused by fifteen current and former models of subjecting them to unnecessary nudity and coercive sexual behaviour. American photographer Terry Richardson, another regular British *Vogue* fashion photographer, had been dropped by the magazine in 2017 after multiple allegations of inappropriate sexual behaviour towards female models at photoshoots going back almost two decades. It would have been considered bad enough for any magazine to have been associated with three photographers facing such allegations, but there was soon to be a fourth. French photographer Patrick Demarchelier, another regular British *Vogue* fashion photographer, was called out for similar behaviour, alleged to have engaged in repeated sexual misconduct with models. He too was dropped from the magazine. This was all part of an important moment for the fashion industry connected to the rise in late 2017 of the global #MeToo movement, which saw women speak out about sexual harassment in all parts of their lives. In 2018, a report on sexual misconduct within the fashion industry by the *Boston Globe* newspaper identified twenty-five fashion industry professionals as being engaged in and culpable for multiple acts of harassment over the previous three decades. The four photographers included in the report had been responsible for one hundred and sixteen British *Vogue* covers and attached fashion stories within the magazine between 1990–2018. *Vogue* needed to make a statement distancing the magazine from these photographers and the hunt was quickly on to find new talent to work with.

In 2018, the aristocracy made its own statement, one that was felt within Vogue House across all of the magazines that still employed those with aristocratic connections. A campaign was started named 'Daughters' Rights' and a case submitted to the European Court of Human Rights, led by Charlotte Carew Pole, the daughter of Sir Richard Carew Pole, a baronet, whose title was bestowed on his family by King Charles I in 1628. Alongside four other similarly connected women, Carew Pole was challenging the tradition of male primogeniture, by which titles automatically pass over first-born daughters to the next male in line, no matter how distantly related. If no male relative exists, then the title is allowed to die out. One of those within Vogue House who was to speak out about this was *House & Garden* editor Hatta Byng, herself the eldest of Viscount Torrington's three daughters.

Byng argued in an article in the *Daily Mail* that, "this is not about having the grandeur of a title or even inheriting the manor, because there isn't one, it was sold off during World War II... There is just a real sadness that when my father, 75, dies, his title will go to a distant cousin in Canada whom we've never met... My father, an only child, has always taken an active role in the House of Lords and would like to see the title pass to me." At the time of writing, the law still allows for hereditary peerages to pass only to male successors.

One of the great figures of publishing and fashion who found a home within Vogue House, whose name you may not be as familiar with as Grace Coddington, Marc Boxer, Tina Brown, Anna Wintour and Michael Roberts, is Lucinda Chambers, fashion director on *Vogue* for twenty-five years. I can speak with a little authority when it comes to Lucinda, as I worked with her when I was at *Elle* magazine in the 1980s. I have always thought that there are two types of fashion editor, those that like shopping and understand the commercial requirements of featuring certain brands, and those who, in addition to the first requirement, have innate style, class and taste as well. Chambers definitely falls into the second category. In my forty years working within the magazine world, I have never seen anyone dress as creatively and with such nonchalance.

Born in 1959 in Notting Hill, West London, Chambers developed a passion for textiles at an early age, collecting fabrics at Portobello Market before trying to design and make her own bags and clothing. A self-proclaimed 'underachiever' at school, she planned on becoming a secretary and getting married. However, after her father left the family home, there wasn't enough money for her to enrol on a secretarial course, so her mother suggested that they both attend art school. Chambers enrolled on a foundation course at Hornsey College of Art and her mother went to the London College of Printing to learn bookbinding. Chambers hated Hornsey and began making plastic jewellery, selling her work to friends and through local shops. After college she worked as a sales assistant in the high-street fashion chain Topshop and continued to make her own jewellery and clothes. It was at this time that she met Mario Testino, who was trying to make a name for himself and was photographing new hairstyles. Her multicoloured hair with bleach-blonde parts had caused Testino to notice her from the top of a London double-decker bus and she modelled for him. They soon became close friends, working together throughout the early 1980s.

In 1980 Chambers was interviewed by British *Vogue* for a secretarial job and was employed to work for Beatrix Miller, which she did for three years before becoming Grace Coddington's assistant. *In a Guardian* article in 2018 she recalled that one of the questions she was asked was "And who do you know here?" The answer was no one, but this didn't stop her from being employed: "That was one of the first things that I actively sought to change when I became fashion director. I couldn't see another CV with 'godchild of so-and-so' on it. It just wasn't interesting."

In her book *Grace*, Coddington speaks fondly of Chambers at this time and encapsulates her eclectic approach to work, fashion and responsibilities, an approach that would only be accepted somewhere like Vogue House: "She would arrive each morning looking like a flower in outfits she made herself and sat at her desk outside Bea's office sprouting petals of organza. I have never known anyone more passionate about clothes. Nor more blissfully scatty... Despite that, the girl was so cute to have around." (In contrast, Chambers' replacement as Coddington's assistant was to be Sophie Hicks, now an acclaimed architect, of whom Coddington said: "Everything about Sophie had to do with being a boy. No make-up, hair cut like a boy's. She even wore men's underwear.")

The first shoots Chambers was allowed to undertake were for the beauty editor Felicity Clark, before she was commissioned by Beatrix Miller to undertake the styling for a main fashion shoot. Unusually, Chambers was given full creative freedom to go wherever she wanted and photograph whoever she wished. Chambers chose the photographer Patrick Demarchelier, whom she had worked with before as an assistant. Both Miller and Coddington loved the resulting images. When *Elle* launched in the UK in September 1985 she joined as one of the fashion editors, but when Tilberis took over from Wintour at *Vogue* in 1987 she asked Chambers to return to Vogue House. Chambers was made fashion director in 1997, but her work and fashion influence was not restricted to the magazine. She worked on the closing ceremony for the 2012 London Olympics, was a consultant at the fashion brand Prada and designed and influenced the creative direction of another Italian fashion brand, Marni, for over twenty years.

"I would pass through the fashion department, and I befriended Lucinda, and she would often bring me clothes that she was sent as gifts that she didn't want. I would find these things left on my desk. Then she did a story on me in *Vogue*, which she titled 'Bronwyn Chic.' She took me over to the rack of clothes that she had called in for the story and said, 'This is all about you!' Well, I wore suits to work at *Vogue*, a lot of Chanel, Moschino, a lot of Missoni, coordinated separates to make it easy to dress for work. When I looked at what she had called in it was nothing like what I wore. It was so far removed, and I was like Wow! It's like me through her eyes."
Bronwyn Cosgrove
Vogue

Chambers' departure from *Vogue* was controversial, and the controversy intensified when she decided to tell the online fashion magazine *Vestoj* exactly how her departure was handled. The original article saw lawyers on behalf of both Condé Nast and Edward Enninful, the editor of *Vogue*, request changes, however it remains online and evidences Chambers' steely spirit and fearless character, in her refusal to back away from what she saw as the truth of the matter: she was fired.

"The wonderful Ateh Damachi, now Jewel, was an absolute angel. Ateh has since spoken out about how she felt about working at *Tatler*, the only black woman – and woman above a size 12, now that I think about it. It wasn't easy for her at times and I'm sorry I didn't do more to protect her from the ignorance and entitlement she politely confronted on a regular basis. I employed her because she was the best at her job, and

because her smile lit up the room. Looking back though, I didn't even think about how the environment might affect her. It was just the way it was."
Kathleen Baird-Murray
Tatler, Vogue

Edward Enninful was born in Ghana, the fifth of six children to Major Crosby Enninful of the Ghanaian Army. In 1985, after the country's coup d'état, the family emigrated to Britain and settled in Ladbroke Grove, West London. The sixteen-year-old Enninful was spotted on a train by the influential fashion stylist Simon Foxton and just a few weeks later he was modelling for Foxton at his house, with photographer Nick Knight. It's a story not too dissimilar from that concerning the meeting of Chambers and Testino. Enninful was then introduced to Terry Jones, the former *Vogue* art director and founder of *i-D* magazine, and began assisting the *i-D* fashion director Beth Summers. He finished college, earning a degree from Goldsmiths, University of London whilst still modelling and assisting on photoshoots with Foxton and Summers. When Summers left the magazine a few weeks after Enninful's eighteenth birthday, Terry Jones gave him her position on the magazine.

Enninful's promotion made him the youngest ever fashion director of an international publication. But that was just the start. In 1998 he became a contributing editor to Italian *Vogue,* and in 2006 became a contributing fashion editor for US *Vogue.* In 2011 he was made style director and immediately made the struggling Condé Nast magazine's editorial riskier and more challenging, thanks to collaborations with model Kate Moss and the photographer Steven Meisel. The magazine's advertising revenue grew by 16.7 per cent by May 2012, with 453 pages compared to 388 pages for the same period the year before. It was clear that Enninful was closely associated with a successful period for the magazine, though the film *The September Issue* would seem to belie this, in which he came over as somewhat lost and reliant on Coddington's experience and generous support as he failed to meet Wintour's expectations. Documentary performance aside, Enninful was considered by management to be a big part of the US magazine's success and in April 2017 he was appointed as the new editor-in-chief at British *Vogue*. In an article in the *Independent* newspaper, Condé Nast international chairman and chief executive Jonathan Newhouse announced him as the successor to Shulman, calling Enninful "an influential figure in the communities of fashion, Hollywood and music which shape the cultural zeitgeist" and adding that "by virtue of his talent and experience, Edward is supremely prepared to assume the responsibility of British *Vogue*." Shulman remembered in a *Daily Mail* article in 2023 that Newhouse wanted 'evolution not revolution' and that together they "mulled over a list of contenders – some *Vogue* insiders, other outsiders – as we tucked into mineral water and chicken salad, and then suddenly he stopped and looked at me like a child seeing their tower of shiny, wrapped Christmas presents. 'Edward,' he said excitedly, 'Everybody loves Edward!'"

This was a big moment for Vogue House, for many reasons. Enninful did not come from a public-school background, he did not have old-family connections, and he was black. In fact he was the first editor of colour in the history of Condé Nast, let alone within Vogue House. In a time of Black Lives Matter and growing demands for more diverse representation and inclusivity in all areas of society, such an appointment made a powerful statement. He was also not slow in coming forward in expressing his feelings concerning *Vogue* under Shulman. In his 2022 book *A Visible Man*, Enninful expressed his opinion that the magazine had "languished creatively and tonally, speaking exclusively to an upper-middle to upper-class pocket of Britishness" and went on to say that as each year passed it seemed to be "drifting ever further from the beating heart of the country – to say nothing of the world at large." I can say from personal experience that there is no shortage of opinions, controversial or otherwise, in the world of magazine publishing, but in expressing this view it seemed to many that what Eninnful was reacting against was the very essence of every magazine that had been created within Vogue House for the last six decades and a criticism of how his fellow editors continued to work. It was guaranteed to upset the status quo. In 2023, reflecting on Enninful's tenure, Shulman commented that "Edward's vision for *Vogue* was not mine, just as mine was not my predecessor's. It's no secret that it has been a sadness and frustration for me that he positioned himself and his vision by portraying my tenure at *Vogue* as if it were a crucible of white privilege. But in the intervening years I have learnt this sort of thing can happen."

Enninful openly championed diversity both on and off the pages of British *Vogue* and, from the moment his appointment was announced, a rear mirror was placed on his predecessor's editorship. Supermodel Naomi Campbell criticised the historical lack of diversity at the publication by posting on social media a photograph of *Vogue* staff under Shulman's leadership, which showed there were no black employees in a workforce of approximately fifty, whilst also thanking Enninful for appointing her as a contributing editor to the magazine. Today, twenty-five per cent of the *Vogue* editorial staff are people of colour.

"It was very different. There were still several familiar faces. But in the place of that posh girls' boarding-school froideur, there were faces that looked up from desks and smiled at the new girl. Many of those faces were black or Asian, and the effect it had on the content of the magazine, and on the atmosphere in general, was the biggest breath of fresh air, both liberating and exciting. Some of the walls had come down – both physically and psychologically."
Kathleen Baird-Murray
Tatler, Vogue

For his first issue, Enninful made a bold statement of what his 'New *Vogue*' would be featuring, choosing British mixed-heritage model and feminist activist Adwoa Aboah for the cover. However, things are rarely exactly what they seem within Vogue House. Although Enninful's description of his first issue's cover star as a Ghanaian model and media activist is accurate, Aboah is also a well-connected member of the London fashion community, the daughter of photography super-agent Camilla Lowther, herself the daughter of a Viscount. Aboah is also the goddaughter of Ronnie-Cooke Newhouse, wife of Jonathan Newhouse, chairman of Condé Nast International. Some things at Vogue House may never change.

Subsequent covers under Enninful have indeed made good on his promise, featuring musicians, entertainers and sportspeople of colour, including international superstars Beyoncé and Rihanna, global household name Oprah Winfrey, and the footballer Marcus Rashford. For the September 2020 issue, Enninful commissioned Misan Harriman, and the Nigerian photographer became the first black person to shoot a British *Vogue* cover in its 104-year history. These were editorial choices that were filled with PR potential for the title, raising its profile outside of its traditional and established readership, as it became very clear that Enninful's intention was to reshape the century-old publication and transform it into a contemporary fashion platform more reflective of the current global audience as he saw it. These efforts led to a 51 percent increase in digital traffic to the *Vogue* website and the signing of 140 new advertisers. In addition, the use of celebrity editors saw the magazine achieve record single issue sales.

"Edward was treated with the utmost deference and was involved in every detail. Meetings with him where I had fallen back on my default setting of 'better-get-through-this-before-they-get-bored' now took more than their allocated time. Instead, it wasn't uncommon to get:

'Wait, that idea about ageing, let's go back to it for a second. How about you ask Helena if she can shoot it?'

'Helena … Christensen?'

'Here's her number.'

I had thought I didn't care about magazines any more. I really thought those days of loving them were gone. [But under Edward] I loved seeing the shoots laid out in the art room, the creative process of discussing stories and then bringing them to life. The shoots. There were actual beauty shoots! And parties! Even better – parties that I was actually invited to, because I was a valued team member. This was a first!"

Kathleen Baird-Murray

Tatler, Vogue

The September 2019 issue, guest edited by the Duchess of Sussex, became the fastest-selling issue in the magazine's history, selling out its print run in ten days. It was also the biggest-selling issue of the decade. There is no doubt that Enninful had injected a new sense of purpose into the magazine, and his success pointed to a new future for *Vogue* and similar luxury-based magazines, but it was one that some traditionalists baulk at. In fact, in the course of writing this book I spoke to many who felt that the *Vogue* of today was not a success; many I spoke with felt that the title had lost its way and they therefore no longer bought it, despite many loyal years supporting the title. The problem seemed to be that in making a new version of the magazine, Enninful had lost sight of the essence of the magazine and what it meant to so many.

From a business perspective, the plan for *Vogue* today appears to focus primarily on its global website, with an acceptance that online readers will never buy the print edition. This leaves the printed magazines as a vehicle for advertising and brand-informed content, with greatly reduced space given to traditional original editorial content. There is no space in the modern magazine for the age-old battle between advertising and editorial integrity. Today the successful magazine editor must be willing to be a commercial animal, and able not only to meet and greet the advertiser but also to work with them as an important contributor. In the early 1960s Ailsa Garland had struggled with the commercial considerations of being the British *Vogue* editor; in the 2010s these considerations were now necessities.

Vogue House has always been a conservative publishing environment, with the very occasional short-lived moment of anarchy mainly confined to *GQ* and *Tatler*. It was therefore not difficult for Enninful to make his way through a list of 'firsts' with *Vogue* within a short period of time. The question is how divisive those 'firsts' were, including cover stars of advanced age and disability, and how alienating they were to the magazine's traditional readership as he encouraged his readers to become a 'force for change'. No one would criticise his intention, but his reliance on celebrities to make his point, alongside £2,000 Gucci dresses, has led many to discuss whether or not *Vogue* was the right platform for such a debate. Enninful's iteration of *Vogue* embraced a 'woke' global political awareness aimed at attracting a younger audience to the magazine. Young people unfortunately are not a large magazine-buying demographic, preferring to find their inspiration and information online through blogs, influencers, branded websites and social media like Instagram, Pinterest and TikTok.

To appeal to this untapped pool of potential readers, Enninful allegedly let go of highly skilled members of staff to pay for celebrity contributors with massive social media followings and the resultant expensive photoshoots. His personal Instagram account was filled with photographs of him with models and celebrities, and he placed considerable importance on the magazine's online presence, some say to the detriment of the printed magazine's authority in the marketplace. He also refocused the magazine as being fashion-centred, inviting criticism from those who perceived it to be over-interested with the fashion industry. In an interview with *The Times* in 2020, Shulman commented that "the reason why I was given the job was because I was outside the industry, and I was brought in to broaden it. I think now it's reverted more to how it was prior to my being there." Eninnful claims to have looked to the magazine in the 1970s under Bea Miller for inspiration when building a mission statement to secure the editorship, perhaps confirming Shulmans observation. Either way, it is clear that there is no love lost between the current and former editor-in-chief.

"The future was uncertain again, but this time not just for me, for everyone. A new direction was afoot, the globalisation of *Vogues*, and with it, talk of merging stories with other international *Vogues*. Those critics of 'old' *Vogue*, who'd hated the way it was too elitist, too alienating, too cliquey, now complained there was nothing to read, and why were there so many black models? I heard this from several people, sadly. But whatever the negatives, the determination to make changes that counted for something remained the driving force of British *Vogue*."
Kathleen Baird-Murray
Tatler, Vogue

I have spoken about the love felt within Vogue House for 'the Peters', two of the guardians of the reception desk, and the same could be said for their replacement, the equally beloved Arsenal fan, John. Another story that reached the newspapers concerning issues entering the building after the death of the *Tatler* dog was the arrival of Enninful into the building on a day just like any other.

The famous revolving door faced onto Hanover Square, but the building's loading bay was accessed via Maddox Street; it was a scruffy location where the mail office was situated, and deliveries were made. On his first day as editor, walking up to the front entrance of Vogue House carrying a *Vogue* tote bag containing his laptop, Enninful was accosted by a security guard who refused him entry to the building. He continued walking inside, presuming this was a mistake, only to be told that deliveries were to be taken to the loading bay. Eninnful let the security guard know who he was speaking to in no uncertain terms, and she apologised profusely, but he was not placated and told his team and human resources what had happened when he got to his office. He also posted about the experience on social media and made his position very clear, seeing the event as a case of racial profiling.

Enninful's voice was echoed within Condé Nast, which wanted to openly address any concerns that had been or could be voiced over potential or actual racism within the company. A global chief diversity and inclusion officer, Yashica Olden, was employed, and a diversity report was released in September 2020, alongside the 'Condé Code', a five-pronged set of values that states that "diversity is our strength". (This desire for inclusivity continued into a new decade: the May 2023 issue of British *Vogue* focused on disability, justice, accessibility and pride and was published as a Braille edition, the first time this had happened in the magazine's 107-year history. The issue was also made available in audio format to increase access for blind and partially-sighted readers.)

At this point in the story, I must issue a warning. Until now this book has been mainly focused on the characters and stories of the magazine staff who populated Vogue House; their eccentricities, their backgrounds and memories. However, during the 2010s the narrative becomes more corporate. The truth is that Vogue House was losing its island status and would no longer be left unaffected by the global decisions of its publisher or the impact of the storms of digital disruption and wider economic challenges that were facing all of the creative industries. Its wildness (and occasional inappropriateness) no longer fitted into a global picture. Therefore, to paint the picture, I need to place the story of the building and its staff into a new, more business-focused context. But stay with me, I hope not to bore you.

> "You'd go to parties, you'd host events, and you'd have a champagne glass with sparkling mineral water in it, because you had so many to get through in just one evening. I used to go to lunches, dinners and for cocktails, usually with my publisher, and we did this fabulous double-act together. I remember people saying, "Why do you that? Why are you so interested in the commercial aspects?" Well, as far as I was concerned, if I'm the editor, I have to be interested in the commercial as well as the editorial."
> **Sarah Miller**
> **Condé Nast Traveller**

When magazines approach advertisers they give their newsstand and subscriber numbers as proof of both their potential reach and popularity. To ensure that these numbers have some sense of reality, publishers submit their figures in the UK to the 'ABC', the Audit Bureau of Circulations, which will then audit these numbers and issue the official statistics. There has always been a sense of smoke and mirrors concerning the submission of these numbers, a black art in massaging the message when it comes to hiding dips in circulation, but some drops are too large to hide. At the time of writing, the 2022 ABCs were the most recent published figures, and they show the challenge facing magazines today. In 2022, *GQ*'s circulation (measured as an average per issue) was announced as being 74,900, *World of Interiors* 54,000, *House & Garden* 112,400, *Tatler* 78,300, *Traveller* 76,100 and *Vogue* 190,200. However, these figures are based on the sales promoted to advertisers, figures released by Vogue House. Only magazines purchased at newsstands are recognised by advertisers as being true sales, and so from this perspective the figures above are often inflated. There are many reasons for the drop in magazine purchasing and reading over the last ten years but the most obvious is the rise of the internet as a source of information, aspiration and inspiration.

Condé Nast has, unlike many other magazine publishers, established separate digital teams to create and oversee their online content for British *Vogue* and *GQ*. This may seem to make sense to editorial teams founded in old-school magazine production who are already stretched to meet print deadlines, but it can also produce two very separate products and experiences, each vying against each other. The printed magazine needs to validate its cost without being able to plan to benefit from interactive functionality. Most importantly, it cannot use the moving image to enhance the content it is producing in its edition. Meanwhile, the digital team points to the future and rapidly realises that it can exist without the magazine journalists. The US-based Condé Nast entertainment team, producing both digital content for online and social media use, describes itself as working 'in parallel' with Condé Nast editorial, creating, developing and producing thousands of videos, including video series like *Architectural Digest*'s *Open Door, WIRED*'s *Autocomplete, Vogue*'s *73 Questions*, and the *Bon Appétit Test Kitchen* for the magazine's websites, social media platforms and YouTube channels. They may see themselves as working in parallel, but the trajectory and speed of content-delivery certainly gives the digital team the upper hand. As does the ease by which they can evidence the audience numbers engaging with their content.

In 2015 Jonathan Newhouse made a decision to address the digital future for the titles within Vogue House and employed the company's first Chief Digital Officer, Wolfgang Blau, who would be the second German to take control at Vogue House in its history. Condé Nast announced it was merging the American and international versions of *Condé Nast Traveler* onto a new single platform. Fashion week coverage production from *Vogue* would also be centralized. Photography production, backstage videos, social media posts and selected features concerning fashion shows would now be handled by *Vogue* International from new offices between The Strand and Victoria Embankment, in London not in its historic HQ.

After graduating, Blau had worked for a radio station in Munich as its head news anchor, then as a freelance journalist in San Francisco and in Washington DC, in addition to developing the online audio edition of the German newspaper *Die Zeit* and Amazon's audiobook portal Audible. In 2008, Blau was made editor-in-chief of *Zeit Online* often commenting on politics and journalism. In 2013, he joined the *Guardian* newspaper as their Director of Digital Strategy and became a member of the board of Guardian News & Media in London. At Condé Nast, Blau began hiring enthusiastically, setting up digital, engineering and product teams and hiring people with titles such as 'Growth Editor', 'Data and Insight Analyst, 'Director of Product and Innovation' and 'Director of Data and Insight'. Unfortunately, a knowledge and experience of magazine publishing was not a pre-requisite of employment in any of these roles. Blau had been asked to initiate the London 'digital transformation' fifteen years after the dot-com boom, far too late to be ahead of the game. Despite this, in a 2018 *New York Times* article he confidently stated that, "We are in a state of transformation ... After years of operating with many highly autonomous magazine businesses all over the world – an approach that historically worked very well – C.N.I. is moving our titles toward a new way of thinking."

In 2017 the announcement was made that Blau would be taking over from the long-standing managing director Nicholas Coleridge on his retirement, with the new title of president of Condé Nast International. Newhouse said on his appointment that "Wolfgang Blau is a rare executive who can combine digital mastery with the journalistic talent and experience needed to redefine excellence in the digital age." The new guard were replacing the old, and Blau's new way of thinking could now be implemented across both digital and traditional printed media. His history as a digital evangelist presented a concerning direction for the Vogue House staff, although Blau did attempt to reassure by re-defining his past comments, saying that the "whole end-of-print narrative, which I have sung myself in different circumstances, doesn't hold the same weight with a highly visual title like *Vogue* as it does with, say, newspapers."

So, in a digital-first age, how can publishers encourage readers to buy printed magazines? Well, they can either incentivise them by cutting the cover price, usually done for individual issues through specific retailers, or they can enhance the desire to make the purchase through collectability. The idea of a monthly magazine as an artefact of value beyond its cover price is central to encouraging the twenty-first century reader to dip into their pocket and purchase a printed magazine at the full cover price. *Vogue* and *GQ* have employed the widely used concept of multiple cover choices for the same issue to achieve this feeling of collectability, and to increase 'repeated issue' magazine purchasing. In a *New York Times* article in 2021, Wintour spoke about this idea of the magazine as a collectable purchase: "I feel that print is our runway... It should be collectible. It should be something that you want to hold on to."

Unfortunately, such a strategy has also been repeatedly implemented by the independent niche sector of the market, that publish high cover price, high quality printed magazines on a quarterly or annual basis. These are usually pitched to the consumer as an alternative to the digital world. Although those magazines often have small circulations, they can be attractive to luxury brands keen to connect with niche high-income readers, therefore diluting advertising revenue available to the established mass-market monthly titles such as *Vogue*.

The other trend in magazine publishing sits in direct opposition to creating an aura of exclusivity and collectability: the increasing homogenisation of magazines. Homogenisation of design, writing and photography is led by a desire to resell and syndicate 'content', including the writing and photography that magazines commission. Commissioning is expensive and can be risky, and publishing today is risk averse. Budgets constrain creativity and mistakes are discouraged. The maverick is rarely given an opportunity to experiment; market research and data analysis have become the gatekeepers of editorial creation. Vogue House had always been a home for the maverick, as the stories in this book have shown, but the next decade will not see its revolving door continue to welcome those who want to bring a sense of individuality to the magazines created across its floors.

The concept of expanding brands such as *Vogue* and *GQ* outside of their magazine format had been a constant consideration for Condé Nast since the turn of the millennium. Direct to consumer retail was an element of this strategy that they had addressed back in 2000 with the launch of Style.com. This website was to be a digital resource that would serve as the online home for *Vogue* specifically, despite the fact that a *Vogue* website had already been set up eight years previously. However, the choice not to use the *Vogue* brand to launch this venture felt like a mistake to many. The reality was that it soon became an unloved home for runway footage only and in 2015 it was announced that it would undergo a multimillion-dollar rebranding.

The new idea for Style.com was to bring the pages of *Vogue* to life for the readers by allowing them to buy what they saw directly from one website, and their orders would be fulfilled by the new company that had been incorporated to facilitate this. Considerable investment was made into the site, and a staff of 75 employed to run it. Style.com's president, Franck Zayan, who came from the upmarket French department store Galeries Lafayette, was recruited to launch the new company and re-launch the website. He proclaimed that "What you see on the pages of the magazine may help you to make a decision on your future purchases. Style.com is the connection between the inspiration and the transaction to create a bridge between editorial and commerce." This idea of linking magazine product-placement with retail selling was a regularly discussed desire in the early 2000s, when the website was originally launched, but now, instead of linking to third-party sites, Style.com would link to a publisher-controlled site. Zayan went on to state that: "For a very long time, e-commerce was just about selling products and now what we're doing is bringing that whole experience together: we inspire, we guide, we offer, and we sell. Ultimately, the plan is to extend Style.com's reach into all the areas that Condé Nast covers worldwide, such as design, travel, grooming and technology, to make it a true lifestyle destination." These were big ideals that were a long way from the traditional publication of magazines in

Vogue House, but they spoke of the continued desire for diversification from the core Condé Nast business model of the past six decades.

Despite the fine words, Style.com did not fulfil its promise. In 2017 it ceased trading after a reported $100 million investment. In a *New York Times* article Matt Starker, the general manager of digital strategy at Condé Nast, claimed that it had been successful in many ways, saying "Our experience with Style.com taught us that content is a powerful driver of commerce, and the combination of great editorial with a great shopping experience creates a great user experience and revenue upside," but he also acknowledged that the skill sets required to create engaging content and those required to run a seamless e-commerce shopping site were different. I would suggest that anyone who had ever worked on a magazine or in retail would have been able to tell him that before the money had been spent and lost.

The closure of Style.com saw the beginning of a partnership with Farfetch, a French online retail business based in London. The company acts as a digital marketplace and middleman between brands, independent stores and consumers, builds and maintains the websites for labels, connects them to customers and then takes a percentage. However, unlike its rivals matches.com and net-a-porter.com, it did not have its own content-creation arm and so Jonathan Newhouse joined the Farfetch board of directors. How did this relate to Vogue House, I hear you cry? Well, two of its former inhabitants were then drafted in. Natalie Massenet, the one-time work experience on *Tatler* under Jane Procter's editorship and more recently founder of Net-a-Porter, also joined the Farfetch board to bring some editorial experience and online retail experience to the new initiative alongside Anna Wintour. Today the Farfetch website looks no different to any other luxury clothing retail site.

When looking to make economies in magazine production, those in management positions who have never worked on an individual title see multiple staff across different magazines with the same job titles and see savings. 'Hubs' of designers, sub-editors and production staff would be more cost-effective, and so they believe that the same people could and should be working across multiple magazines at the same time. This is of course the death knell for the personality of individual magazines, and the point where a publishing house becomes a page-factory, an editorial production line based on quantity rather than quality of output. This may seem obvious to you – it does to me! – but the world is full of publishers who have followed this cost-saving path and introduced hubs, only to see the quality of their magazines drop and staff begin to leave. Hubs can be local, national or international, but whichever is chosen identity is inevitably lost. The hubs are then usually removed or restructured completely in order to return to a more traditional staffing structure, but they never go back fully to how they were. Invariably this is because the staff have lost confidence in their management, which has demonstrated its ignorance as to what staff actually do and what skills they bring to their positions. I have rarely heard anyone in editorial suggest that a 'hub' is a good idea.

This sense of staff dissatisfaction has been made clear in the US with employees across the company pushing for change. Staff at the *New Yorker, Wired, Arts Technica* and *Pitchfork* have formed unions and Condé Nast were forced to reach a pay and conditions deal with three of the unions in 2022 after heated and public negotiations, which included a protest outside of Wintour's Greenwich Village townhouse. The US office was always a very different beast to Vogue House, as Wintour discovered during her tenure at British *Vogue*, but with the development of a global company with central leadership it becomes impossible to disconnect the limbs from the central nervous system.

Condé Nast is a global publishing company and thus cultural individualism, tradition and sentimentality are second at best to profit and loss. Many of the magazines within Vogue House had struggled over the years, but it was only in the second decade of the twenty-first century that titles which faced difficulties were closed. A magazine cannot survive without some autonomy over its content. The international franchised titles, by contrast, who had been allowed to define their own identities and create their own content as a result became the magazines within the Condé Nast stable that are the most editorially interesting and adventurous.

In 2021, Wintour spoke in defence of having spent the previous year turning *Vogue, GQ, Wired, Architectural Digest, Vanity Fair, Condé*

Nast Traveler and *Glamour* into global brands, each under one leader, cutting costs and streamlining the sharing of content across both print magazines and digital platforms: "Instead of having twenty-seven *Vogues* or ten *Vogues* go after one story, we have one global *Vogue* go after it," she stated. "It's more like a global newsroom with different hubs." There is that word 'hub' but in this case seen as a positive rather than a negative. Despite this defence of the structure, there were others from Wintour's generation of Vogue House incumbents who spoke out against it, including Tina Brown, who described the plan as "suicidal" in an interview with *The Times*. I think that it is clear that Wintour herself realised that the 'hub' model was not an easy fix: "Obviously there are some stories that work, particularly if you think about fashion, that's a global language, and music, so there are stories that will work across all territories and then those that absolutely won't, we're very aware of that."

In August 2018, British *Condé Nast Traveller* and American *Condé Nast Traveler* were combined under a single editorial structure, led by Melinda Stevens. Then, in 2020 Condé Nast announced a new global leadership structure, with key editors taking over titles across different markets. Anna Wintour became the chief content officer and *Vogue's* global editorial director, in addition to being editor-in-chief of US *Vogue* and artistic director of Condé Nast. (Some title! I wonder if she has a business card with all of that on.) Enninful was appointed *Vogue* European editorial director, overseeing the magazine in the UK, France, Italy, Germany and Spain, in addition to remaining editor-in-chief of British *Vogue*. The territory covers a wide range of cultural differences and, I would suggest, few similarities. Simone Marchetti, the editor of Italian *Vanity Fair,* was also made a European editorial director and given control of the French and Spanish versions of the magazine, as well as remaining in control of her own title. *Architectural Digest's* Amy Astley, *GQ's* Will Welch and *Condé Nast Traveler's* India editor Divia Thani all became global editorial directors of their titles, with Oliver Jahn of *Architectural Digest* Germany, Adam Baidawi of *GQ* Middle East and Jesse Ashlock of *Condé Nast Traveler* US as their global deputies. (This sense of global publishing was however somewhat contradicted a few years later in 2020 by the international *Vogue's* response to the global Covid-19 pandemic when they all 'came together' for their September 2020 issue to mark the impact Covid was having on the world. As part of a global response each editor of every *Vogue* was allowed to respond to the universal theme on their covers by doing whatever they wanted that was appropriate for their readers.)

In 2018 Jonathan Newhouse was appointed as chairman of the group's newly merged international and US businesses. He had a huge challenge on his hands in his new role. Circulation across the combined Condé Nast's US titles had declined by five million in one year, yet despite this Newhouse had ensured that the international arm of the business had recorded considerable profits. In 1989 he had moved from the US to Paris to work on the company's global expansion, and subsequently made it his life's work. With Newhouse in charge the future was always going to be global. In 2021 the long established and respected editors of both French and Italian *Vogue* were replaced and their new editors were instructed to report directly to Anna Wintour in New York. The first names you now see at the top of the mastheads of Condé Nast titles is the global team, with the local teams dramatically reduced in staff numbers. Whilst many publishers had adopted the 'hub' approach to editorial teams, Condé Nast took it to an international level.

An unexpected outcome of globalisation can be a disconnect with local or national reality. As Vogue House had always insisted through its employment of staff who knew the people, places and unwritten rules of the society their titles reflected, this sort of intimate understanding of a society or culture is important. This growing disconnect with a British outlook was certainly evident in 2022 when the New York based Condé Nast legal team sent a cease and desist letter with the threat of legal action to a small pub in Cornwall. The Star Inn is over 200 years old, and the village of Vogue much older still. This did not stop Condé Nast from trying to stop the pub from using the word 'Vogue' in their advertising. The owner of the pub replied to Conde Nast: "I presume your magazine bases its name on the dictionary term for being in fashion which is uncapitalised as used in the Oxford English Dictionary … If a member of your staff had taken the time to investigate, they would have discovered that our company, the Star Inn, is in the small village of Vogue, near St Day, Cornwall... Yes, that's right, Vogue is the name of our village, which has been in existence for hundreds of years and in fact is a Cornish word, not English... I note in your letter that you have only been in existence since 1916 and I presume that at the time when you chose the name *Vogue* in the capitalised version you didn't seek permission from the villagers of the real Vogue." Condé Nast replied: "Many thanks for your letter... and for responding with more information about your business and the hamlet of Vogue... you are quite correct to note that further research by our team would have identified that we did not need to send such a letter on this occasion."

This disconnect between the global and the local was referenced by Alexander Shulman in her column for the *Daily Mail* in 2023. "To understand the changes now happening in the *Vogue* empire you have to look back at how *Vogue* expanded throughout the world during my time there... last month... a multi-page Annie Leibovitz shoot, commissioned by Wintour as a tribute to the Karl Lagerfeld show at the New York Metropolitan Museum Costume Institute, commandeered most of the editorial space in most of the *Vogues*. Did the Editors really think all the different international readerships shared the same interest in Lagerfeld or the Met? I make this point because, during my tenure at *Vogue*, I was always passionately guarding my magazine's independence."

"The internet changed everything. A great issue of *Vogue*, no matter how old, is still something you can hold, flick through, look at the incredible images and read great stories from famous writers. It sits in its own time and is a tangible part of history. It looks as good as the day it was printed, even if that day was in the 1960's. Yet the online delivery of 'content' has replaced it... a continuous pipe spewing out 'information' in a moment in time. Readers have become consumers."
Geoff Waring
Vogue, Tatler

The internet is a global product, an international juggernaut that eats content hour by hour, minute by minute. The editorial teams within Condé Nast were now expected to respond to this demand and embrace its possibilities. Similarly, fashion and luxury brands, magazine's main advertisers and their essential source of revenue, now saw their customer bases as global. Advertising spend was now being set on the basis of territories rather than cities or countries. Publishers began to speak of portfolios of titles and not individual magazines, of reach and not readers, of data and not 'spirit'. The future of Vogue House had to be in jeopardy; Big Brother had its cameras trained on a small corner of a London square.

Chapter 7: 2020–2024
Turn Out the Lights

In a 2020 article in the *Financial Times*, Roger Lynch, a former Morgan Stanley investment banker, physicist, founder of Sling TV, president of Pandora Media and Condé Nast outsider, spoke of the future for the publisher. Lynch had been brought in to steer the company through an extremely difficult time for magazines: the global pandemic had seen print advertising revenue drop dramatically but according to the article Condé Nast been making losses for years. The Newhouse family told the *Financial Times* they had hired Lynch because they needed someone who was "steeped in dealing with disruption." Lynch was not a magazine man.

His plan was to invest approximately ten per cent of the company's revenues into technology and content creation, in order to boost online subscriptions and e-commerce propositions, as well as focusing on initiatives such as movie and television licensing deals, in an attempt to find new ways to make money from the magazine brands away from selling print advertising. Although Condé Nast claimed not to be affected by the global advertising downturn, they did see a need to cut costs and laid off or furloughed hundreds of employees, reducing pay for those earning more than £100,000 by between ten to twenty per cent, which affected nearly half the global workforce. Despite this, Lynch said that in 2021 the company would be hiring approximately three hundred engineering and product roles, and he had been responsible for hiring top executives from Disney and Google. Lynch was not bringing in experienced magazine people or using the language previously associated with publishing. He accepted that the magazine's readers had an attachment to the printed page but insisted that the traditional magazine distribution model had to change. He also saw the future as being one where revenue was no longer dependent on advertisers but on the readers themselves. This was a direct reversal of the established magazine-publishing status quo, and more aligned to broadcast streaming networks such as Netflix, Spotify or Apple TV.

Throughout this book I have repeatedly mentioned advertising revenue as the fuel that magazines need to exist. Newsstand sales and subscriptions are part of the overall revenue stream for any magazine, but it is through selling advertising pages that profit is made. To this end, Condé Nast has always been the leader within the luxury goods and brands market, claiming successfully that their readers were the potential purchasers that high-end brands needed to get their products in front of. Interiors magazines sell kitchens, furniture, paint, wallpaper, doors and windows. Fashion magazines sell clothes, cars, accessories, watches, perfume and beauty products. Interiors titles boomed during the Covid-19 pandemic in 2020–21, as people stuck at home under government-mandated lockdowns decided to spend on improving their immediate environments, whilst the fashion magazines suffered as people could no longer go out to work, parties or events. Leisure-wear was the only fashion story to tell. Readers turned to online or digital for their cultural entertainment and information, as people could no longer purchase a physical magazine from a physical shop. Post-Covid many magazines would struggle to re-establish themselves as a required purchase.

Whilst fashion advertising is crucial to magazines, beauty product revenue is also a key income for any fashion magazine via product placement within its editorial pages. When you read the long list of make-up apparently used on a shoot to 'get the look' do not be misled.

Any make-up artist will tell you that they use whatever lipstick, blusher, foundation and mascara that is at hand and it is only when the magazine page is designed and written that the product list is compiled to keep the brands happy and willing to buy advertising pages. I'm sorry if this comes as a revelation to you, but at the end of the day a magazine is a business. I should add that exactly the same approach to product placement is adopted by every magazine you look at and read, whatever its subject matter.

> "It's important to remember that beauty is always a poor relation to fashion at Condé Nast. It may bring in the advertising money and be a huge industry incorporating cosmetics, skin care, hair care, health, spa treatments and more but it's always considered peripheral to clothing."
> **Kathy Phillips**
> **Tatler, Vogue**

> "Beauty constantly had to fight for budgets to shoot; it was very much the poor relation, despite being such a major source of advertising revenue. As a department, you often felt like an afterthought. It wasn't uncommon to be handed an image – a fashion image – and be told, "She's wearing red lipstick, maybe write a story about red lipstick?"
> **Kathleen Baird-Murray**
> **Tatler, Vogue**

Whilst on the subject of advertising revenue, it might be worth briefly taking a sense-check on the advertising market globally as the magazine world came out of the Covid-19 pandemic. In a 2022 article in the *Guardian* a senior media industry executive saw little positivity in the future: "Conventional wisdom would suggest that next year will be a car crash … consumers are being squeezed harder than at any time since the 1970s. Many things will become secondary to essential spending, all of which creates a nasty cocktail for the ad industry." The article went on to state that "advertising budgets make for a quick cost-cutting strategy to boost, or at least salvage, a company's balance sheet as demand dries up." In a 2023 *Press Gazette* article dealing specifically with print advertising revenue, the stark reality of the situation for magazines was made even clearer: "The global print advertising market has halved in the past six years but a growing online 'oligopoly' of tech giants and retailers mean digital ad revenues are still insufficient to plug the gap." It goes on to note that "relatively modest" increases in digital advertising revenue cannot compensate for the level of print advertising income loss. It is within this environment that the closure of Vogue House was made.

> "*Vogue* seeps into your identity in a way that other magazines just cannot do. It's only when you leave that you realise that most people could not care less about it, and that you're inhabiting some sort of magic bubble for the time that you're there."
> **Kathleen Baird-Murray**
> **Tatler, Vogue**

> "If you were chosen to work regularly for *Vogue* you felt as if you were in the first eleven and were very privileged. Along with this went an intense sense of loyalty."
> **Tessa Traeger**
> **Vogue**

In addition to advertising revenue and product placement, subscriptions have always been an important source of magazine revenue, providing financial security and guaranteed sales. The subscriptions model has traditionally been one reliant on gift-purchases and heavily discounted new reader offers, giving considerable discounts on the cover price to entice readers with the hope that they will remain with the title on a monthly payment schedule after the initial offer has ended and the price is increased. It is a hope not always delivered upon. It is possible that a digital subscription model could be a more successful and less expensive format with which to build subscription audiences and it is this model that perhaps points most effectively to the future for magazines and newspapers who have already or intend to adopt a pay wall model.

This is not guesswork on my part, the London-based Telegraph Media Group is a publisher best known for its newspapers, many of which have been training grounds and employers of Vogue House journalists, but it also has a magazine publishing arm. The group's mission statement very clearly outlines their view of the future of publishing, which seems to align with that of Condé Nast (although without the risks that international 'hubs' could bring):

"In 2018 [...] we set out a bold vision to become a subscriber-first business, with quality journalism at our heart, building deeper connections with our subscribers at scale. We stated then, and reiterate now, that this requires us to think and act differently. This is essential if we want to continue to operate at the forefront of the industry [...] There are now many ways readers can engage with our journalism: via our newspaper and website, our app and newsletters, liveblogs, podcasts, video and social media [...] Alongside audience growth will come increased subscriber revenue to maintain and grow our business."

A 'paywall' – a digital content-blocker only bypassed by paying for a subscription – is used by the *Telegraph*, *The New Yorker*, *The Times* and the *New York Times* to monetise their output, but a magazine is not a newspaper. It lacks the urgent imperative of 'breaking news' that means its consumers fear missing out on vital information if they do not subscribe. Moreover, a magazine is a luxury item and therefore that much easier to cancel when economic times get tough and similar content is available online for free.

The idea of paying for streaming services raises an interesting transatlantic difference in expectation. Those in the US are used to paying for everything from radio to healthcare, from cable television to education. In the UK we have become used to receiving these services for free. Therefore, although there has been an acceptance of the 'pay-to-view' model for US television streaming systems, it is a much harder sell to UK audiences who have, on the whole, excellent free-to-access alternatives. This may or may not be fully understood by US-based decision makers.

In an April 2021 memo to Condé Nast employees, Lynch said that the company would increase its investment in "content capabilities" by twenty-five percent over the following four years, and that "parts of our workforce will evolve as we transition from outdated modes of publishing and build a digital-first content company for the future". He continued: "As we implement each brand's specific vision, by the end of the year, our global workforce is anticipated to grow." How this was received by staff employed to create what he considered to be "outdated modes of publishing" within Vogue House can easily be imagined.

In 2021, after editing the magazine for twenty-two years, GQ editor Dylan Jones left Vogue House, to be replaced by Adam Baidawi, the new Condé Nast deputy global editorial editor. Although Baidawi was named editor the 'strategy' for the magazine was to be led by Will Welch, editor of the US edition and the new global editorial director, whose focus was to bring a more progressive vision of masculinity across both editions. Baidawi, an Iraqi-Australian writer and photographer, was the first editor-in-chief of GQ Middle East, a licensed edition launched in 2018. He moved from Dubai to London and Vogue House to take control of GQ and announced that he wanted to bring "a fresh set of eyes" to the magazine, telling the *Evening Standard* that he wanted UK GQ to tap into the UK's "world-conquering talents" and be "more involved with [...] cultural moments and more connected with our consumer, our creative community and the zeitgeist". It is perhaps strange that the globalisation of editorial content and editorial staff was being presented with such a national and local focus, unless of course this was being done to calm the existing staff's nerves concerning the loss of the title's national identity and the much-loved eccentric nature of the magazine. Echoing the mantra that Enninful had bought to *Vogue,* Baidawi stated that he wanted to make the magazine "more inclusive and communal". Although Baidawi may have seemed like a complete outsider, as was so often the way at Vogue House, its revolving doors had once again performed their duty. In 2011, Baidawi had briefly moved to the UK to do work experience on GQ: "I transcribed interviews, did research, stacked magazines and spent an afternoon washing dishes in the kitchen," he said. "I loved it."

Dylan Jones was professional when leaving, issuing a statement that talked with affection of the title and the company. "I have had such a brilliant time working for Condé Nast these last twenty-two years. It has been one of the most rewarding professional adventures of my career, and it has been one hell of a ride [...] I am hugely, immensely proud of the fantastic team I have been lucky enough to build around me, a team that has won eighty awards, more than any other magazine in the country. There is no greater recognition of journalistic integrity." The facts back up Jones' claims. UK *GQ* had the largest average circulation among men's magazines in 2020 with 95,298 copies sold each month. Jones also claimed that *GQ*'s website was reaching 5 million potential readers. These are all signs that the magazine was in rude health under Jones, so why did he leave? Well, as any editor will tell you, twenty-two years is a long time on any magazine, and Jones had a multitude of outlets for his writing outside of *GQ* in newspapers and books. However, I think that it is clear that Condé Nast's global ambitions were also impacting directly on members of its staff within Vogue House.

Shortly before Jones' resignation staff had been informed of the company's plans to merge editorial teams around the world, changes that would affect editorial and commercial staff at *Vogue, Condé Nast Traveller* and *GQ* and require some staff to reapply for their roles under the new structure. It may have been the catalyst for his decision. Interestingly, seven years previously Jones had remarked to the *Press Gazette* that, "It's terrible what's happened to our industry. However, there are lots of people running around like headless chickens complaining that the world is over. But there will be winners and losers. And you have to adapt. And if you don't adapt, you die."

Another long-standing member of the *GQ* team worth mentioning at this point is Bill Prince, who left the magazine just one year after Jones' departure. Price joined *GQ* in 1997 and remained as a loyal features editor and then deputy editor under Jones. He shared a similar background to Jones, having worked in music journalism as the assistant editor of *Q* magazine and as a writer on the *NME*. He was also a member of the Grand *Prix d'Horlogerie de Genève* Academy – very useful if you want to attract big-spending luxury watch brands to buy advertising space.

There is no doubt that Jones' *GQ* was as steady as any magazine could be, and so without the usual dramas it provided few stories for this book, as I chose not to include stories from the Annual Awards night as they would have taken up a book on their own! However, it did produce a number of outstanding journalists who continue to work in the magazine world. One of these is Nick Sullivan, who arrived at *GQ* after stints at *Arena* and British *Esquire*. Sullivan was a fashion director with a degree in French from the University of Warwick, who left *GQ* in 2004 to work at US *Esquire*. In a 2018 interview with *Business of Fashion*, Sullivan spoke of his time in London and in Vogue House: "I did a long stint with Dylan, which was probably the best experience and most formative part of my life. I'd crossed from *Esquire*, which was in its infancy, to *Arena*, which was very cool, and I wasn't very cool, so it was a bit like being in the deep end. But I wrote a lot, and I started shooting more. Working on those magazines was the best experience, because we had no budget and not enough people, we just got on with it."

The world of magazines is filled with uncertainty, as there is such a strong sense of job insecurity amongst editorial teams. Changes of staff is part of the deal, sometimes editors are dismissed and occasionally they are promoted, although the latter happens less than the former as there are very few places you can progress to without moving into management. Those positions are few and far between, and usually only become an option due to an unexpected death or age-related retirement. The process of publishing the written word in physical print requires the completed text to be submitted to give time for layout, printing, binding and distribution. For a magazine, it usually takes a week to print, dry and bind. A book takes a lot longer. It is inevitable that some of the names I have spoken about in this chapter and the following one will change roles before you sit down to read this book. Whilst I was writing, it was announced in June 2023 that Edward Enninful would leave British *Vogue* in 2024 to take on a role as global creative and cultural advisor for *Vogue* and editorial advisor at British *Vogue*. It's an announcement that echoes the position created for Anna Wintour when she left British *Vogue*, eventually taking control of US *Vogue* in the late 1980s. Enninful's new position invited speculation that he would one day take over from Wintour, a rumour that had been circulating for the previous year. When he was asked if he had ambitions to succeed Wintour, Enninful told the *New York Times* that "I'm happy working in Europe but you never know what the future holds."

In a letter to the British *Vogue* staff in Vogue House, Enninful wrote: "I am excited to share that from next year I will be stepping into the newly appointed position of editorial advisor of British *Vogue* and global creative and cultural advisor of *Vogue*, where I will continue to contribute to the creative and cultural success of the *Vogue* brand globally while having the freedom to take on broader creative projects." That word 'global' front and centre once again. Enninful said that his promotion had come after discussions with Wintour and chief executive officer of Condé Nast Roger Lynch, about how he could "play a broader role in enhancing *Vogue* globally". An argument that the future for magazine publishing is not global would be difficult to make when met with such evangelism.

The saddest outcome of this announcement was that it indicated the end of a publishing institution: there would no longer be an editor-in chief of British *Vogue*, instead there would be a "head of editorial content", a title that does not traditionally exist within the publishing world, but which resonates clearly within multi-media offices. As Shulman put it in the *Daily Mail*: "Whoever is bleakly titled 'editorial content director' will have little, if any, autonomy and will report to a bureaucratic tangle of 'leads' in New York." 2024 will not only be the year that sees the end of Conde Nast's occupancy of Vogue House, but also the end of the position of editor of *Vogue*. I can only imagine what Withers, Miller and Tilberis would make of such a decision. Anna Wintour, however, I presume was in support. This means that the only remaining editors-in-chief, not including Wintour, are those at *Vogues* published under license.

As we came to the end of the process of proofing this book the new head of editorial content was announced. Chioma Nnadi was perhaps not surprisingly the editor of US vogue.com before moving to British *Vogue*. The 44-year-old London-born journalist is the daughter of a Swiss-German mother who works as a nurse and a Nigerian father, both of whom moved to the UK in the 1960s. Nnadi grew up in central London and started her career on the features desk at the *Evening Standard Magazine*, before she moved to New York and began working at independent style magazines such as *Trace* and at *The Fader* as a style director. In 2010 she joined *Vogue* and began working on the magazine's website, writing for the magazine and presenting its podcast. In a 2023 interview with the *Guardian*, she stated that her focus will be on "digital storytelling" and keeping *Vogue* "interactive" with readers. In a statement offered to the press on the announcement of her new position she further indicated where her priorities would lie: "I'm looking forward to engaging a loyal and inspired digital community that is energised by our access, point of view, and storytelling." Anna Wintour added that Nnadi had proved herself as being "adept at speaking to our digital audience" and finding "ways to extend *Vogue's* reach, authority, and influence across all of our platforms". There was no mention of the importance of the printed magazine by either of them. Nnadi also commented on working in Vogue House, "When I started out, there was one other Black person working in the building, and we both went to the same college. It wasn't the same place it is now."

I started in magazines in 1986. At that time magazine pages were designed with scalpels, Cow Gum glue, hot wax and lighter fuel on what were called grid sheets. Photographs were edited on light boxes through a Lupe eye glass and then made into prints on a Photo Mechanical Transfer machine. Headlines were ordered as text over the phone and then sent to the office on motorbikes as glossy print-outs, ready to be cut and re-sized; text came to us the same way. This process required designers to be ordered in how they tackled their workload as they waited for the components they needed to be delivered. Photocopier machines were then used to resize type and images to the required scale; creating the pages was a form of design-jigsaw-come-collage. The pages were then signed off by the art director and editor in pen on the grid sheets, which were then sent to the reprographic companies somewhere in London (usually the East End) to make what were called 'bromides'. These arrived at the office a day or so later as toxic-smelling blueprints, which were laid onto the grid sheets on a light box to ensure that they were accurate to the original design. Bromides did not have images on so for the designers, writers and sub-editors this was a text-checking process only. Once checked these were motor biked back to the repro company. A few days later a Cromalin would be sent back. This was a glossy, expensive proof and the first time that photographs would be seen in colour with colour type. Corrections could be made at this point, but they were expensive and to be avoided. Everyone involved in the page would take a look at this stage before the art director and production director signed it off to go to print. All of this process required communication, collaboration and physical hands-on work to meet the relatively short production schedule of approximately three weeks that ensures any monthly magazine meets its on-sale date.

The arrival of the Apple Macintosh in the early 1990s saw the art departments move away from physical 'cut and paste' and having to order text from printers, but it did not have a great impact on the everyday world of the magazine office. Photographers would still come in to show their work, models would arrive for castings, journalists and writers still delivered copy. The reception would fill up from twelve thirty as people arrived to go 'out for lunch' with friends and those commissioning them, and for some 'lunch' could continue well into the mid-afternoon. As long as you were back by three o'clock it never seemed to be a problem. The magazine office was based on an informal acceptance of the requirements of taking blank pages to the printed bound page every month – as long as deadlines were met there was day-to-day flexibility. There were no strict rules but there was a sense of comradery and teamwork, with the occasional tantrum, falling out or professional resentment thrown in for good measure. Everyone needed to be available in one space at one time. Email, fast internet and meeting software such as Zoom, Teams and Google Meet have now changed all of that.

Digitally-created magazines do not need staff to all be in one office and perhaps this shift also points to one of the reasons for the end of Conde Nast's tenancy of Vogue House. The Covid-19 pandemic saw many people begin to work from home and magazines were no different, proving that a monthly magazine could be created with members of staff in their own offices in kitchens, bedrooms, or even the shed – if that shed was in the Cotswolds or Tuscany! Or as *House & Garden* editor Hatta Byng revealed, "I'm not sure I dare own up to this, but I'm at a desk in my bedroom in a cottage my parents have at the bottom of their garden in Wiltshire." The staff on the magazines within Vogue House had rarely visited each other's offices – there had always been a sense that each title was like an independent island where travel to another territory was rarely considered or undertaken. Now it was even less likely to happen.

> "I think I went into Alex's (Shulman's) office twice, the entire time I was in the building. I went into Dylan's (Jones) office once, with Angus (MacKinnon) never, maybe once with James (Brown), never did I visit Rupert's (Thomas). I think I went into Sue Crewe's. *Tatler* I never went into even though it was opposite 'the hatch'. God no! I mean, no way!
> **Sarah Miller**
> **Condé Nast Traveller**

Vogue House was no different than any other office during the Covid-19 pandemic: in 2020, for the first time since 1958, it was silent and empty. An expensive piece of real estate in the centre of the West End of London was no longer being used, although the rent was still being paid. In a post-Covid world many people have reassessed their relationship with work, the office and commuting. I certainly would have done if I was still working at Condé Nast and doing a two-and-a-half-hour commute each way, each day. However, the buzz and excitement that a busy magazine office can generate cannot be beaten, a fact that siloed management often find difficult to appreciate. Neither can the mix of experienced and inexperienced staff sharing knowledge, opinions and ways of working as part of an informal learning exchange. It was this very experience that had seen so many interns at Vogue House progress in their careers. Working from home does not offer this opportunity and this is a serious problem for the magazine industry in the future. Hybrid working has many positive aspects, but it can easily lead to templated magazines being created without soul, spirit and a sense of adventure.

"'If someone offers you a fee for a piece, put the phone down, and wait for them to ring back,' advised Vicky Woods, the magazine's deputy editor, who definitely did not get out of bed for less than £800. In the 80s journalists could still command proper fees (though I don't remember putting the phone down on Anna Wintour when agreeing to write *Vogue's Modern Style*). The treasure came in other ways: time poring over a light box, training my eye to choose this photograph over that one, to juxtapose images on a spread, writing stand-firsts, editing other people's texts, resisting PR pressure (in spite of grand hotel lunches and perfumed gifts); learning how long you needed to wait for a person to reveal their real selves; how the intensity of a deadline and pursuit of excellence made those sentences miraculously appear. I didn't know it at the time, but it was the kind of self-wrought apprenticeship you can only find when immersed in certain workplaces."

Charlotte du Cann
Vogue

"I look back on my time and in a way I took it for granted but I wonder if magazines can be that creative again. I worked through the 90s at a golden time and it was really fun, and I think that has gone. I don't think that will come again. We had the bandwidth to be quirky and *Vogue* could take risks. I thought if *Vogue* can't do it then no one can do it and if it didn't work out it wasn't the end of the world."

Isabella Kullman
Vogue

"Working in Vogue House was like being at college again. It was a learning environment as much as a publishing house. Every day was different and every day someone interesting would visit, whether it was the whirlwind that was Manolo Blahnik or milliner Philip Treacy or photographers such as Snowdon or Mario Testino or Nick Knight. Creativity was king and respected beyond all else. It gave us freedom. Sales figures were important, but you never felt pressured to increase sales."

Geoff Waring
Vogue, Tatler

The conflicted positivity towards such hybrid working by Vogue House employees was evidenced by British *Vogue* on their own website in 2020 when they asked members of staff to divulge how their July issue came together during lockdown. Laura Ingham, the fashion market director said: "I have learnt that so much can be achieved remotely: a shared screen on Zoom, pop-up fashion cupboards from our houses and flats across London and virtual styling have become the new way to prepare and execute shoots." Contributing fashion director Venetia Scott explained that "the positive has been having spare time to think more laterally. It's opened up a different way of living and working." Managing editor Mark Russell also saw positives in working from home: "As someone who usually spends three hours a day commuting, it's also been a joy to use some of that time to watch the spread of spring. I would love to think that technology such as Zoom and Slack will allow us to build more flexibility into our working lives after lockdown."

Ingham also commented on the downsides of working from home: "I am grateful for the time with my family, but I do miss the office, the hustle and bustle of central London, the conversations that we have together at Vogue House." Jessica Diner, beauty & lifestyle director, added: "I was itching to get back to Vogue House, to reconnect with the team as well as feed off the creative energy that abounds there." However, it was perhaps features editor Olivia Marks who most clearly identified the appeal of working at Vogue House: "Vogue House has slightly more glamour than an office borne from, say, Ricky Gervais' imagination – after almost four years working there, I can attest there's still a thrill to be found from walking through those glass revolving doors – but nevertheless, I never expected to feel this yearning for it. But I do.

I miss my desk; the too-small kitchen where there are never any teaspoons; a printer that picks and chooses when to work like an insolent teenager [...] It's the atmosphere I miss the most, though. Rails of clothes for shoots lining the corridors; editors gathered around a screen to look at an anticipated set of photographs; morning conferences after a big news event. Even inane chatter can often (okay, sometimes) lead to brilliant ideas, and as much as Zoom has served us well these past months, nothing can beat the buzz of a face-to-face meeting."

"Great, I thought to myself, working from home is my thing, I can do this. However, we were unprepared for Edward's relentless zeal. He wanted to somehow find any glimmer of positivity from the situation, despite the lack of resources available and restrictions imposed, to transform this moment into something British *Vogue* -worthy. There were covers with brave women tube-drivers, beautiful British landscapes by photographers and artists such as David Hockney. And there were 5.30pm Friday Zoom meetings where seemingly on a whim Edward would ask me to round up a selection of staff and get them to take selfies of their most happy or confident beauty moment. It was back-to-back Zooms. We even called on beauty brands to donate products that might cheer up the nurses so that we could donate them."
Kathleen Baird Murray
Tatler, Vogue

In 2021, in a co-signed letter, Anna Wintour and Edward Enninful at *Vogue*, Gideon Lichfield at *Wired*, Divia Thani and Jesse Ashlock at *Condé Nast Traveller* and Amy Astley and Oliver Jahn at *Architectural Digest* shared Condé Nast's "collective vision" for the future. They wrote that their magazines' brands had previously worked in "self-defeating" silos that competed against each other and that the future would see their brands working together resulting in "bigger gets, bigger scoops, and more ground-breaking storytelling". The letter went on to outline how they perceived the pandemic years could be an insight into the future where operations could be "more decentralised, more democratic, open to more voices than we've been in the past" with a goal "to be a more 21st century media company, and a more community-minded one as well" with local stories given wider distribution. The relevance of such local stories to a wider audience was not however addressed.

Not all of the staff returned to Vogue House post-Covid and many of those that did have done so on a hybrid basis, only going in a few days a week at most. The 1990s and 2000s had seen the building overflowing with staff and the company seeking additional office space from Bond Street to Clerkenwell. Since then, magazines had closed, staffing had been reduced and hybrid working introduced. Despite this, the official Condé Nast email to staff announcing the departure from Vogue House came as a shock to many staff and former employees. It said this: "There's no other way to say it – leaving our iconic Vogue House will be hard. After many attempts to find a way to expand and redesign the space to meet our needs, there were just too many challenges to be able to do so."

The announcement came shortly after the news that US *Vogue* was to reduce its print issues from eleven to ten each year, having dropped from twelve issues in 2020. It is perhaps the fact that *Vogue* needs to reduce its published issues that points to a more accurate reason for Vogue House to go dark.

"The building was too small to contain so many big personalities, everyone passed through those doors."
Bronwyn Cosgrove
Vogue

Condé Nast gave no details as to what their needs are from a building or what challenges they faced at Vogue House may have been. It could be argued that such an old building could not meet the requirements of a 21st-century communications company, but if that was truly the case then their move into the Adelphi building on the Embankment between the Strand and the River Thames would seem to be a very strange decision. The Adelphi was built in the early 1930s, nearly thirty years before Vogue House and, despite having undergone a complete refurbishment, it remains a monumental Art Deco building that would not look out of place in Chicago or Manhattan. It is an impressive building that would appeal to any US-based company, but it also shows that an old building can be adapted to meet modern needs if the money and the desire is there. Condé Nast's international digital teams had moved into the building in 2018 and a film is available on YouTube of the '*Blade Runner*-esque' spaces that were created for the staff. With the benefit of hindsight, this was probably a very visible sign that Vogue House's days were numbered.

> "Times change, jobs change, desks change and now it seems that buildings change too."
> **Kathy Phillips**
> **Vogue, Tatler**

> "I'm very worried about the move to the Strand, that area is never going to be Bond Street, it is never going to have the Caprice on its doorstep. It's never going to have a Royal Academy, John Lewis or Marylebone High Street. Or, let's face it, Claridges. You've got the Savoy, but that's a bit kind of frosty compared to Claridges, which is quite sexy."
> **Sarah Miller**
> **Condé Nast Traveller**

These may seem like shallow reasons to be concerned about the move of an office space, but Condé Nast have previously made a similar series of moves that indicate how a change of physical environment can impact negatively on their own staff. In 1996 Condé Nast in New York announced that they would be moving away from their long-time Madison Avenue headquarters into a new architect-designed building on the northeast corner of 42nd Street and Broadway. Effectively Times Square, the epicentre of Manhattan. Condé Nast occupied at least 500,000 square feet of the offices and moved all of its staff under one roof. This was a prestigious address and certainly one that met the expectations of the aspirational staff, particularly those on *Vogue*. But in 2014 they left, despite having four years remaining on their lease, and moved to One World Trade Center in Lower Manhattan. Wintour was certainly unhappy with the move, telling *New York* magazine "It's dreadful!" On Broadway she had been at the centre of everything, as had the rest of the Condé Nast staff; now they were in a sterile corporate district, the antipathy of the lives evidenced in the magazines pages they were producing. The move had been a financial decision, but it had misunderstood the needs of its staff in responding to difficult economic conditions. In 2020 rumours began to circulate about a return to midtown New York; at the time of writing they remain downtown.

"I think that it's no coincidence that the heartland of Condé Nast, New York, suffered September 11th. I think that is all part of the story. Caution crept in, as nobody knew what the future would be like, and they made the fatal move downtown for cheaper rent. I think that was the beginning of the 'not feeling in the centre of the universe' and being slightly disconnected. They were part of Wall Street and that whole area, it wasn't 'uptown girl' any more."
Sarah Miller
Condé Nast Traveller

Magazine publishing was once filled with people fascinated and intrigued by creative expression in all its forms, mavericks that would have had no time for an Excel spreadsheet. Those who worked in the art departments of Vogue House were also photographers, cartoonists, sculptors, illustrators, stylists, typographers and artists. Many of the art directors went on to become successful photographers including Paul Bowden, Richard Burbridge, Michael Roberts, Robin Derrick, Geoff Waring, Eric Boman and, dare I say, myself! The fashion and features departments were filled with those who embraced every form of artistic practice from film to music, from literature to architecture. Many have gone on to become successful novelists, entrepreneurs, academics, curators, architects and television personalities. In this book I have dealt purely with the time in which the UK Condé Nast magazines were produced within Vogue House, but a sense of the bohemian, and a desire to challenge societal norms, has always been embedded within the DNA of the magazines and *Vogue* in particular.

During the 1920s UK *Vogue* had been transformed from what was seen as a society paper into a magazine of high modernism and the avant-garde under the editorship of Dorothy Todd, who was ably assisted by her protégée and lover, the Australian-born Madge Garland. The two professional journalists had expertise in the worlds of both fashion and art. Todd and Garland lived together in a house just off the King's Road, Chelsea, an area of London that remained the heartland for Vogue House employees throughout the twentieth century and into the twenty-first. Garland and Todd were friends with the novelist Virginia Woolf and other members of the Bloomsbury Group, which included artists and writers who all lived sexually adventurous and unconventional lives for the time. Amongst many other famous names, Todd employed Aldous Huxley as a *Vogue* staff writer, contributing theatre and book reviews. Such spirit informed the pages of the magazine, but as I mentioned earlier in this book, creative experimentation is rarely embraced by publishers and Todd was sacked in 1926 after just four years, as it was perceived by Condé Nast that the magazine had become a little too bohemian. Garland left shortly after. Todd planned to sue Condé Nast for a breach of contract for £5,000, however, this never happened, perhaps because Nast had reportedly threatened to reveal Todd's private life if she sued. It is believed that Todd accepted £1,000 to leave quietly. A very Condé Nast solution to a problem.

Magazines that too closely challenge the status quo are rarely left alone for long, but nevertheless I believe it is important for magazines to employ mavericks and independent thinkers. Corporate thinking produces corporate products, and this squeezes the sense of fun and entertainment from something that should at its heart be enjoyable to read and look at. A good magazine should not only tell you what and where to buy things, it should also open your eyes, ears and mind to cultural experiences that challenge and inform.

"Matt Gibberd was a sub editor at the time and with the *World of*

Interiors. For a few months he was my work experience, and then six years later, we got together and now we're married, and he runs a business called The Modern House and Imago. I thank the Lord for Vogue House. Everything that we learned at the *World of Interiors* has made the life that we have now, quite literally in terms of our relationship, but also in terms of the businesses that we have."
Faye Toogood
House & Garden, World of Interiors

"At least one child was born from an inter-office liaison."
Dafydd Jones
Tatler

Successful work relationships within Vogue House have also led to multiple couplings over the years, both formal and long-lasting and informal or brief in nature. I will not refer to the brief affairs in this book, but there are many long-lasting couplings including fashion editors marrying features editors, art directors marrying make-up artists, magazine designers marrying beauty editors, art directors marrying interiors editors and interiors editors marrying sub-editors. I can even include myself in this list as an art director who married his work experience intern. Most of these relationships are to be expected when working long hours and socialising together. However, there was one relationship formed in the building that saw the paparazzi camped outside of Vogue House and made the newspapers in 2004. Kimberly Quinn held multiple roles within the building, including on *GQ* and as a press officer (after working as the publisher of *The Spectator*, alongside its editor at the time Boris Johnson). When I worked with her in the late 1990s, she was still Kimberley Fortier. In 2001 she married the *Vogue* publisher Stephen Quinn but shortly after met the Labour MP David Blunkett and they began an affair. The Quinns had a son in 2002 and the affair ended. However, in 2003 Blunkett raised the possibility that he could be the child's father and a DNA test proved that this was indeed the case. Blunkett was then accused of having fast-tracked a visa application for the Quinns' nanny, which he denied; in 2004 he was forced to resign from the government due to the row. The family courts then ordered a paternity test of the Quinns' second son, born in 2005. This time the DNA tests established that the child was not Blunkett's. Meanwhile, it transpired that Blunkett had not been Kimberley Quinn's only lover since the marriage. Stephen Quinn had joined Condé Nast in 1988 to launch British *GQ* and moved onto British *Vogue* in 1992 where he remained for the following twenty-six years, retiring in 2018. During Quinn's time at British *Vogue*, he oversaw the publication of 312 issues, selling of 42,500 display advertising pages and secured advertising revenues of more than 430 million pounds.

Despite such advertising revenues, budgets within Vogue House were small, editorial teams even smaller in size if not stature, and with a fashion shoot rarely consisting of more staff than a fashion editor, a photographer and a model happy to do their own make-up. I once art directed a six-page beauty/jewellery shoot that was just myself, the supermodel Elle Macpherson and the photographer Jean Loup Sieff with one camera and twelve rolls of 35mm black and white film! Today a fashion shoot on *Vogue* is believed to require a dozen or so people to make it happen, with the associated costs. Where once magazines were produced with scalpels, glue and hot-wax, and I have the scars to prove it, today Adobe InDesign is the go-to tool for screen-based designers. Long lunches in Soho have been replaced with a quick sandwich at the desk. Morning hangovers have been replaced by gym workouts.

"There wasn't much inter-floor mingling... Although I remember people would often gather in the sick bay, which was on the *Vogue* floor. Everyone in there was usually nursing a huge hangover."
Pip Blaszkowski
Vogue, Tatler, Vanity Fair

"There was a small cupboard in the corridor with a bed you could lie down on if you felt sick, and I was in there so often I almost had a spare key cut. I had to wear large, dark shades, to offset the light streaming through the windows, which would

trigger my migraines, much to the amusement of one intern who thought I was trying to out-*Vogue* Anna Wintour. While stress definitely didn't help, I'm not blaming *Vogue* for the migraines; I was perimenopausal, I just didn't know it!"
Kathleen Baird Murray
Tatler, Vogue

The much loved and used basement archive of magazines and prints has been moved to a warehouse facility in Stockwell, south London, and is no longer available to staff to access by just dropping into the library. The past has been locked away, disconnected from the present and the future. A new building could have incorporated at least the magazine archive, but it is clear that the future is not musty, dusty bound magazines. There is little space for nostalgia in big business unless it is repackaged as heritage.

"The library was a cavern of discovery where leather-bound volumes going back to the very beginnings of *Vogue* were stored. Now, of course, everything is stored digitally, Korean *Vogue's* all-digital archive is a wonder to behold, but in those days, the bound books with their yellowing pages on rolling-shelves which could be pulled in and out to reveal French, Italian, US and British editions of all of the Condé Nast titles going back to the very beginning were the starting point and creative resource of many memorable shoots."
Kathy Phillips
Vogue, Tatler

"I've really missed looking through our iconic *Vogue* archive that's just a few floors down in the building, which is full of photography, fashion and art books as well as every copy of British *Vogue* and other Condé Nast titles."
Cai Lunn
Vogue
"Hours were spent in the chilly basement library pouring

through old editions of *Vogue* in search of arresting images and inspiration. I remember doing a piece on poses through the ages, from the leaping sixties via the striding seventies to the power stances of the eighties and nineties."

Laura Campbell
Vogue

The globalisation of the magazine business model has led to templates being constructed and followed, and an unhealthy desire to use past glories to create 'heritage brands' means that titles have lost their spirit and become ghosts of their former selves. Edward Enninful has spoken of looking back to the heyday of Bea Miller's *Vogue* for inspiration and in a 2018 interview with *Women's Wear Daily*, *Tatler* editor Richard Dennen presented this with positivity: "What's really exciting in the 21st century is to have these old heritage brands... One of the things that I felt strongly about was that *Tatler* had to have very recognizable faces on the cover to really take you in... That's not to say that we can't launch new people... It might be a new 'It' girl. I like a mix." The problem with Dennen's seemingly reasonable intentions for his contemporary magazine is that his vision is exactly that of Jane Procter on the same magazine twenty-eight years previously – except that the 'It' girl is no longer created by a magazine. That is the domain today of Instagram, TikTok or a reality television series. Procter's plan worked then but times have changed, and new ambitious editorial ideas are needed today to differentiate the magazine from its competitors.

The "heritage brands" Dennen refers to were not created by people who had any interest in creating such a thing – they were living in the moment, creating for their present time. To repeat mantras of the past speaks to me of a lack of new ideas. The incumbents of Vogue House never lacked ideas or a sense of anarchy in bringing their ideas to fruition. There was no fear of failure in its eclectic ramshackle offices. I wonder what Procter, Boxer and Brown would think of Deneen's minimalist white office decorated with a poster of one of Norman Parkinson's iconic historic *Tatler* covers. Perhaps it is a metaphor for where publishing finds itself today, with one foot in the corporate world whilst the other remains planted firmly in the past. Interestingly, the previous editor Kate Reardon hung an iconic *Tatler* image behind her desk in the same office, hers chosen from Tina Brown's time as editor of the magazine and shot by photographer Dafydd Jones. Perhaps nostalgia for the magazines of the past is a twenty-first century obsession for the editor unsure of their publication's future. The past is important in informing the present and the future but is not a template to be copied. It can give inspiration, but needs some perspiration to remain relevant. Liz Tilberis encapsulated this notion in her autobiography: "Working for Condé Nast was more than a job ... Even the lowliest person on the masthead felt 'chosen' and outsiders admitted that just entering the lobby, they felt short of breath, seeing the elite few who somehow knew in their bones how to wear a strand of pearls with a white t-shirt and look fabulous."

"I loved the approach to the building from across Hanover Square. It was a building many of us grew up in. I started working there in my late twenties and left on the eve of my fifty-first birthday. Many of us stayed a long time and we made lifelong friendships. We have an emotional attachment to Vogue House, which is hard to explain to anyone who hasn't worked there. It wasn't just the building it was the people and the characters who worked and who had worked there, and it always seemed extremely glamorous to hop into a taxi and say, 'Vogue House'."
Susannah Coe
Vogue, GQ, Tatler

"Sometimes I tell people I started at the top and have been going down ever since. They always laugh. Self-amusement is perhaps the greatest gift I've taken with me into a century that takes itself very seriously indeed. Norman Parkinson taught me that by the lifts. We emerged at the same time on the ground floor, laughing, and headed out to Hanover Square through the spinning glass doors."
Charlotte du Cann
Vogue

Vogue House was the home for British Condé Nast, and it had all of the quirks, eccentricities, personality and sense of tradition that the magazines produced there demonstrated. The new space in the Adelphi building may be impressive, but it is generic: big open spaces, huge digital projections, brightly coloured cushions and lots of industrial steel painted in dark colours with polished concrete floors. It could be any industrial design-influenced advertising agency, architects' practice or exclusive chain hotel. British Condé Nast is no more, International Condé Nast is now in town. The future of the printed magazine is walking a tightrope. Paper, printing and distribution costs are at an all-time high, sales are at an all-time low and advertisers have a multitude of options in how they wish to connect and engage with potential purchasers. Options with which they can collect and track data and build subscriber bases rather than rely upon a third party's promise that sales will come from advertising with them.

It would be easy and trite to say that the end of Condé Nast's time at Vogue House is the end of luxury magazine publishing in the UK, but I do believe that it can be seen as a metaphor. It is a sign, a message to those involved or once involved in producing magazines that the glossy printed page has a limited shelf life. There will always be a need for readers to be informed, inspired and to have something to aspire to, but the ways in which these needs are fulfilled will no longer be confined to one printed artefact, published and purchased on a monthly basis with a sense of excitement and anticipation.

> "My lasting memory of Vogue House is as a world unto itself, a little community of perfectly mixed talent, dedicated, maverick, conformist, rebellious, posh individuals with the odd 'bampot' all included and housed at a work address that screamed respect."
> **David Eustace**
> **Vogue, GQ, Tatler**

Condé Nast had a seventy-eight-year lease on the building that displays the name Vogue House in an elegant gold serifed font, and they are getting out whilst they still have something to sell. That makes commercial sense if they can find someone to take on the lease. Shortly after the email announcement of the proposed decamp, a meeting for the one hundred and twenty London-based staff was held at the Adelphi with a champagne reception and free food.

"When I started [at Vogue], I truly hated it, what had I done, it felt to me like landing on Mars. I told myself to stick it out for twelve months so that way I could use it on my CV. One morning, about six months in, on the bus ride to Vogue House, I realised I no longer felt sick. This was huge, a real turning point that led to a very happy eighteen-year career at both *Vogue* and *Glamour*. Once I conquered my fear of the job itself and learnt to navigate and indeed appreciate the extraordinary and uniquely talented, at times almost mythical people within Vogue House, the world became my fashion oyster. There are so many extraordinary tales to tell across two decades in Vogue House but not many that could be printed…"
Racheal Reavley
Vogue

"The atmosphere was terrific, everyone seemed to like each other. I left in 1972 and all my good friends from there then are my good friends today."
Geoffrey Aquillina Ross
Vogue

"It was the most extraordinary place to work. It was always dramatic, eccentric behaviour was positively encouraged, long lunches were allowed and yet we all managed to create a monthly magazine, usually on time."
Emma White Turle
Vogue, Tatler

"Whilst I have so many memories of the covers, the shoots, the perfume launches and fashion shows, the memories I hold most dear are of my colleagues. They were (are!) some of the most driven, industrious, creative and determined people I've ever met, but kind and thoughtful too. Vogue House was often called 'the velvet coffin' as people would start and end their careers there because it was so comfortable. But the reality is, and was, that it incubated ideas and many businesses were no doubt developed over lunch breaks. If you add up the number of people that companies such as This Works, Net-A-Porter and Nails Inc employ, and their annual turnovers, that's a great contribution to the British economy."

Carmel Allen
Vogue, Tatler

"I will be so sad to say goodbye to this incredible building, who held us all safe under its gilded lettering for so many years."
Kathleen Baird Murray
Tatler, Vogue

"My desk was always on the fifth floor, the *Vogue* floor. I started rather fortuitously with a window seat looking out over Hanover Square and then we moved around from the front to the side of the building overlooking St George Street. At that point I had a huge beautiful red geranium called Marcello which thrived on the sunny windowsill as that side of the building was extremely hot in the summer. Next, I moved a little way along when the floor was having one of its many refurbishments and re-configurations, still keeping my view until my department was moved to the back of the building with a rather depressing view of grey buildings and fire escapes. When I left the building in 2018, I was back where I had originally started, at the front of the building, overlooking the square."
Susannah Coe
Vogue, GQ and Tatler

In October 2023 it emerged that the property agent Knight Frank had been appointed by Condé Nast to sell the leasehold of Vogue

House, for a proposed £70 million. It was also revealed that one option a buyer might look at was the potential to work on a scheme designed by architects and designers at Orms, London to refurbish and extend the building to approximately 88,000 square feet from its current 62,777 square feet. This seems further proof that the building could have been adapted and developed, if the will had been sufficient. It only took until January 2024 for a buyer to be found: the Monaco-based Israeli shipping billionaire Eyal Ofer, through his business Global Holdings Management Group, which owns a number of properties in London, including Sea Containers House, as well as an extensive portfolio of New York properties. The *Telegraph* reported that Ofer paid £75 million for the property, £5 million more than the price it was listed at. They also suggested that Vogue House would be renamed 1 Grosvenor Square.

When I began working on this book, I reached out to a number of people I knew that had worked on and for the Vogue House magazines, and further research revealed many others whom I was not previously aware of who also had stories to tell. Many came from *Tatler*, and *Vogue*, some from *Brides*, *House & Garden*, *World of Interiors* and *Traveller*, less from *GQ*. I am grateful for those voices I did hear from, now that Vogue House is silent. I am also grateful to the people I contacted who recommended others to me. This process of research and discussion allowed me to speak with many people whose stories informed the narrative I have constructed here, although, sadly, it was not possible to include them all. However, the response to my communications painted their own picture of the ways in which Vogue House had influenced the lives of its inhabitants, both positive and negative.

My intention was always to focus on interesting stories rather than document careers of people that you may already be aware of. The loudest voices do not always tell the best stories. I hope the stories I have included here have been of interest whether you have worked on a magazine or not, whether you are an academic or a student, a magazine reader or a former Vogue House employee. I focused on speaking with interns rather than managers, creatives over administrators. Some of the people I reached out to did not respond to my emails, others were too busy to contribute, some others felt that their time in the building was too painful to revisit.

When I started in Vogue House, I was always aware that I was an outsider, a visitor given a permit to view but not to stay. I never felt that I would be accepted, and, in many ways, I was not, but that was okay with me. It has not left me feeling bitter – I was grateful for the permit. Twenty-three years since I last walked out of the building, I still remember the telephone number, 070-499-9080, and the building's postcode, W1R 0AD.

Over six decades, Vogue House has been a container for a strata of life that I never aspired to be part of. I started writing this book over two decades after I left *Tatler*, at a point in my life when I was able to reposition myself as the observer I always was, and, with the benefit of hindsight, reflecting my own experiences alongside the memories of others. During my research I was regularly asked if I had the permission of Condé Nast to write this book and if members of management of the past and present had given their agreement for the project to go ahead. I did not and I had not; there was no reason to do so. However, that these questions were so frequently asked indicates to me the power of the connections many still have, not only with the positions they held or the magazines they worked on but with the publishers and the perceived power they had and have over their employees. Many people were only willing to speak with me off-line rather than be directly quoted. To many, what happened in Vogue House stays in Vogue House.

I always wanted this book to be a positive, humorous look at life within Vogue House, based on first-person experience with no axes to grind. I hope that it has achieved that outcome. The publishing world is filled with insecurity and ego, and those two ingredients can make a dangerous cocktail. You need a thick skin to work on a magazine and an ability to maintain a sense of perspective, two things that I learnt very early on in my time at Vogue House. It had not been such a priority before I went through the revolving door.

On 7 February 2024 the *Daily Mail Online* reported on Condé Nast's final day at Vogue House, and described the farewell as a "champagne-fuelled soirée." In many ways the final day echoed much of the building's history, including a champagne bucket descending from a second-floor window outside the building, though more sedately than the one thrown by James Brown in the 1990s. Loud music could be heard from the street as staff danced on tables, with a hole supposedly being made in one of the ceilings. Claridge's, the unofficial canteen for the more senior staff, delivered a trolley loaded with champagne, sweets and burgers. According to the *Sunday Times* one insider hailed it as the "best party I've ever been to" – the use of hyperbole perfectly in line with magazine speak. The newspaper also reported that an employee claimed that the day had been like a "Bridget Jones office party but cooler" that "felt like what the office must have been like in the Nineties heyday". Many took to the seventh-floor rooftop to photograph each other, themselves and the sunset as others took selfies in front of the building's revolving door. Again, according to the *Sunday Times*, "Others left messages scrawled on door frames, including one insider who wrote of the legendary fashion empire: 'A million girls would kill for this job.'"

Reflecting now on the story that I have told here it seems clear to me that the 1960s and 70s were a time of fun, adventure and informality, when working in the building seemed to have very few rules if you were young and new determined to create a different world inside an old conservative environment. Those whom I spoke with confirmed this conclusion with their openness and warmth in sharing their stories. This seems to have remained the case until the late 1980s, when a new desire for professionalism and increased hunger for sales entered the building, resulting in a growing sense of personal ambition. Despite this, those I spoke with still had tales to tell of fun and eccentric characters. The 1990s were the years of high emotion, drama, drink and drugs, and the 2000s were the come-down from a decade of excess. Whilst different magazines in each decade proved to be the exceptions to my very broad rules, what I am suggesting is that there was a sense of something in the air – a spirit, an attitude, an eclectic anarchy. The 2010s was the decade when all of the magazines faced the same issues: closures, sell-offs and insecurity. It was also the decade when the magazines within Vogue House had to become truly global online; in so doing, they came under scrutiny from those who had never stepped foot inside its hallowed halls. This resulted in a loss of that anarchic spirit and a focus on corporate agendas.

To me it was obvious from 2000, and the first sparks of the digital age, that Vogue House was under threat. Traditional publishing has been endangered for much of this century and Vogue House was a stone and brick symbol to what publishing had always been – it could not last. To many in management positions, who have not come from publishing backgrounds, that past needed to be left behind, rejected and replaced by innovative but untried business models to secure a financial future for the companies looking to them for an answer. That answer does not seem yet to be well defined, confused by a fear of losing the very heritage they are trying to sell, whilst attempting to embrace new ways of connecting with new audiences. Despite this, long-lasting decisions have been made and one of these is that the iconic Hanover Square address of Condé Nast's magazines in London will no longer be their home. One of the most important physical representations of heritage Condé Nast had, Vogue House, is no more, and an era has ended. It's time to turn out the lights. Condé Nast have left the building.

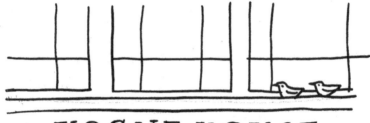

VOGUE HOUSE

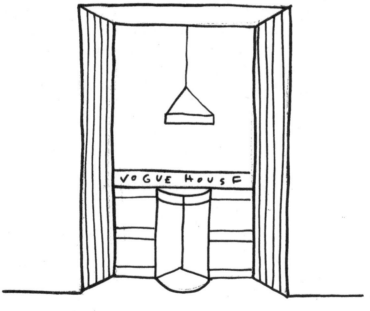

VOGUE HOUSE

Epilogue

I left Vogue House and *Tatler* in the spring of 1999 but, as you can probably tell, it didn't leave me. I never art directed a mainstream magazine again, but I did go on to art direct and photograph editorial and commercial photographic shoots. I edited photography magazines, worked as a consultant creative director and even launched my own magazine, *Hungry Eye*, acting as editor, writer and designer. In the early 2010s I started to teach within a university setting and I now find myself existing within a multi-platform environment as a lecturer, writer, podcaster and photographer. The experiences I had on magazines informs all of these endeavours.

I can't remember ever taking stock and thinking about what I was learning during my time in Vogue House. It was a process of osmosis. At *Elle* I had learnt what to do and how to do it, at *Tatler* I was able to put that learning into practice. I was given the freedom to do so and that is a precious gift that should not be underestimated within a creative environment. I have been given such freedom since I left Vogue House, but it has become a rarer and rarer commodity. I am not someone who feels that the past is always cast with a golden glow of perfection. However, the magazine publishing world did have a sense of continuity based upon a passing on of knowledge from generation to generation, a form of creative baton-passing. Those who made their mark on each decade were trained, informed and influenced by those who had done the same in years past.

There was nepotism, and sexism, and I am sure that there was racism and perhaps other forms of discrimination, although I never personally witnessed any. In any case, the lack of cultural diversity told its own story to a boy from South London. There were certainly drugs and excessive drinking, lots of both at different times. But it was not a party atmosphere: it was hard work. Not hard like working down a mine or doing shiftwork in A&E, but in other ways. Conversation and feedback could be brutal, unfair and personal. The pressure to succeed and meet extremely short deadlines with minimal support was a monthly reality. Sales figures were used as a barometer of success, with no allowance for contributing factors outside of the editorial team's control. Today, 'hits and views', alongside social media follower numbers, act as the Sword of Damocles that swings above the heads of 'content providers'. In that sense little changes; the expectation is to build and retain an audience of readers, purchasers, and subscribers.

The transferable skills of those schooled in the 'old ways' of publishing could, should and would be valuable to anyone looking to publish aspirational and inspirational material. Sadly, in a rush for a 'quick win' the new and untried is too often venerated over the established and proven. In this sense, this book acts as a metaphor for the death of publishing, not only as the history for those who worked in a particular building.

In December 2023 Condé Nast announced staffing cuts in multiple departments globally, as the advertising market continued to decline, with five per cent of its staff being let go, more than 300 employees. In a company-wide memo announcing the news, the Condé Nast CEO, Roger Lynch, said: "There is no easy way to share this news and our focus will be on making this transition as easy as possible for our dedicated colleagues with enhanced severance packages and career service offerings."

In an article in the *Guardian* a Condé Nast employee who requested anonymity stated that we have been "through multiple restructures over the years, but this one is feeling particularly unpleasant …There is little transparency or clear strategy, creating a culture of fear and drastically damaging morale across the staff. It's increasingly hard to believe that the leaders of the company care about the quality of the work we do when resources keep getting stripped away, and revenue targets continue to increase."

The book didn't start out to explore the death of publishing, however, although its evolution took me in that direction. In fact, this book was ignited by an Instagram post by my long-term friend Geoff Waring and the comments many others made beneath his post. Geoff and I have known each other for nearly forty years. We first met working at *Elle* and our paths have intertwined and diverged over the years, but it was an obvious decision to ask him to provide the illustrations for this tale. I should also add that Geoff was the art director of UK and Australian *Vogue, Elle, Tatler, Red,* UK *Glamour, Easy Living* and *Good Housekeeping* magazines. He is also a very talented illustrator.

That spark of an idea was fully ignited by the good people at Orphans Publishing, and another good friend, gardener and writer Tamsin Westhorpe. Debbie and Helen at Orphans saw something in my enthusiasm for the project and gave me some of that elusive freedom and much needed proofing expertise to bring the project to fruition in record time. In publishers these are qualities to be treasured.

I started off this book by saying that this was not the story of a building and I remain true to that belief in these final words. Its story is bigger than bricks and mortar. The story is one of progress and communication, society and economics, global expansion and expectation. It's bigger than one corner of Hanover Square.

I will end by asking you three questions. How often did you buy a magazine in the past? When was the last time you bought a magazine? And when will you next buy a magazine? Your answers will dictate the future of the magazine publishing industry. It really is that simple.